At Sylvan, we believe that everyone can master math skills, and we are glad you have chosen our resources to help your children experience the joy of mathematics as they build crucial reasoning skills. We know that time spent reinforcing lessons learned in school will contribute to understanding and mastery.

Success in math requires more than just memorizing basic facts and algorithms; it also requires children to make connections between the real world and math concepts in order to solve problems. Successful problem solvers will be ready for the challenges of mathematics as they advance to more complex topics and encounter new problems both in school and at home.

We use a research-based, step-by-step process in teaching math at Sylvan that includes thought-provoking math problems and activities. As students increase their success as problem solvers, they become more confident. With increasing confidence, students build even more success. The design of the Sylvan workbooks lays out a roadmap for mathematical learning that is designed to lead your child to success in school.

Included with your purchase of this workbook is a coupon for a discount at a participating Sylvan center. We hope you will use this coupon to further your children's academic journeys. Let us partner with you to support the development of confident, well-prepared, independent learners.

The Sylvan Team

Sylvan Learning Center
Unleash your child's potential here

No matter how big or small the academic challenge, every child has the ability to learn. But sometimes children need help making it happen. Sylvan believes every child has the potential to do great things. And, we know better than anyone else how to tap into that academic potential so that a child's future really is full of possibilities. Sylvan Learning Center is the place where your child can build and master the learning skills needed to succeed and unlock the potential you know is there.

The proven, personalized approach of our in-center programs deliver unparalleled results that other supplemental education services simply can't match. Your child's achievements will be seen not only in test scores and report cards but outside the classroom as well. And when he starts achieving his full potential, everyone will know it. You will see a new level of confidence come through in everything he does and every interaction he has.

How can Sylvan's personalized in-center approach help your child unleash his potential?

• Starting with our exclusive Sylvan Skills Assessment®, we pinpoint your child's exact academic needs.

• Then we develop a customized learning plan designed to achieve your child's academic goals.

• Through our method of skill mastery, your child will not only learn and master every skill in his personalized plan, he will be truly motivated and inspired to achieve his full potential.

To get started, included with this Sylvan product purchase is $10 off our exclusive Sylvan Skills Assessment®. Simply use this coupon and contact your local Sylvan Learning Center to set up your appointment.

And to learn more about Sylvan and our innovative in-center programs, call 1-800-EDUCATE or visit www.SylvanLearning.com. ***With over 900 locations in North America, there is a Sylvan Learning Center near you!***

5th Grade
Super Math Success

Published in the United States by Random House, Inc., New York, and in Canada by Random House of Canada Limited, Toronto.

www.tutoring.sylvanlearning.com

Created by Smarterville Productions LLC
Producer & Editorial Direction: The Linguistic Edge
Producer: TJ Trochlil McGreevy
Writer: Amy Kraft
Cover and Interior Illustrations: Shawn Finley, Tim Goldman, and Duendes del Sur
Layout and Art Direction: SunDried Penguin
Director of Product Development: Russell Ginns

First Edition

ISBN: 978-0-307-47921-1

This book is available at special discounts for bulk purchases for sales promotions or premiums.
For more information, write to Special Markets/Premium Sales, 1745 Broadway, MD 6-2,
New York, New York 10019 or e-mail specialmarkets@randomhouse.com.

PRINTED IN CHINA

10 9 8 7

Basic Math Success Contents

Basic Math Success Contents

Measurement & Geometry

Math Games & Puzzles Contents

Math Games & Puzzles Contents

Measurement & Geometry

Math in the Environment

Math in Action Contents

Math in Action Contents

5th Grade
Basic Math Success

Pattern Patch

MULTIPLY each number by the first number, and WRITE the missing numbers in each pattern.

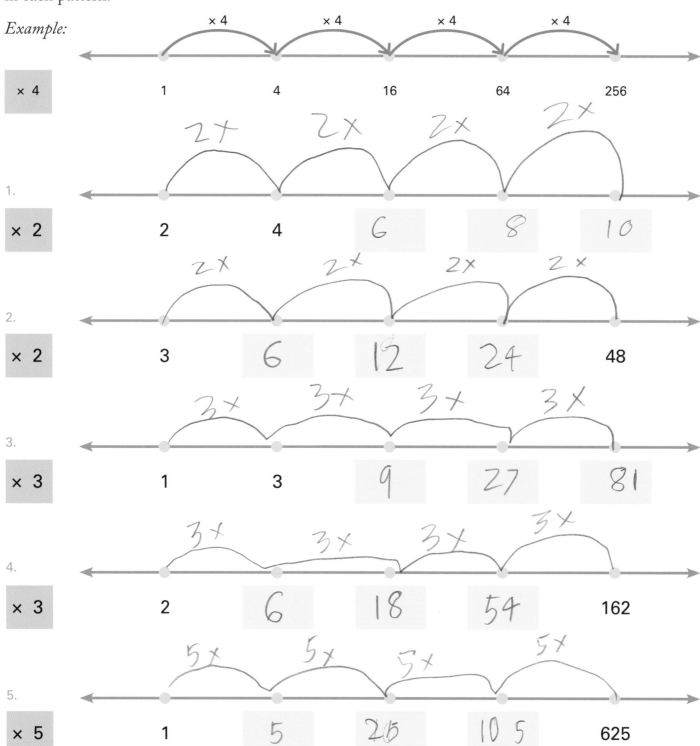

Example:

| × 4 | 1 | 4 | 16 | 64 | 256 |

1.

| × 2 | 2 | 4 | 6 | 8 | 10 |

2.

| × 2 | 3 | 6 | 12 | 24 | 48 |

3.

| × 3 | 1 | 3 | 9 | 27 | 81 |

4.

| × 3 | 2 | 6 | 18 | 54 | 162 |

5.

| × 5 | 1 | 5 | 2⑮ | 10 5 | 625 |

3

Multiplication Patterns

So Many Zeros

Factors are numbers that are being multiplied together, and the **product** is the result.

Find the product of the first number in each factor. Next, count the total number of zeros in both factors. Write the same number of zeros after the product of the first numbers.

30	×	500	=	_____
3	×	5	=	15
30	×	500	=	_____
30	×	500	=	15,000
3	×	5	=	15
3	×	50	=	150
30	×	50	=	1,500
30	×	500	=	15,000
300	×	500	=	150,000
300	×	5,000	=	1,500,000

WRITE the products.

1.
8 × 1 = 8
8 × 10 = 80
80 × 10 = 800
80 × 100 = 8000
800 × 100 = 80000
800 × 1,000 = 800000

2.
6 × 7 = 42
6 × 70 = 420
60 × 70 = 4200
60 × 700 = 42000
600 × 700 = 420000
600 × 7,000 = 4200000

3.
2 × 3 = 6
2 × 30 = 60
20 × 30 = 600
20 × 300 = 6000
200 × 300 = 60000
200 × 3,000 = 600000

4.
4 × 9 = 36
4 × 90 = 360
40 × 90 = 3600
40 × 900 = 36000
400 × 900 = 360000
400 × 9,000 = 3600000

Picture It

Use the pictures to help you answer the problems. WRITE each product.

Example: 43 × 6 = ___240___

4 tens and 3 ones

4 tens × 6 ones = 24 tens, or 240   3 ones × 6 ones = 18 ones, or 18

When multiplying a two-digit number, think of it as tens and ones.
240 + 18 = 258
43 × 6 = 258

1. 56 × 3 = _168_

50 + 6

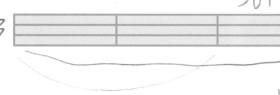

50 × 3 = 150   6 × 3 = 18

2. 65 × 7 = _455_

60 + 5

60 × 7 = 420   7 × 5 = 35

3. 49 × 8 = _392_

40 + 9

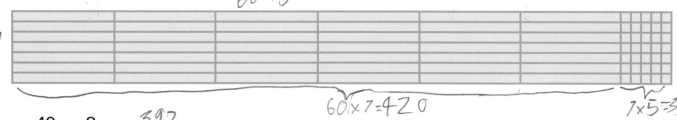

40 × 8 = 320   9 × 8 = 72

Computation Station

Multiply a three-digit number by a one-digit number.

$\overset{2}{283}$	$\overset{6\ 2}{283}$	$\overset{6}{283}$
$\times\ \ \ 8$	$\times\ \ \ 8$	$\times\ \ \ 8$
$\overline{\quad 4}$	$\overline{\quad 64}$	$\overline{\ 2{,}264}$
Multiply the ones.	Multiply the tens.	Multiply the hundreds.
$3 \times 8 = 24$	$80 \times 8 = 640$	$200 \times 8 = 1{,}600$
	$640 + 20 = 660$	$1{,}600 + 600 = 2{,}200$

WRITE each product.

1. $45 \times 3 = 135$

2. $52 \times 6 = 312$

3. $13 \times 7 = 91$

4. $74 \times 4 = 296$

5. $68 \times 8 = 544$

6. $34 \times 5 = 170$

7. $227 \times 7 = 1589$

8. $589 \times 2 = 1178$

9. $644 \times 5 = 3220$

10. $356 \times 8 = 2848$

11. $995 \times 7 = 6965$

12. $447 \times 4 = 1788$

13. $739 \times 9 = 6651$

14. $253 \times 6 = 1518$

15. $172 \times 8 = 1376$

16. $929 \times 4 = 3716$

17. $684 \times 5 = 3420$

18. $865 \times 9 = 7785$

Computation Station

Multiply a two-digit number by a two-digit number.

4 9 7 × 4 6 ‾‾‾‾‾ 5 8 2	2 9 7 × 4 6 ‾‾‾‾‾ 5 8 2 8 0	2 9 7 × 4 6 ‾‾‾‾‾ 5 8 2 3,8 8 0	9 7 × 4 6 ‾‾‾‾‾ 5 8 2 + 3,8 8 0 ‾‾‾‾‾‾‾ 4,4 6 2
Multiply 97 by 6.	Multiply 97 by 40, starting with the ones place. 7 × 40 = 280	Next, multiply the tens place. 90 × 40 = 3,600 3,600 + 200 = 3,800	Then add 582 and 3,880.

WRITE each product.

1.
$$\begin{array}{r} 27 \\ \times\ 20 \\ \hline 00 \\ 540 \\ \hline 540 \end{array}$$

2.
$$\begin{array}{r} 66 \\ \times\ 32 \\ \hline 132 \\ 1980 \\ \hline 2112 \end{array}$$

3.
$$\begin{array}{r} 45 \\ \times\ 14 \\ \hline 180 \\ 450 \\ \hline 630 \end{array}$$

4.
$$\begin{array}{r} 56 \\ \times\ 28 \\ \hline 448 \\ 1120 \\ \hline 1568 \end{array}$$

5.
$$\begin{array}{r} 92 \\ \times\ 19 \\ \hline 828 \\ 920 \\ \hline 1748 \end{array}$$

6.
$$\begin{array}{r} 31 \\ \times\ 36 \\ \hline 186 \\ 930 \\ \hline 1246 \end{array}$$

7.
$$\begin{array}{r} 72 \\ \times\ 47 \\ \hline 504 \\ 2880 \\ \hline 3384 \end{array}$$

8.
$$\begin{array}{r} 87 \\ \times\ 53 \\ \hline 261 \\ 4350 \\ \hline 4611 \end{array}$$

9.
$$\begin{array}{r} 50 \\ \times\ 26 \\ \hline 300 \\ 1000 \\ \hline 1300 \end{array}$$

10.
$$\begin{array}{r} 44 \\ \times\ 39 \\ \hline 396 \\ 1320 \\ \hline 1716 \end{array}$$

11.
$$\begin{array}{r} 68 \\ \times\ 58 \\ \hline 544 \\ 3400 \\ \hline 3944 \end{array}$$

12.
$$\begin{array}{r} 18 \\ \times\ 17 \\ \hline 126 \\ 180 \\ \hline 306 \end{array}$$

13.
$$\begin{array}{r} 94 \\ \times\ 52 \\ \hline 188 \\ 2000 \\ \hline 2188 \end{array}$$

14.
$$\begin{array}{r} 81 \\ \times\ 34 \\ \hline 324 \\ 2430 \\ \hline 2754 \end{array}$$

15.
$$\begin{array}{r} 75 \\ \times\ 15 \\ \hline 315 \\ 750 \\ \hline 1125 \end{array}$$

16.
$$\begin{array}{r} 67 \\ \times\ 65 \\ \hline 335 \\ 4020 \\ \hline 4355 \end{array}$$

17.
$$\begin{array}{r} 99 \\ \times\ 59 \\ \hline 891 \\ 4950 \\ \hline 5841 \end{array}$$

18.
$$\begin{array}{r} 84 \\ \times\ 78 \\ \hline 672 \\ 5880 \\ \hline 6552 \end{array}$$

Computation Station

Multiply a three-digit number by a two-digit number.

$\begin{array}{r} 3\ 1 \\ 963 \\ \times\ \ 56 \\ \hline 5{,}778 \end{array}$	$\begin{array}{r} 1 \\ 963 \\ \times\ \ 56 \\ \hline 5{,}778 \\ 50 \end{array}$	$\begin{array}{r} 3\ 1 \\ 963 \\ \times\ \ 56 \\ \hline 5{,}778 \\ 150 \end{array}$	$\begin{array}{r} 3\ 1 \\ 963 \\ \times\ \ 56 \\ \hline 5{,}778 \\ 48{,}150 \end{array}$	$\begin{array}{r} 3\ 1 \\ 963 \\ \times\ \ 56 \\ \hline 5{,}778 \\ +48{,}150 \\ \hline 53{,}928 \end{array}$
Multiply 963 by 6.	Multiply 963 by 50, starting with the ones place. $3 \times 50 = 150$	Next, multiply the tens place. $60 \times 50 = 3{,}000$ $3{,}000 + 100 = 3{,}100$	Next, multiply the hundreds place. $900 \times 50 = 45{,}000$ $45{,}000 + 3{,}000 = 48{,}000$	Then add 5,778 and 48,150.

WRITE each product.

1.
$$\begin{array}{r} 1\,3 \\ 325 \\ \times\ 61 \\ \hline 325 \\ 19500 \\ \hline 19825 \end{array}$$

2.
$$\begin{array}{r} 2\ 2 \\ 478 \\ \times\ 93 \\ \hline 1434 \\ 43020 \\ \hline 44454 \end{array}$$

3.
$$\begin{array}{r} 2\ 1 \\ 932 \\ \times\ 58 \\ \hline 7456 \\ 46600 \\ \hline 44056 \end{array}$$

4.
$$\begin{array}{r} 1\ 9 \\ 215 \\ \times\ 87 \\ \hline 1505 \\ 17200 \\ \hline 19005 \end{array}$$

5.
$$\begin{array}{r} 2\ 3 \\ 559 \\ \times\ 74 \\ \hline 2236 \\ 39130 \\ \hline 41366 \end{array}$$

6.
$$\begin{array}{r} 2\ 4 \\ 737 \\ \times\ 67 \\ \hline 5159 \\ 43220 \\ \hline 48379 \end{array}$$

7.
$$\begin{array}{r} 2 \\ 530 \\ \times\ 49 \\ \hline 4770 \\ 21200 \\ \hline 25970 \end{array}$$

8.
$$\begin{array}{r} 3\ 2 \\ 197 \\ \times\ 34 \\ \hline 788 \\ 5910 \\ \hline 5698 \end{array}$$

9.
$$\begin{array}{r} 812 \\ \times\ 91 \\ \hline 812 \\ 73080 \\ \hline 73892 \end{array}$$

10.
$$\begin{array}{r} 7\ 4 \\ 385 \\ \times\ 29 \\ \hline 3465 \\ 7700 \\ \hline 11165 \end{array}$$

11.
$$\begin{array}{r} 4\ 3 \\ 497 \\ \times\ 55 \\ \hline 2485 \\ 24850 \\ \hline 28335 \end{array}$$

12.
$$\begin{array}{r} 1\ 1 \\ 664 \\ \times\ 83 \\ \hline 1992 \\ 53120 \\ \hline 54112 \end{array}$$

13.
$$\begin{array}{r} 2\ 2 \\ 344 \\ \times\ 96 \\ \hline 2064 \\ 30960 \\ \hline 33024 \end{array}$$

14.
$$\begin{array}{r} 3\ 7 \\ 939 \\ \times\ 78 \\ \hline 7512 \\ 69730 \\ \hline 77242 \end{array}$$

15.
$$\begin{array}{r} 1 \\ 502 \\ \times\ 27 \\ \hline 3514 \\ 10040 \\ \hline 13554 \end{array}$$

16.
$$\begin{array}{r} 2\ 1 \\ 463 \\ \times\ 54 \\ \hline 1852 \\ 23150 \\ \hline 25002 \end{array}$$

17.
$$\begin{array}{r} 2\ 2 \\ 689 \\ \times\ 33 \\ \hline 2067 \\ 20670 \\ \hline 22737 \end{array}$$

18.
$$\begin{array}{r} 1 \\ 925 \\ \times\ 62 \\ \hline 1850 \\ 55500 \\ \hline 57350 \end{array}$$

Computation Station

Multiply a four-digit number by a three-digit number.

$\overset{1\ 2\ 2}{4,378}$ × 253 ‾‾‾‾‾ 13,134	$\overset{1\ 3\ 4}{4,378}$ × 253 ‾‾‾‾‾ 13,134 218,900	$\overset{1\ 1}{4,378}$ × 253 ‾‾‾‾‾ 13,134 218,900 875,600	4,378 × 253 ‾‾‾‾‾ 13,134 218,900 +875,600 ‾‾‾‾‾ 1,107,634
Multiply 4,378 by 3.	Multiply 4,378 by 50.	Multiply 4,378 by 200.	Then add 13,134 + 218,900 + 875,600.

WRITE each product.

1. 1,546
× 84
‾‾‾‾
6184
123680
‾‾‾‾‾‾
129864

2. 6,115
× 27
‾‾‾‾
42805
122300
‾‾‾‾‾‾
165105

3. 4,923
× 66
‾‾‾‾
29538
295380
‾‾‾‾‾‾
324918

4. 8,354
× 52
‾‾‾‾
16708
417700
‾‾‾‾‾‾
434408

5. 3,694
× 93
‾‾‾‾
11082
332460
‾‾‾‾‾‾
343542

6. 677
× 352
‾‾‾‾
1354
33850
203100
‾‾‾‾‾‾
238304

7. 962
× 175
‾‾‾‾
4810
67340
96200
‾‾‾‾‾‾
968350

8. 407
× 486
‾‾‾‾
2442
32560
322800
‾‾‾‾‾‾
357802

9. 726
× 296
‾‾‾‾
4356
6534
145200
‾‾‾‾‾‾
214896

10. 595
× 510
‾‾‾‾
5950
297500
‾‾‾‾‾‾
293450

11. 5,204
× 268
‾‾‾‾
41632
132240
1040800
‾‾‾‾‾‾
1214672

12. 7,328
× 350
‾‾‾‾
366400
2198400
‾‾‾‾‾‾
2564800

13. 3,831
× 193
‾‾‾‾
11493
344790
383100
‾‾‾‾‾‾
739383

14. 2,456
× 679
‾‾‾‾
22104
171920
1473600
‾‾‾‾‾‾
1668624

15. 9,197
× 437
‾‾‾‾
64379
295910
367600
‾‾‾‾‾‾
727889

Many Miles

WRITE the answers.

HINT: Multiply the number of miles by the number of days in the month.

If Marissa rides the same number of miles each day for
a month or a year, how many miles would she ride?

1. 8 miles × 31 days = __**248**__ miles

2. 11 miles × 28 days = __308__ miles

3. 26 miles × 31 days = __806__ miles

4. 32 miles × 30 days = __960__ miles

5. 40 miles × 31 days = __1240__ miles

6. 45 miles × 30 days = __1350__ miles

7. 4 miles × 365 days = __1460__ miles

8. 15 miles × 365 days = __5795__ miles

9. 24 miles × 365 days = __8760__ miles

10. 29 miles × 365 days = __10585__ miles

11. 37 miles × 365 days = __11680__ miles

12. 50 miles × 365 days = __18250__ miles

Round About

Rounding numbers can help you estimate a product.

6,893	→	7,000
× 795	→	× 800
		5,600,000

6,893 rounded to the nearest thousand is 7,000.

795 rounded to the nearest hundred is 800.

7,000 × 800 = 5,600,000

6,893 × 795 = 5,479,935

ESTIMATE each product by rounding to the first digit and multiplying. WRITE the actual product to check your estimate.

1.
$$\begin{array}{r} 296 \\ \times\ 24 \\ \hline 7104 \end{array}$$
$$\begin{array}{r} 300 \\ \times\ 20 \\ \hline 6000 \end{array}$$

2.
$$\begin{array}{r} 814 \\ \times\ 96 \\ \hline 78144 \end{array}$$
$$\begin{array}{r} 800 \\ \times 100 \\ \hline 80000 \end{array}$$

3.
$$\begin{array}{r} 571 \\ \times\ 935 \\ \hline 533885 \end{array}$$
$$\begin{array}{r} 600 \\ \times 900 \\ \hline 540000 \end{array}$$

4.
$$\begin{array}{r} 707 \\ \times\ 682 \\ \hline 482174 \end{array}$$
$$\begin{array}{r} 700 \\ \times 700 \\ \hline 490000 \end{array}$$

5.
$$\begin{array}{r} 4,338 \\ \times\ 472 \\ \hline 2047536 \end{array}$$
$$\begin{array}{r} 4000 \\ \times 500 \\ \hline 2000000 \end{array}$$

6.
$$\begin{array}{r} 9,566 \\ \times\ 343 \\ \hline 3281138 \end{array}$$
$$\begin{array}{r} 10000 \\ \times 300 \\ \hline 3000000 \end{array}$$

The Mighty Marlock

The Mighty Marlock will guess any product, but he sometimes guesses incorrectly. ESTIMATE each product, and CROSS OUT any product that is clearly wrong.

775 × 91 = 70,525

6,323 × 972 = 6,145,956

199 × 485 = 96,515

611 × 281 = 1,821,851

2,594 × 312 = 2,637,208

836 × 17 = 44,952

Tic-Tac-Toe

CIRCLE any number that is a factor of the blue number. PUT an X through any number that is not a factor. DRAW a line when you find three factors in a row. The line can go across, down, or diagonally.

Example:

50

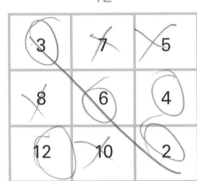

1	×	50	=	50
25	×	2	=	50
5	×	10	=	50

The factors of 50 are 1, 2, 5, 10, 25, and 50.

12

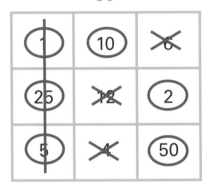

18

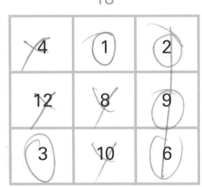

24

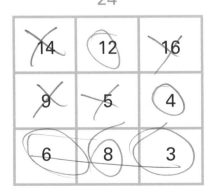

40

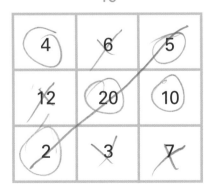

So Much in Common

A factor shared by two or more numbers is called a **common factor**. The **greatest common factor** is the largest number in a set of common factors.

Example: The factors of 12 are 1, 2, 3, 4, 6, and 12.
The factors of 30 are 1, 2, 3, 5, 6, 10, 15, and 30.

The common factors of 12 and 30 are 1, 2, 3, and 6.
The greatest common factor is 6.

WRITE the factors of each pair of numbers followed by the common factors and the greatest common factor.

14: 1 , 2 , 7 , 14

49: 1 , 7 , 49

Common factors: 1 , 7

Greatest common factor: 7

20: 1 , 2 , 4 , 5 , 10 , 20

32: 1 , 2 , 4 , 8 , 16 , 32

Common factors: 1 , 2 , 4

Greatest common factor: 4

24: 1 , 2 , 3 , 4 , 6 , 8 , 12 , 24

60: 1 , 2 , 3 , 4 , 5 , 6 , 10 , 12 , 15 , 20 , 30 , 60

Common factors: 1 , 2 , 3 , 4 , 6 , 12

Greatest common factor: 12

Pattern Patch

DIVIDE each number by the first number, and WRITE the missing numbers in each pattern.

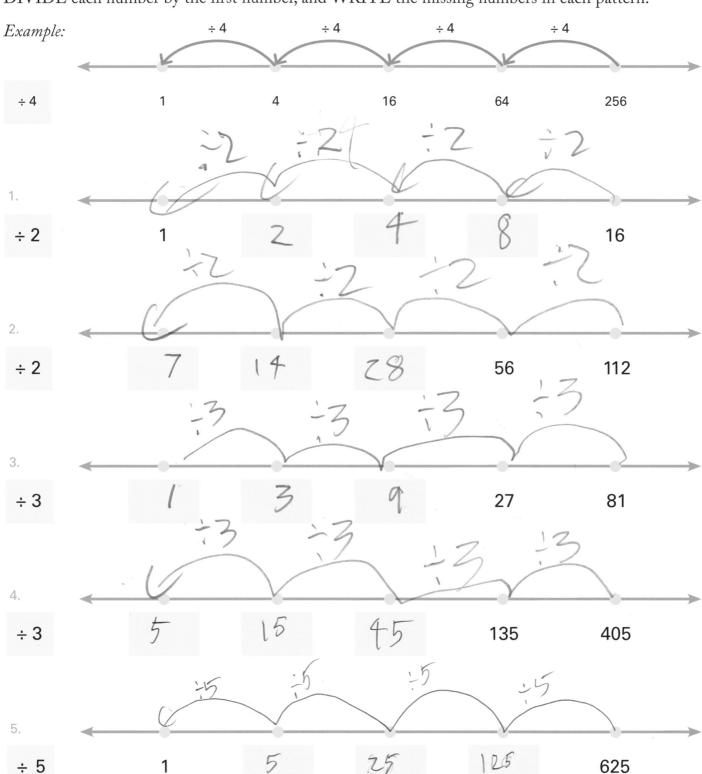

Example:

| ÷ 4 | ÷ 4 | ÷ 4 | ÷ 4 |

÷ 4   1   4   16   64   256

1.

÷ 2   1   2   4   8   16

2.

÷ 2   7   14   28   56   112

3.

÷ 3   1   3   9   27   81

4.

÷ 3   5   15   45   135   405

5.

÷ 5   1   5   25   125   625

Division Patterns

So Many Zeros

When one number (the **dividend**) is divided by another number (the **divisor**), the resulting number is called the **quotient**.

HINT: Try multiplying the quotient by the divisor to check your work.

Find the quotient of the first number in the dividend and divisor.

Next, subtract the number of zeros in the divisor from the number of zeros in the divided.

Write the difference of zeros after the quotient of the first numbers.

9,000 ÷ 30	=	___	
9 ÷ 3	=	3	
9,000 ÷ 30	=	___	
9,000 ÷ 30	=	300	

9 ÷ 3	=	3
90 ÷ 3	=	30
900 ÷ 30	=	30
9,000 ÷ 30	=	300
90,000 ÷ 300	=	300
900,000 ÷ 300	=	3,000

WRITE the quotients.

1.
   8 ÷ 2 = *4*
   80 ÷ 2 = *40*
   800 ÷ 20 = *400*
   8,000 ÷ 20 = *4000*
   80,000 ÷ 200 = *4000*
   800,000 ÷ 200 = *400000*

2.
   12 ÷ 4 = *3*
   120 ÷ 4 = *30*
   1,200 ÷ 40 = *300*
   12,000 ÷ 40 = *3000*
   120,000 ÷ 400 = *30008*
   1,200,000 ÷ 400 = *300000*

3.
   10 ÷ 5 = *20*
   100 ÷ 5 = *200*
   1,000 ÷ 50 = *2000*
   10,000 ÷ 50 = *20000*
   100,000 ÷ 500 = *200000*
   1,000,000 ÷ 500 = *2000000*

4.
   63 ÷ 7 = *9*
   630 ÷ 7 = *90*
   6,300 ÷ 70 = *900*
   63,000 ÷ 70 = *9000*
   630,000 ÷ 700 = *9000*
   6,300,000 ÷ 700 = *900000*

Computation Station

Divide a four-digit number by a one-digit number.

$8\overline{)6{,}048}$	$8\overline{)6{,}048}$ $5\,6$ quotient 7	7 $8\overline{)6{,}048}$ $-5\,6$ $\overline{4\,4}$	$7\,5$ $8\overline{)6{,}048}$ $-5\,6$ $\overline{4\,4}$ $4\,0$	$7\,5$ $8\overline{)6{,}048}$ $-5\,6$ $\overline{4\,4}$ $-4\,0$ $\overline{4\,8}$	$7\,5\,6$ $8\overline{)6{,}048}$ $-5\,6$ $\overline{4\,4}$ $-4\,0$ $\overline{4\,8}$ $-4\,8$ $\overline{0}$
6 cannot be divided by 8, so look to the next digit. Think of a multiple of 8 that is near 60 but not greater than 60.	$8 \times 7 = 56$	Subtract 56 from 60. Bring 4 down next to the 4.	Now divide 44 by 8. $8 \times 5 = 40$	Subtract and bring down the 8.	Divide 48 by 8.

WRITE each quotient.

1. $3\overline{)105}$ quotient 035

2. $7\overline{)413}$ quotient 059

3. $4\overline{)388}$ quotient 097

4. $6\overline{)114}$ quotient 019

5. $8\overline{)4{,}480}$ quotient 0560

6. $2\overline{)1{,}838}$ quotient 0919

7. $9\overline{)3{,}429}$ quotient 0381

8. $3\overline{)2{,}262}$ quotient 0754

9. $5\overline{)40{,}355}$ quotient 08071

10. $4\overline{)29{,}372}$ quotient 07343

11. $7\overline{)11{,}536}$ quotient 01648

12. $8\overline{)36{,}736}$ quotient 04592

Last Number Standing

Sometimes a number is not divided evenly. A number left over that is smaller than the divisor is called the **remainder**.

7)3,755	5 7)3,755 −3 5 ⎯⎯ 2	53 7)3,755 −3 5 ⎯⎯ 25 −21 ⎯⎯ 4	536 7)3,755 −3 5 ⎯⎯ 25 −21 ⎯⎯ 45 −42 ⎯⎯ ③	536 r3 7)3,755 −3 5 ⎯⎯ 25 −21 ⎯⎯ 45 −42 ⎯⎯ 3
			3 cannot be divided by 7. It is the remainder.	The answer is written as 536 r3.

WRITE each quotient.

1. 8)649

2. 3)236

3. 2)117

4. 5)474

5. 6)3,227

6. 4)1,375

7. 7)5,613

8. 8)2,873

9. 7)68,576

10. 8)51,323

11. 5)43,871

12. 9)14,659

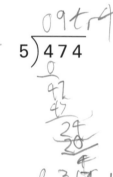
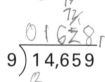

Computation Station

WRITE each quotient.

HINT: Try writing multiples of the divisor before you begin.

$$17\overline{)638}$$

$$\begin{array}{r} 3 \\ 17\overline{)638} \\ -51 \\ \hline 12 \end{array}$$

$$\begin{array}{r} 37 \\ 17\overline{)638} \\ -51 \\ \hline 128 \\ -119 \\ \hline 9 \end{array}$$

$$\begin{array}{r} 37\ r9 \\ 17\overline{)638} \\ -51 \\ \hline 128 \\ -119 \\ \hline 9 \end{array}$$

1. $$\begin{array}{r} 044 \\ 13\overline{)572} \\ 0 \\ \hline 57 \\ 52 \\ \hline 52 \\ 52 \\ \hline 0 \end{array}$$

2. $$\begin{array}{r} 017\ r\ 225 \\ 39\overline{)663} \\ 0 \\ \hline 66 \\ 31 \\ \hline 273 \\ 273 \\ \hline \end{array}$$

3. $$\begin{array}{r} 022 \\ 34\overline{)748} \\ 0 \\ \hline 74 \\ 68 \\ \hline 68 \\ 68 \\ \hline 0 \end{array}$$

4. $$\begin{array}{r} 039 \\ 21\overline{)819} \\ 0 \\ \hline 81 \\ 63 \\ \hline 189 \\ 189 \\ \hline 0 \end{array}$$

5. $$\begin{array}{r} 015\ r2 \\ 62\overline{)932} \\ 0 \\ \hline 93 \\ 62 \\ \hline 312 \\ 310 \\ \hline 2 \end{array}$$

6. $$\begin{array}{r} 071\ r\ l \\ 12\overline{)853} \\ 0 \\ \hline 85 \\ 84 \\ \hline 13 \\ 12 \\ \hline 1 \end{array}$$

7. $$\begin{array}{r} 021\ r8 \\ 17\overline{)365} \\ 0 \\ \hline 36 \\ 34 \\ \hline 25 \\ 17 \\ \hline 8 \end{array}$$

8. $$\begin{array}{r} 026\ r22 \\ 24\overline{)646} \\ 0 \\ \hline 64 \\ 48 \\ \hline 166 \\ 144 \\ \hline 22 \end{array}$$

9. $$\begin{array}{r} 034\ r5 \\ 26\overline{)889} \\ 0 \\ \hline 88 \\ 78 \\ \hline 109 \\ 104 \\ \hline 5 \end{array}$$

10. $$\begin{array}{r} 014\ r4 \\ 55\overline{)774} \\ 0 \\ \hline 77 \\ 55 \\ \hline 224 \\ 220 \\ \hline 4 \end{array}$$

11. $$\begin{array}{r} 027\ r26 \\ 33\overline{)917} \\ 0 \\ \hline 91 \\ 66 \\ \hline 257 \\ 231 \\ \hline 26 \end{array}$$

12. $$\begin{array}{r} 013\ r14 \\ 45\overline{)599} \\ 0 \\ \hline 59 \\ 45 \\ \hline 149 \\ 135 \\ \hline 14 \end{array}$$

Multidigit Division

Computation Station

WRITE each quotient.

| $25\overline{)5{,}429}$ | $\begin{array}{r} 2 \\ 25\overline{)5{,}429} \\ -50 \\ \hline 4 \end{array}$ | $\begin{array}{r} 21 \\ 25\overline{)5{,}429} \\ -50 \\ \hline 42 \\ -25 \\ \hline 17 \end{array}$ | $\begin{array}{r} 217 \\ 25\overline{)5{,}429} \\ -50 \\ \hline 42 \\ -25 \\ \hline 179 \\ -175 \\ \hline 4 \end{array}$ | $\begin{array}{r} 217 \text{ r4} \\ 25\overline{)5{,}429} \\ -50 \\ \hline 42 \\ -25 \\ \hline 179 \\ -175 \\ \hline 4 \end{array}$ |

1. $\overset{177}{20\overline{)3{,}540}}$

2. $\overset{486}{16\overline{)7{,}776}}$

3. $\overset{113}{43\overline{)4{,}859}}$

4. $\overset{212}{32\overline{)6{,}784}}$

5. $\overset{226 \text{ r2}}{41\overline{)9{,}268}}$

6. $\overset{304\text{r5}}{23\overline{)6{,}997}}$

7. $\overset{184 \text{ r8}}{54\overline{)9{,}944}}$

8. $\overset{425\text{r4}}{19\overline{)8{,}079}}$

9. $\overset{326\text{r3}}{24\overline{)7{,}827}}$

10. $\overset{135\text{r6}}{13\overline{)1{,}761}}$

11. $\overset{194\text{r12}}{33\overline{)6{,}414}}$

12. $\overset{367\text{r11}}{27\overline{)9{,}920}}$

Computation Station

WRITE each quotient.

	1	1,7	1,70	1,707	1,707 r11
46)78,533	46)78,533 −46 32	46)78,533 −46 325 −322 3	46)78,533 −46 325 −322 33 −0 33	46)78,533 −46 325 −322 33 −0 333	46)78,533 −46 325 −322 33 −0 333 −322 11

1. 30)38,430   *1281*

2. 14)23,618   *1687*

3. 22)50,952   *2316*

4. 39)49,257   *1263*

5. 28)96,938   *3462 r2*

6. 42)67,124   *1598 r8*

7. 51)52,502   *1029 r23*

8. 18)15,346   *852 r40*

9. 12)28,783   *2398 r7*

10. 33)46,352   *1404 r20*

11. 74)87,651   *1184 r35*

12. 55)78,993   *1436 r13*

Safe Speeds

WRITE the answers.

HINT: Divide the number of miles by the number of hours.

If a car always travels at the same speed, how many miles per hour is it traveling?

1. 60 miles in 2 hours = _____30_____ miles per hour

2. 132 miles in 3 hours = _____44_____ miles per hour

3. 435 miles in 15 hours = _____29_____ miles per hour

4. 576 miles in 24 hours = _____24_____ miles per hour

5. 1,040 miles in 20 hours = _____52_____ miles per hour

6. 1,098 miles in 18 hours = _____61_____ miles per hour

7. 1,344 miles in 32 hours = _____42_____ miles per hour

8. 2,688 miles in 48 hours = _____56_____ miles per hour

9. 3,575 miles in 65 hours = _____55_____ miles per hour

10. 5,785 miles in 89 hours = _____65_____ miles per hour

11. 5,278 miles in 91 hours = _____58_____ miles per hour

12. 3,663 miles in 99 hours = _____37_____ miles per hour

Rounding Estimates

Rounding numbers can help you estimate a quotient. With division, think about how you can round the dividend and divisor to make a problem that you can do in your head.

$4{,}264 \div 13 =$ To estimate, think about basic division facts.
You know $45 \div 15 = 3$, so estimate this problem by rounding the dividend to 4,500 and the divisor to 15.
$4{,}500 \div 15 = 300$
The answer is around 300.
$4{,}264 \div 13 = 328$

$4{,}792 \div 63 =$ $48 \div 6 = 8$
$4{,}800 \div 60 = 80$
The answer is around 80.
$4792 \div 63 = 76 \ r4$

ESTIMATE each quotient by rounding and then dividing. WRITE the actual quotient to check your estimate.

1.
$$5\overline{)97}$$
      $5 \div 100 = 20$
        19
        5
        47
        45
        3

2.
$$6\overline{)5{,}415}$$
      $6 \div 5400 = 900$
        0902
        0
        54
        54
        06
        15
        12
        3

3.
$$11\overline{)408}$$
      $10 \div 400 = 40$
        031
        0
        40
        33
        78
        77
        1

4.
$$67\overline{)2{,}079}$$
      $7100 \div 7000 = 030,20$
        0031
        0
        28
        207
        201
        69
        67
        3|41 r)2

5.
$$82\overline{)55{,}691}$$
      $80 \div 56000 = 70000$
        0679
        0
        556
        492
        0649
        574

6.
$$29\overline{)91{,}101}$$
      $30 \div 90,000 = 3000$
        3|41 r)2
        87
        1

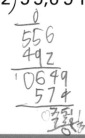

The Mighty Marlock

The Mighty Marlock will guess any quotient, but he sometimes guesses incorrectly.
ESTIMATE each quotient, and CROSS OUT any quotient that is clearly wrong.

$827 \div 4 = 206\ r3$

$75{,}733 \div 26 = 2{,}912\ r21$

$637 \div 88 = 45\ r2$

$4{,}954 \div 51 = 212\ r6$

$12{,}275 \div 38 = 4{,}323\ r1$

$3{,}569 \div 9 = 396\ r5$

Pathfinder

A **prime number** can only be divided evenly by itself and one. A **composite number** has more factors than itself and one.

Example: 13 is a prime number. The only factors of 13 are 1 and 13.

12 is a composite number. The factors of 12 are 1, 2, 3, 4, 6, and 12.

BEGIN at Start. FOLLOW the arrows. When you get to a box with two arrows, CHOOSE the box with a prime number. If you make all the right choices, you'll end up at Finish.

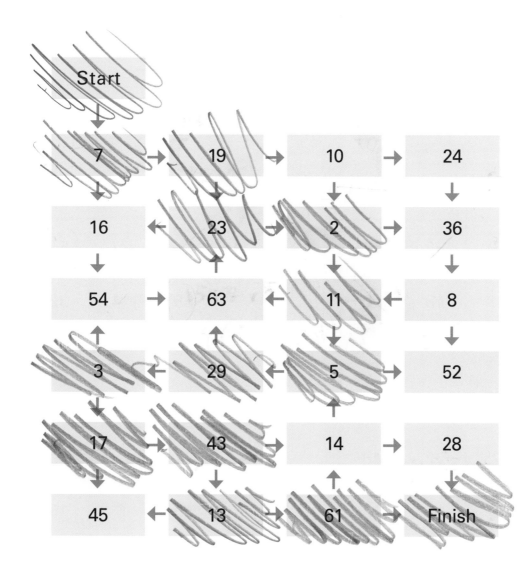

Prime & Composite

Tic-Tac-Toe

CIRCLE each composite number. PUT an X through any prime number. DRAW a line when you find three composite numbers in a row. The line can go across, down, or diagonally.

Example:

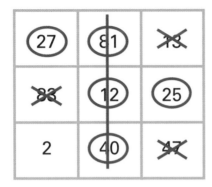

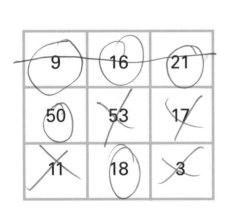

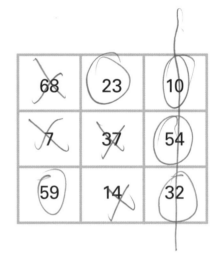

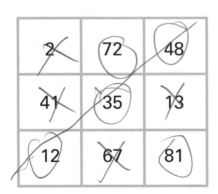

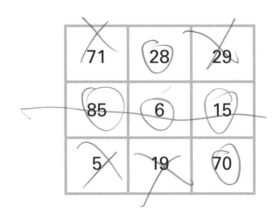

Find Your Place

A **decimal point** separates the part of the number that is one or greater than one from the part of the number that is less than one. IDENTIFY the place of each digit. Then WRITE the digit.

Example:

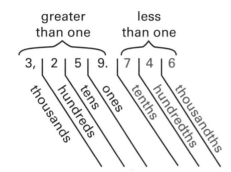

1. 7,361.248

7	thousands
3	hundreds
6	tens
1	ones
2	tenths
4	hundredths
8	thousandths

2. 9,482.156

9	thousands
4	hundreds
8	tens
2	ones
1	tenths
5	hundredths
6	thousandths

3. 3,024.817

3	thousands
0	hundreds
2	tens
4	ones
8	tenths
1	hundredths
7	thousandths

4. 8,210.539

8	thousands
2	hundreds
1	tens
0	ones
5	tenths
3 9	hundredths
9	thousandths

5. 4,194.682

4	thousands
1	hundreds
9	tens
4	ones
6	tenths
8	hundredths
2	thousandths

6. 1,576.041

1	thousands
5	hundreds
7	tens
6	ones
0	tenths
4	hundredths
1	thousandths

Place Value

High Fives

FIND the 5 in each number. WRITE the place of each 5.

1. 9,529.697 _____hundredths_____ place

2. 6,339.548 _____tenths_____ place

3. 3,068.195 _____hundredths_____ place

4. 7,915.403 _____ones_____ place

5. 5,209.821 _____thousends_____ place

6. 8,344.254 _____hundredths_____ place

7. 2,653.717 _____tens_____ place

8. 1,994.576 _____tenths_____ place

9. 4,587.014 _____hundreds_____ place

10. 6,772.825 _____hundredths_____ place

Getting Bigger

Line up decimals when comparing numbers, and look at the size of the numbers of each place working left to right.

Example:

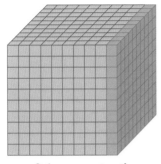 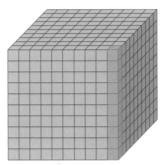 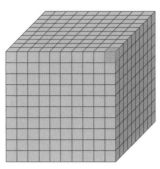

| 0.1 or one tenth | 0.01 or one hundredth | 0.001 or one thousandth |

0.1 is bigger than 0.01, which is bigger than 0.001.

WRITE the numbers from smallest to biggest.

1. 5.279   4.914

    4.914   4.952

    5.836   5.279

    4.952   5.836

2. 7.156   7.156

    8.442   7.159

    7.159   7.671

    7.671   8.442

3. 0.694   0.482

    0.617   0.533

    0.482   0.617

    0.533   0.694

4. 1.208   1.208

    1.265   1.228

    1.228   1.232

    1.232   1.265

5. 4.006   4.003

    4.014   4.006

    4.053   4.014

    4.003   4.053

6. 0.932   0.239

    0.322   0.322

    0.329   0.329

    0.239   0.932

Matched or Mismatched?

COMPARE each pair of decimals, and WRITE >, <, or = in the box.

Example: 0.56 < 0.71

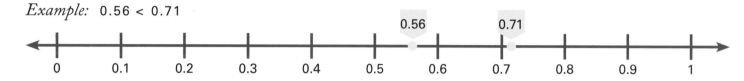

0.6 **>** 0.3

1

0.4 **=** 0.4

2

1.9 **>** 0.8

3

3.5 **<** 5.3

4

6.03 **<** 7.2

5

3.92 **>** 2.1

6

4.3 **<** 4.65

7

1.52 **<** 1.8

8

1.39 **>** 0.21

9

5.04 **<** 6.33

10

7.72 **=** 7.72

11

0.37 **>** 0.25

12

0.292 **≠** 0.45

13

9.832 **>** 9.75

14

6.402 **>** 6.02

15

3.114 **<** 3.54

16

7.675 **<** 7.933

17

5.118 **>** 5.102

18

8.234 **<** 8.247

19

4.593 **=** 4.593

20

Round About

Rounding makes numbers easier to work with.

Numbers that end in 0.001 through 0.499 get rounded **down** to the nearest one.

Numbers that end in 0.5 through 0.999 get rounded **up** to the nearest one.

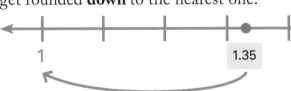
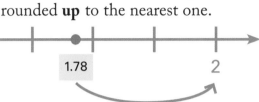

ROUND each number to the nearest one.

1. 1.2   _1_

2. 8.6   _9_

3. 6.1   _6_

4. 3.7   _4_

5. 4.9   _5_

6. 3.5   _4_

7. 5.4   _5_

8. 9.8   _10_

9. 2.63   _3_

10. 9.24   _9_

11. 0.47   _0_

12. 7.96   _8_

13. 6.104 _6_

14. 2.859 _3_

15. 0.621 _1_

16. 7.482 _7_

Cash Crunch

WRITE the decimal for each picture. Then ROUND to the nearest dollar.

1.

$ __11.79__ $ __12.00__

2.

$ __3.12__ $ __3__

3.

$ __9.85__ $ __10__

4.

$ __20.28__ $ __20__

5.

$ __5.41__ $ __5__

6.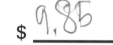

$ __10.50__ $ __11__

Round About

When rounding, look at the digit to the right of the place you're rounding to. If that digit is less than 5, round down. If it is 5 or greater, round up.

Example:

3.43 rounded to the nearest tenth is 3.4.

3.48 rounded to the nearest tenth is 3.5.

7.282 rounded to the nearest hundredth is 7.28.

7.286 rounded to the nearest hundredth is 7.29.

ROUND each number to the nearest tenth.

1. 2.23   _2.2_

2. 5.67   _5.7_

3. 8.18   _8.2_

4. 1.84   _1.8_

5. 3.29   _3.3_

6. 7.71   _7.7_

7. 4.05   _4.1_

8. 0.02   _0.0_

ROUND each number to the nearest hundredth.

9. 9.549   _9.55_

10. 4.477   _4.48_

11. 1.915   _1.92_

12. 4.534   _4.53_

13. 2.382   _2.38_

14. 5.174   _5.17_

15. 3.086   _3.09_

16. 6.903   _6.90_

Rounding Decimals

Rather Rounded

ROUND each number to the nearest one, tenth, and hundredth.

	Nearest One	Nearest Tenth	Nearest Hundredth
25.158	25	25.2	25.16
1.372	1	1.4	1.37
83.614	84	83.6	83.61
390.293	390	390.3	390.29
7.872	8	7.9	7.87
14.426	14	14.4	14.43
5.555	6	5.6	5.56
0.307	0	0.3	0.31

Cash Crunch

ADD or SUBTRACT the dollar amounts.

Example:

$21.25
+ 5.62
$26.87

1. $ 7.14
    + 2.62
    $ 9.76

2. $ 20.03
    + 9.52
    $ 29.55

3. $ 56.31
    + 31.17
    $ 87.48

4. $ 34.02
    + 24.23
    $ 58.75

5. $171.66
    + 18.21
    $189.87

6. $521.40
    +454.23
    $ 975.63

7. $ 8.79
    − 3.48
    $ 5.31

8. $ 64.29
    − 2.06
    $ 62.25

9. $ 56.97
    − 11.95
    $ 45.02

10. $ 37.47
    − 13.03
    $ 29.44

11. $584.97
    − 73.07
    $511.90

12. $668.88
    −431.31
    $237.57

Adding & Subtracting Decimals

It All Adds Up

When adding decimals, add and regroup as you normally would, keeping the decimal between the ones place and the tenths place.

36.274 $+ 18.85$ _____ 4	$\overset{1}{3}6.274$ $+ 18.85$ _____ 24	$\overset{1\ 1}{3}6.274$ $+ 18.85$ _____ $.124$	$\overset{1\ 1\ 1}{3}6.274$ $+ 18.85$ _____ 5.124	$\overset{1\ 1\ 1}{3}6.274$ $+ 18.85$ _____ 55.124
Add the thousandths. Think of this as $4 + 0 = 4$.	Add the hundredths. $7 + 5 = 12$	Add the tenths. $1 + 2 + 8 = 11$	Add the ones. $1 + 6 + 8 = 15$	Add the tens. $1 + 3 + 1 = 5$

WRITE the sum.

1.
$\quad 6.7$
$+ 2.8$
$\overline{9.5}$

2.
$\quad 8.92$
$+ 2.7$
$\overline{11.62}$

3.
$\quad 36.35$
$+ \quad 4.49$
$\overline{40.84}$

4.
$\quad 52.9$
$+ 34.12$
$\overline{87.02}$

5.
$\quad 48.28$
$+ 60.27$
$\overline{108.55}$

6.
$\quad 91.257$
$+ 14.13$
$\overline{105.387}$

7.
$\quad 121.98$
$+ \quad 29.577$
$\overline{151.557}$

8.
$\quad 455.91$
$+ 219.40$
$\overline{675.31}$

9.
$\quad 779.04$
$+ 587.8$
$\overline{1366.84}$

10.
$\quad 494.292$
$+ 244.07$
$\overline{938.362}$

11.
$\quad 2,717.152$
$+ \quad 213.23$
$\overline{2,930.382}$

12.
$\quad 8,212.67$
$+ 1,831.75$
$\overline{10,044.42}$

What's the Difference?

When subtracting decimals, subtract and regroup as you normally would, keeping the decimal between the ones place and the tenths place.

⁵¹⁷ 4 4 1.6̷7̷ − 2 6 2.4 9 ――――― 8	⁵¹⁷ 4 4 1.6̷7̷ − 2 6 2.4 9 ――――― 1 8	³¹¹ ⁵¹⁷ 4 4 1̷.6̷7̷ − 2 6 2.4 9 ――――― 9.1 8	³¹³¹¹ ⁵¹⁷ 4 4̷ 1̷.6̷7̷ − 2 6 2.4 9 ――――― 7 9.1 8	³¹³¹¹ ⁵¹⁷ 4̷ 4̷ 1̷.6̷7̷ − 2 6 2.4 9 ――――― 1 7 9.1 8
Subtract the hundredths. 17 − 9 = 8	Subtract the tenths. 5 − 4 = 1	Subtract the ones. 11 − 2 = 9	Subtract the tens. 13 − 6 = 7	Subtract the hundreds. 3 − 2 = 1

WRITE each difference.

1.
$$
\begin{array}{r}
^{7\ ^{1}2}\ \ \\
8.\!\!\!/2 \\
-\ 4.8 \\
\hline
3.4
\end{array}
$$

2.
$$
\begin{array}{r}
^{7\ ^{1}3}\ \\
9.8\!\!\!/3 \\
-\ 7.05 \\
\hline
16.78
\end{array}
$$

3.
$$
\begin{array}{r}
^{5\ ^{1}_{\!+\!2}12}\ \\
6\!\!\!/0.2\!\!\!/6 \\
-\ \ 1.3 \\
\hline
58.96
\end{array}
$$

4.
$$
\begin{array}{r}
^{15}\\
^{3_{+6}14}\ \\
46.491 \\
-\ 28.56 \\
\hline
17.931
\end{array}
$$

5.
$$
\begin{array}{r}
^{14}\\
^{8_{+5}\ 10}\ \\
79.5\!\!\!/0 \\
-\ 30.99 \\
\hline
48.51
\end{array}
$$

6.
$$
\begin{array}{r}
^{9\ 11}\\
^{4_{+2\ +2}11}\ \\
550.21 \\
-\ 14.74 \\
\hline
535.47
\end{array}
$$

7.
$$
\begin{array}{r}
^{5\ 12}\ \\
96\!\!\!/2.97 \\
-\ 208.6 \\
\hline
754.37
\end{array}
$$

8.
$$
\begin{array}{r}
^{12}\\
^{5_{+3}14}\ \\
16\!\!\!/3.469 \\
-\ 135.82 \\
\hline
027.649
\end{array}
$$

9.
$$
\begin{array}{r}
^{4\ 11}\ \\
79\!\!\!/5.1\!\!\!/8 \\
-\ 323.62 \\
\hline
471.56
\end{array}
$$

10.
$$
\begin{array}{r}
^{7\ 17\ 6\ 11}\ \\
8\!\!\!/7\!\!\!/7.1\!\!\!/8 8 \\
-\ 293.94 \\
\hline
583.248
\end{array}
$$

11.
$$
\begin{array}{r}
^{13\ 13\ 14\ 14}\\
^{3_{3\ +4\ +4\ +5}13}\ \\
4,445.53 \\
-\ 2,465.75 \\
\hline
1,979.78
\end{array}
$$

12.
$$
\begin{array}{r}
^{9\ 11}\\
^{8_{+0\ +2}10\ 9\ 10}\ \\
9,020.9\!\!\!/0 \\
-\ 1,252.75 \\
\hline
7,768.15
\end{array}
$$

Adding & Subtracting Decimals

Round About

Rounding numbers can help you estimate a sum or difference.

$$
\begin{array}{r}
5.93 \\
- 2.16 \\
\hline
\end{array}
\quad\longrightarrow\quad
\begin{array}{r}
6 \\
- 2 \\
\hline
4
\end{array}
$$

5.93 rounded to the nearest one is 6.

2.16 rounded to the nearest one is 2.

6 − 2 = 4

5.93 − 2.16 = 3.77

ESTIMATE each answer by rounding to the first digit and and then adding or subtracting. WRITE the actual sum or difference to check your estimate.

1.
$$
\begin{array}{r}
3.42 \\
+ 5.6 \\
\hline
9.02
\end{array}
\qquad
\begin{array}{r}
3.00 \\
+ 6.00 \\
\hline
9
\end{array}
$$

2.
$$
\begin{array}{r}
1.84 \\
+ 4.95 \\
\hline
6.79
\end{array}
\qquad
\begin{array}{r}
2 \\
+ 5 \\
\hline
7
\end{array}
$$

3.
$$
\begin{array}{r}
4.068 \\
+ 6.75 \\
\hline
10.818
\end{array}
\qquad
\begin{array}{r}
4 \\
+ 7 \\
\hline
11
\end{array}
$$

4.
$$
\begin{array}{r}
6.17 \\
- 2.9 \\
\hline
3.27
\end{array}
\qquad
\begin{array}{r}
6 \\
- 3 \\
\hline
3
\end{array}
$$

5.
$$
\begin{array}{r}
9.81 \\
- 5.66 \\
\hline
4.15
\end{array}
\qquad
\begin{array}{r}
10 \\
- 6 \\
\hline
4
\end{array}
$$

6.
$$
\begin{array}{r}
12.691 \\
- 4.32 \\
\hline
8.371
\end{array}
\qquad
\begin{array}{r}
13 \\
- 4 \\
\hline
9
\end{array}
$$

Computation Station

When multiplying decimals, you do not need to line up the decimal points. When writing the product, count how many digits there are to the right of the decimal points in the factors. Then count that many places from the right in the product, and insert the decimal point.

```
  4 1
  4.5 2
×   3.9
───────
  4 0 6 8
```

```
    1
  4.5 2
×   3.9
───────
  4 0 6 8
1 3 5 6 0
```

```
  4.5 2
×   3.9
───────
    4 0 6 8
+ 1 3 5 6 0
───────────
  1 7 6 2 8
```

```
  4.5 2
×   3.9
───────
    4 0 6 8
+ 1 3 5 6 0
───────────
  1 7.6 2 8
```

Solve the problem the same way you would if there were no decimal points.

In the factors, there are a total of three digits to the right of the decimal. Put a decimal point in the product three places from the right.

WRITE each product.

1.
$$\begin{array}{r} 1.9 \\ \times\ \ 7 \\ \hline \end{array}$$
13.3

2.
$$\begin{array}{r} 7.3 \\ \times\ \ 5 \\ \hline \end{array}$$
36.5

3.
$$\begin{array}{r} 8.63 \\ \times\ \ 3 \\ \hline \end{array}$$
25.89

4.
$$\begin{array}{r} 2.7 \\ \times\ 46 \\ \hline \end{array}$$
124.2

5.
$$\begin{array}{r} 9.6 \\ \times\ 2.2 \\ \hline \end{array}$$
21.12

6.
$$\begin{array}{r} 6.7 \\ \times\ 8.4 \\ \hline \end{array}$$
56.28

7.
$$\begin{array}{r} 5.1 \\ \times\ 3.8 \\ \hline \end{array}$$
19.38

8.
$$\begin{array}{r} 7.5 \\ \times\ 1.3 \\ \hline \end{array}$$
9.75

9.
$$\begin{array}{r} 3.8 3 \\ \times\ \ 4.9 \\ \hline \end{array}$$
18.767

10.
$$\begin{array}{r} 1.7 6 \\ \times\ \ 0.2 \\ \hline \end{array}$$
0.352

11.
$$\begin{array}{r} 8.1 6 \\ \times\ \ 5.4 \\ \hline \end{array}$$
44.064

12.
$$\begin{array}{r} 9.22 \\ \times\ 6.5 \\ \hline \end{array}$$
59.93

Multiplying & Dividing Decimals

Computation Station

When dividing decimals, line up the decimal point in the quotient with the same place in the dividend.

$$
\begin{array}{r}
21\overline{)7.476}
\end{array}
\qquad
\begin{array}{r}
3 \\
21\overline{)7.476} \\
-63 \\
\hline
11
\end{array}
\qquad
\begin{array}{r}
35 \\
21\overline{)7.476} \\
-63 \\
\hline
117 \\
-105 \\
\hline
12
\end{array}
\qquad
\begin{array}{r}
356 \\
21\overline{)7.476} \\
-63 \\
\hline
117 \\
-105 \\
\hline
126 \\
-126 \\
\hline
0
\end{array}
\qquad
\begin{array}{r}
0.356 \\
21\overline{)7.476} \\
-63 \\
\hline
117 \\
-105 \\
\hline
126 \\
-126 \\
\hline
0
\end{array}
$$

Solve the problem the same way you would if there were no decimal points.

Put a decimal point in the quotient aligned with the one in the dividend. If there is no digit to the left of the decimal point, add a zero.

WRITE each quotient.

1. $9\overline{)6.3}$ quotient: 0.7

2. $6\overline{)2.4}$ quotient: 0.4

3. $5\overline{)8.35}$ quotient: 1.67

4. $3\overline{)9.81}$ quotient: 3.27

5. $8\overline{)23.28}$ quotient: 02.11

6. $4\overline{)17.28}$ quotient: 04.32

7. $2\overline{)6.234}$ quotient: 3.117

8. $4\overline{)2.296}$ quotient: 0.574

9. $11\overline{)64.46}$ quotient: 05.86

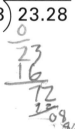

10. $25\overline{)86.25}$ quotient: 03.45

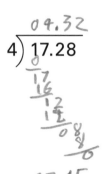

11. $15\overline{)3.945}$ quotient: 0.263

12. $41\overline{)7.134}$ quotient: 0.174

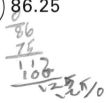

Rounding Estimates

Rounding numbers can help you estimate a product or quotient.

$$
\begin{array}{r}
8.\ 8\ 4 \\
\times\quad 7.\ 3 \\
\end{array}
\longrightarrow
\begin{array}{r}
9 \\
\times\ 7 \\
\hline
6\ 3 \\
\end{array}
$$

8.84 rounded to the nearest one is 9.
7.3 rounded to the nearest one is 7.
$9 \times 7 = 63$
$8.84 \times 7.3 = 64.532$

$3.684 \div 12 =$	Look for a convenient way to round the numbers so that you can use basic facts. Think $36 \div 12 = 3$.	$3.600 \div 12 = 0.300$ The answer is around 0.3. $3.684 \div 12 = 0.307$

ROUND the numbers to estimate each product. WRITE the estimate.

1. 4.2×6.9

   $\underline{4} \times \underline{7} = \underline{28}$

2. 3.8×3.8

   $\underline{4} \times \underline{4} = \underline{16}$

3. 5.106×8.3

   $\underline{5} \times \underline{8} = \underline{40}$

4. 2.94×40.3

   $\underline{3} \times \underline{40} = \underline{120}$

5. 4.281×10.925

   $\underline{4} \times \underline{11} = \underline{44}$

6. 9.237×8.886

   $\underline{9} \times \underline{9} = \underline{81}$

ROUND the numbers to estimate each quotient. WRITE the estimate.

7. $5.9 \div 6$

   $\underline{6} \div \underline{6} = \underline{1}$

8. $4.9 \div 8$

   $\underline{5} \div \underline{8} = \underline{0.6}$

9. $9.288 \div 3$

   $\underline{9} \div \underline{3} = \underline{3}$

10. $1.244 \div 6$

    $\underline{1} \div \underline{6} = \underline{6}$

11. $4.462 \div 5$

    $\underline{4} \div \underline{5} = \underline{0.9}$

12. $109.78 \div 11$

    $\underline{100} \div \underline{10} = \underline{10}$

The Powers of Ten

Notice the movement of the decimal point as numbers are multiplied and divided by multiples of ten.

3.514 × 10 = 35.14	3.514 → 35.14	When multiplying by 10, move the decimal point one place to the right.
3.514 × 100 = 351.4	3.514 → 351.4	When multiplying by 100, move the decimal point two places to the right.
3.514 × 1000 = 3514	3.514 → 3,514	When multiplying by 1,000, move the decimal point three places to the right.
3514 ÷ 10 = 351.4	3514 → 351.4	When dividing by 10, move the decimal point one place to the left.
3514 ÷ 100 = 35.14	3514 → 35.14	When dividing by 100, move the decimal point two places to the left.
3514 ÷ 100 = 3.514	3514 → 3.514	When dividing by 1,000, move the decimal point three places to the left.

WRITE each product.

1. 4.51 × 10 = _____ 45.1

2. 1.983 × 10 = _____ 19.83

3. 7.242 × 100 = _____ 724.2

4. 0.603 × 100 = _____ 60.3

5. 8.599 × 1,000 = _____ 8599

6. 4.217 × 1,000 = _____ 4217

WRITE each quotient.

7. 3.6 ÷ 10 = _____ 0.36

8. 77.38 ÷ 10 = _____ 7.738

9. 936.6 ÷ 100 = _____ 9.366

10. 54,103 ÷ 100 = _____ 541.03

11. 38,249 ÷ 1,000 = _____ 38.249

12. 572 ÷ 1,000 = _____ 0.572

Any Way You Slice It

WRITE the fraction for each picture.

Example:

4 ← The **numerator** represents the number of shaded sections.

9 ← The **denominator** represents the total number of sections.

$\frac{1}{6}$

1

$\frac{5}{8}$

2

$\frac{3}{4}$

3

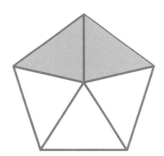

$\frac{2}{5}$

4

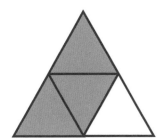

$\frac{7}{8}$

5

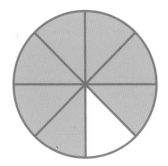

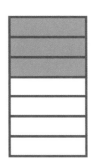

$\frac{3}{7}$

6

7. Which two fractions have the same numerator? $\frac{3}{7}$ $\frac{3}{4}$

8. Which two fractions have the same denominator? $\frac{5}{8}$ $\frac{7}{8}$

Color Sets

COLOR each set of shapes to match the fraction.

Example:

$$\frac{3}{5}$$ ← The **numerator** represents the number of colored objects.

← The **denominator** represents the total number of objects.

1. $\frac{2}{9}$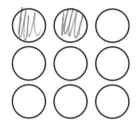

2. $\frac{5}{6}$

3. $\frac{4}{7}$

4. $\frac{3}{10}$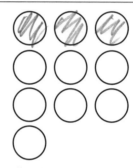

5. $\frac{6}{7}$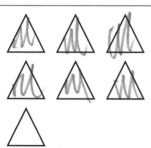

6. $\frac{2}{5}$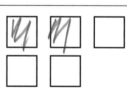

7. Which two fractions have the same numerator?

8. Which two fractions have the same denominator?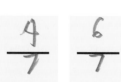

Circle the Same

Equivalent fractions are fractions that have the same value.

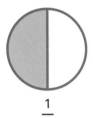 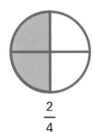 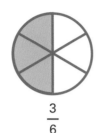

$\frac{1}{2}$ $\frac{2}{4}$ $\frac{3}{6}$

These fractions are different, but the same amount is shaded.

They are equivalent: All are equal to $\frac{1}{2}$ of the circle.

CIRCLE the fraction in each row that is equivalent to the first fraction.

1.  $\frac{1}{3}$  $\frac{2}{4}$  $\frac{3}{7}$  $\frac{3}{9}$

2.  $\frac{9}{12}$ 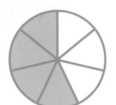 $\frac{4}{7}$ 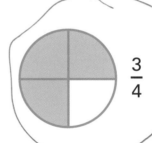 $\frac{3}{4}$ $\frac{4}{6}$

3. 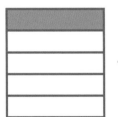 $\frac{1}{5}$ 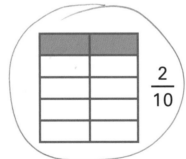 $\frac{2}{10}$ $\frac{3}{9}$ $\frac{3}{8}$

4. 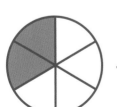 $\frac{2}{6}$ $\frac{2}{7}$  $\frac{1}{3}$ 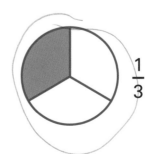 $\frac{4}{9}$

Slicing and Dicing

WRITE the numerator to make a fraction equivalent to the first fraction. Then COLOR the pictures to match the fractions.

HINT: When you color the fractions, they should show the same shaded amount.

Example: $\frac{1}{2}$

If you multiply the same number to the numerator and denominator, the new fraction will be equivalent.

$\frac{2}{4}$

$$\frac{1}{2} \times \frac{2}{2} = \frac{2}{4} \qquad \frac{1}{2} \text{ is equivalent to } \frac{2}{4}.$$

1. 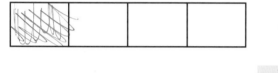 $\frac{1}{4}$

$\frac{2}{8}$

2.  $\frac{2}{3}$

$\frac{6}{9}$

3. 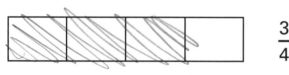 $\frac{3}{4}$

$\frac{9}{12}$

4.  $\frac{2}{5}$

$\frac{4}{10}$

5.  $\frac{1}{3}$

$\frac{2}{6}$

6. 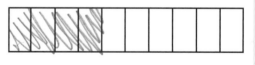 $\frac{1}{2}$

$\frac{5}{10}$

Slicing and Dicing

A fraction is in its **simplest form** if the only common factor of the numerator and the denominator is 1.

Example: $\dfrac{8}{12}$

The common factors of 8 and 12 are 1, 2, and 4. Divide the numerator and the denominator by the greatest common factor, 4.

$\dfrac{2}{3}$

$\dfrac{8 \div 4}{12 \div 4} = \dfrac{2}{3}$ The simplest form of $\dfrac{8}{12}$ is $\dfrac{2}{3}$.

The only common factor of 2 and 3 is 1.

WRITE the fraction in its simplest form. Then COLOR the pictures to match the fractions.

HINT: When you color the fractions, they should show the same shaded amount.

1.
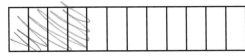

$\dfrac{3}{9}$

$\dfrac{1}{3}$

2.
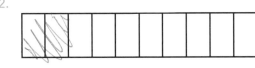

$\dfrac{2}{10}$

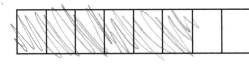

$\dfrac{1}{5}$

3.

$\dfrac{4}{12}$

$\dfrac{1}{3}$

4.

$\dfrac{6}{8}$

$\dfrac{3}{4}$

5.

$\dfrac{3}{6}$

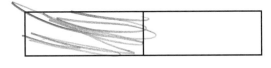

$\dfrac{1}{2}$

6.
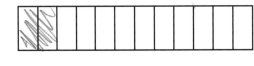

$\dfrac{2}{12}$

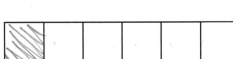

$\dfrac{1}{6}$

Simplifying Fractions

Simply Simplify

WRITE each fraction in its simplest form.

1. $\dfrac{4}{6}$ $\dfrac{2}{3}$

2. $\dfrac{9}{18}$ $\dfrac{1}{2}$

3. $\dfrac{5}{15}$ $\dfrac{1}{3}$

4. $\dfrac{2}{8}$ $\dfrac{1}{4}$

5. $\dfrac{8}{20}$ $\dfrac{2}{5}$

6. $\dfrac{12}{16}$ $\dfrac{3}{4}$

7. $\dfrac{10}{12}$ $\dfrac{5}{6}$

8. $\dfrac{20}{45}$ $\dfrac{4}{9}$

9. $\dfrac{28}{32}$ $\dfrac{7}{8}$

10. $\dfrac{24}{40}$ $\dfrac{3}{5}$

11. $\dfrac{36}{63}$ $\dfrac{4}{7}$

12. $\dfrac{72}{80}$ $\dfrac{9}{10}$

Prim and Proper

An **improper fraction** is a fraction with a numerator larger than its denominator. The simplest form of an improper fraction is called a **mixed number**. WRITE the mixed number for each fraction.

Example:

$$\frac{8}{5} = 1\frac{3}{5}$$

$$\frac{5}{5} = 1$$

$$\frac{3}{5}$$

$$\frac{13}{7}$$ $1\frac{6}{7}$

1

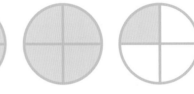

$$\frac{9}{4}$$ $2\frac{1}{4}$

2

$$\frac{13}{9}$$ $1\frac{4}{9}$

3

$$\frac{12}{5}$$ $2\frac{2}{5}$

4

$$\frac{7}{2}$$ $3\frac{1}{2}$

5

$$\frac{29}{8}$$ $3\frac{5}{8}$

6

Improper Fractions & Mixed Numbers

Mix Masters

WRITE the mixed number for each fraction.

To find the mixed number, think of $\frac{31}{5}$ as a way of saying $31 \div 5$.

$$5\overline{)31} \quad 6\text{ r}1$$
$$-30$$
$$1$$

$$1 \div 5 = \frac{1}{5}$$

$$\frac{31}{5} = 6\text{ r}1 = 6\frac{1}{5}$$

1. $\frac{11}{4}$ $2\frac{3}{4}$

2. $\frac{24}{5}$ $4\frac{4}{5}$

3. $\frac{19}{3}$ $6\frac{1}{3}$

4. $\frac{9}{2}$ $4\frac{1}{2}$

5. $\frac{52}{7}$ $7\frac{3}{7}$

6. $\frac{11}{10}$ $1\frac{1}{10}$

7. $\frac{65}{6}$ $10\frac{5}{6}$

8. $\frac{43}{8}$ $5\frac{3}{8}$

9. $\frac{23}{3}$ $7\frac{2}{3}$

10. $\frac{31}{9}$ $3\frac{4}{9}$

11. $\frac{57}{5}$ $11\frac{2}{5}$

12. $\frac{43}{12}$ $3\frac{7}{12}$

Unmixed

When changing a mixed number into an improper fraction, the denominator stays the same. You need to find the numerator. WRITE the improper fraction for each mixed number.

$3\frac{4}{5}$	3 is like having $\frac{5}{5}$ three times, plus $\frac{4}{5}$ left over. Multiply 3 by 5. Then add the 4, which is in the numerator already. $3 \times 5 = 15$ $15 + 4 = 19$	The improper fraction for $3\frac{4}{5}$ is $\frac{19}{5}$.

1. $8\frac{1}{2}$ $\frac{17}{2}$

2. $2\frac{1}{6}$ $\frac{13}{6}$

3. $7\frac{3}{4}$ $\frac{31}{4}$

4. $3\frac{2}{3}$ $\frac{11}{3}$

5. $10\frac{2}{9}$ $\frac{92}{9}$

6. $4\frac{1}{6}$ $\frac{25}{6}$

7. $5\frac{3}{8}$ $\frac{43}{8}$

8. $6\frac{2}{5}$ $\frac{32}{5}$

9. $3\frac{1}{11}$ $\frac{34}{11}$

10. $9\frac{1}{4}$ $\frac{37}{4}$

11. $4\frac{4}{10}$ $\frac{44}{10}$

12. $8\frac{7}{9}$ $\frac{79}{9}$

Improper Fractions & Mixed Numbers

Odd One Out

CROSS OUT the fraction or mixed number in each row that is not equivalent.

1.

$2\dfrac{1}{5}$ $\dfrac{11}{5}$ $1\dfrac{2}{5}$ $\dfrac{22}{10}$

2.

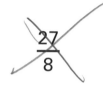 $\dfrac{27}{8}$ $4\dfrac{1}{4}$ $\dfrac{17}{4}$ $4\dfrac{2}{8}$

3.

$\dfrac{5}{3}$ $\dfrac{10}{3}$ $1\dfrac{2}{3}$ $\dfrac{10}{6}$

4.

$2\dfrac{3}{10}$ $\dfrac{61}{10}$ $6\dfrac{1}{10}$ $\dfrac{610}{100}$

5.

$\dfrac{50}{7}$ $7\dfrac{1}{7}$ $\dfrac{100}{14}$ $7\dfrac{3}{7}$

6.

$\dfrac{24}{4}$ 6 $6\dfrac{3}{4}$ $\dfrac{12}{2}$

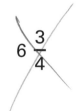

Tiny Tenths

This picture has $\frac{3}{10}$ shaded. In decimal form this is written as 0.3.

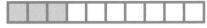

$\frac{3}{10} = 3 \div 10$

$3 \div 10 = 0.3$ Remember, when dividing by 10, move the decimal to the left one place.

WRITE the fraction and decimal for each picture.

HINT: If the number is less than one, put a zero before the decimal point.

1.

$\frac{1}{10}$ 0.1

2.

$\frac{4}{10}$ 0.4

3.

$\frac{9}{10}$ 0.9

4.

$\frac{5}{10}$ 0.5

5.

$\frac{7}{10}$ 0.7

6.

$\frac{6}{10}$ 0.6

Fractions, Decimals & Percents

Handy Hundredths

This picture has $\frac{72}{100}$ shaded. In decimal form this is written as 0.72.

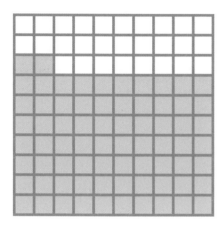

$$\frac{72}{100} = 72 \div 100$$

$$72 \div 100 = 0.72$$

Remember, when dividing by 100, move the decimal to the left two places.

WRITE the fraction and decimal for each picture.

1. 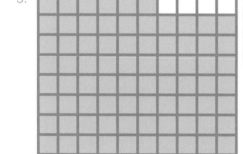 $\frac{55}{100}$ 0.55

2. 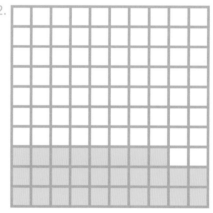 $\frac{38}{100}$ 0.38

3. 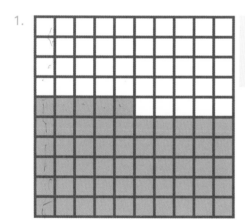 $\frac{99}{100}$ 0.99

4. 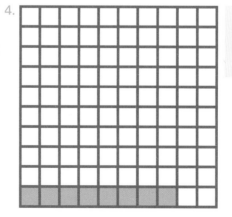 $\frac{8}{100}$ 0.08

Pictured Percent

A **percent** (%) is another way of showing parts of 100. The picture has $\frac{46}{100}$ shaded. It can also be written as 46%.

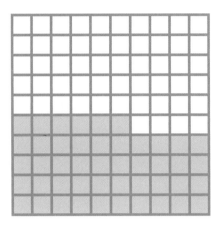

$$\frac{46}{100} = 46\%$$

WRITE the fraction and percent for each picture.

1.

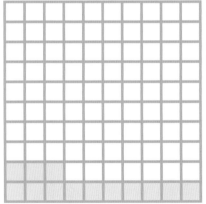

$\frac{13}{100}$ 13%

2.

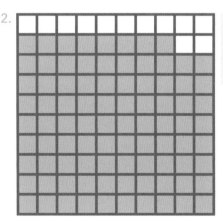

$\frac{88}{100}$ 88%

3.

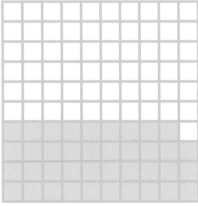

$\frac{39}{100}$ 39%

4.

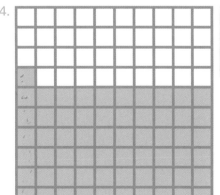

$\frac{61}{100}$ 61%

Paired Parts

WRITE each fraction as a percent and each percent as a fraction in its simplest form.

Examples:

$$\frac{4}{25} \times 4 = \frac{16}{100} = 16\% \qquad 90\% = \frac{90 \div 10}{100 \div 10} = \frac{9}{10}$$

1. $\dfrac{6}{10}$ = 60%

2. $\dfrac{16}{50}$ = 32%

3. $\dfrac{1}{5}$ = 20%

4. $\dfrac{1}{2}$ = 50%

5. $\dfrac{12}{25}$ = 48%

6. $\dfrac{3}{20}$ = 15%

7. 14% = $\dfrac{7}{50}$

8. 40% = $\dfrac{2}{5}$

9. 36% = $\dfrac{9}{25}$

10. 10% = $\dfrac{1}{10}$

11. 35% = $\dfrac{7}{20}$

12. 23% = $\dfrac{23}{100}$

Write It

WRITE each decimal as a percent and each percent as a decimal.

HINT: Thinking about the equivalent fraction may help.

$$0.3 = \frac{3}{10} = \frac{30}{100} = 30\%$$

0.2 = 20%

1

0.45 = 45%

2

0.99 = 99%

3

0.13 = 13%

4

0.51 = 51%

5

0.88 = 88%

6

0.27 = 27%

7

0.06 = 6%

8

0.39 = 36%

9

0.21 = 21%

10

0.72 = 72%

11

0.63 = 63%

12

75% = .75

13

46% = .46

14

32% = .32

15

93% = .93

16

8% = .08

17

15% = .15

18

84% = .84

19

1% = .01

20

51% = .51

21

27% = .27

22

68% = .68

23

82% = .82

24

Pinpoint Percents

To find the percent of a number, change the percent to a decimal and multiply.

Example: 61% of 85 = 0.61 × 85 = 51.85

$$\begin{array}{r} \overset{3}{8}\,5 \\ \times\ 0.6\,1 \\ \hline 8\,5 \\ +5\,1\,0\,0 \\ \hline 5\,1.8\,5 \end{array}$$

WRITE the percent of each number.

75% of 48 = 36

1

30% of 70 = 21

2

25% of 52 = 13

3

50% of 15 = 7.50

4

6% of 91 = 5.46

5

40% of 84 = 33.60

6

16% of 22 = 3.52

7

95% of 37 = 35.15

8

87% of 5 = 4.25

9

Odd One Out

CROSS OUT the number or picture in each row that does **not** have the same value as the others.

1.   0.45 $\frac{1}{2}$ 50%

2.      75% $\frac{3}{4}$ 0.7

3.   30%   0.3 $\frac{3}{10}$

4.   0.10   100% $\frac{1}{10}$

5. $\frac{3}{8}$ 25%   0.25

Matched or Mismatched?

WRITE >, <, or = in the box.

1. $50\% \ = \ \dfrac{1}{2}$

2. $0.6 \ > \ \dfrac{3}{10}$

3. $32\% \ < \ 0.52$

4. $\dfrac{22}{25} \ > \ 75\%$

5. $\dfrac{9}{20} \ < \ 0.98$

6. $0.13 \ > \ 12\%$

7. $\dfrac{39}{50} \ < \ 82\%$

8. $0.8 \ = \ \dfrac{4}{5}$

9. $47\% \ > \ 0.39$

10. $25\% \ = \ \dfrac{4}{16}$

11. $\dfrac{6}{7} \ > \ 0.6$

12. $0.099 \ < \ 99\%$

13. $\dfrac{3}{13} \ < \ 31\%$

14. $0.26 \ < \ \dfrac{7}{25}$

15. $62\% \ = \ 0.62$

16. $78\% \ < \ \dfrac{24}{30}$

Picture It

When fractions have the same denominator, add them by adding only the numerators. The denominator stays the same. ADD the fractions and WRITE the sum.

Example:

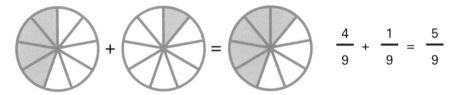

$$\frac{4}{9} + \frac{1}{9} = \frac{5}{9}$$

$$\frac{1}{5} + \frac{3}{5} = \frac{4}{5}$$

1

$$\frac{3}{7} + \frac{3}{7} = \frac{6}{7}$$

2

$$\frac{4}{11} + \frac{6}{11} = \frac{10}{11}$$

3

$$\frac{5}{8} + \frac{3}{8} = \frac{8}{8}$$

4

$$\frac{5}{14} + \frac{4}{14} = \frac{9}{14}$$

5

Adding Fractions

Simplified Sums

WRITE each sum as a fraction in its simplest form.

Examples: $\dfrac{3}{15} + \dfrac{6}{15} = \dfrac{9}{15} = \dfrac{3}{5}$ $\dfrac{5}{6} + \dfrac{8}{6} = \dfrac{13}{6} = 2\dfrac{1}{6}$

$\dfrac{1}{3} + \dfrac{7}{3} = $ $1\dfrac{2}{3}$

1

$\dfrac{3}{16} + \dfrac{5}{16} = $ $\dfrac{8}{16}$

2

$\dfrac{7}{9} + \dfrac{7}{9} = $ $1\dfrac{5}{9}$

3

$\dfrac{4}{18} + \dfrac{11}{18} = $ $\dfrac{15}{18}$

4

$\dfrac{14}{8} + \dfrac{21}{8} = $ $4\dfrac{3}{8}$

5

$\dfrac{5}{21} + \dfrac{9}{21} = $ $\dfrac{14}{21}$

6

$\dfrac{40}{7} + \dfrac{9}{7} = $ 7

7

$\dfrac{27}{45} + \dfrac{8}{45} = $ $\dfrac{35}{45}$

8

$\dfrac{30}{12} + \dfrac{33}{12} = $ $5\dfrac{3}{12}$

9

$\dfrac{14}{15} + \dfrac{10}{15} = $ $1\dfrac{9}{15}$

10

Dueling Denominators

The **lowest common denominator** between two fractions is the smallest number that is a multiple of both denominators.

$$\frac{3}{4} + \frac{2}{3} =$$

Multiples of 4 are: 4, 8, **12**, 16, 20 . . .
Multiples of 3 are: 3, 6, 9, **12**, 15 . . .
12 is the least common multiple of 3 and 4, making it the lowest common denominator.

Multiply the numerator and denominator in each fraction by the number that will make the denominator 12. Then add the two numbers.

$$\frac{3 \times 3 = 9}{4 \times 3 = 12} \qquad \frac{2 \times 4 = 8}{3 \times 4 = 12}$$

$$\frac{9}{12} + \frac{8}{12} = \frac{17}{12} = 1\frac{5}{12}$$

REWRITE the fractions with their lowest common denominators. Then WRITE the sum as a fraction in its simplest form.

$$\frac{1}{2} + \frac{2}{3} = \quad 1\frac{1}{6}$$

1

$$\frac{2}{12} + \frac{1}{6} = \quad \frac{8}{24}$$

2

$$\frac{3}{2} + \frac{13}{8} = \quad 3\frac{2}{16}$$

3

$$\frac{2}{5} + \frac{3}{4} = \quad 1\frac{5}{20}$$

4

$$\frac{4}{3} + \frac{8}{9} = \quad 2\frac{4}{18}$$

5

$$\frac{9}{16} + \frac{7}{8} = \quad 1\frac{17}{16}$$

6

$$\frac{15}{18} + \frac{7}{6} = \quad 2$$

7

$$\frac{8}{9} + \frac{5}{12} = \quad 1\frac{11}{36}$$

8

$$\frac{7}{6} + \frac{23}{24} = \quad 2\frac{1}{8}$$

9

Adding Fractions

Mixed Up

When adding mixed numbers, think of it as two whole numbers plus two fractions. Find the lowest common denominator to add the fractions.

Example: $2\dfrac{1}{6} + 7\dfrac{2}{3} =$

$$(2 + 7) + (\dfrac{1}{6} + \dfrac{2}{3}) = 9 + (\dfrac{1}{6} + \dfrac{4}{6}) = 9\dfrac{5}{6}$$

WRITE each sum as a fraction in its simplest form.

$1\dfrac{3}{7} + 6\dfrac{1}{7} =$ $7\dfrac{4}{7}$

1

$4\dfrac{1}{2} + 2\dfrac{1}{8} =$ $6\dfrac{5}{8}$

2

$3\dfrac{4}{5} + 5\dfrac{2}{15} =$ $8\dfrac{14}{15}$

3

$7\dfrac{2}{3} + 2\dfrac{2}{9} =$ $9\dfrac{8}{9}$

4

$2\dfrac{3}{10} + 1\dfrac{2}{5} =$ $3\dfrac{7}{10}$

5

$3\dfrac{7}{12} + 3\dfrac{1}{4} =$ $6\dfrac{5}{6}$

6

$5\dfrac{1}{9} + 3\dfrac{7}{18} =$ $8\dfrac{9}{18}$

7

$7\dfrac{3}{4} + 4\dfrac{5}{8} =$ $12\dfrac{3}{8}$

8

$6\dfrac{3}{14} + 9\dfrac{6}{7} =$ $16\dfrac{1}{14}$

9

Picture It

When fractions have the same denominator, subtract them by subtracting the numerators only. The denominator stays the same. SUBTRACT the fractions and WRITE the difference.

HINT: Cross out the same number of boxes as the numerator of the second fraction to help you subtract.

Example:

$$\frac{6}{7} - \frac{2}{7} = \frac{4}{7}$$

1.

$$\frac{4}{5} - \frac{3}{5} = \frac{1}{5}$$

2.

$$\frac{9}{10} - \frac{6}{10} = \frac{2}{10}$$

3.

$$\frac{3}{6} - \frac{1}{6} = \frac{2}{6}$$

4.

$$\frac{7}{12} - \frac{2}{12} = \frac{5}{12}$$

5.

$$\frac{8}{8} - \frac{3}{8} = \frac{5}{8}$$

6.

$$\frac{7}{9} - \frac{5}{9} = \frac{2}{9}$$

Simple Differences

WRITE each difference as a fraction in its simplest form.

Examples: $\dfrac{11}{16} - \dfrac{3}{16} = \dfrac{8}{16} = \dfrac{1}{2}$ $\dfrac{15}{7} - \dfrac{2}{7} = \dfrac{13}{7} = 1\dfrac{6}{7}$

$\dfrac{7}{8} - \dfrac{3}{8} =$ $\dfrac{1}{2}$

1

$\dfrac{11}{12} - \dfrac{2}{12} =$ $\dfrac{9}{12}$

2

$\dfrac{17}{21} - \dfrac{10}{21} =$ $\dfrac{7}{21}$

3

$\dfrac{17}{18} - \dfrac{15}{18} =$ $\dfrac{2}{18}$

4

$\dfrac{29}{24} - \dfrac{7}{24} =$ $\dfrac{22}{24}$

5

$\dfrac{24}{17} - \dfrac{7}{17} =$ 1

6

$\dfrac{17}{13} - \dfrac{2}{13} =$ $\dfrac{14}{13} = 1\dfrac{1}{13}$

7

$\dfrac{42}{9} - \dfrac{14}{9} =$ $\dfrac{28}{9}$

8

$\dfrac{34}{25} - \dfrac{4}{25} =$ $\dfrac{30}{25}$

9

$\dfrac{27}{32} - \dfrac{3}{32} =$ $\dfrac{24}{32}$

10

Dueling Denominators

Find the lowest common denominator before subtracting.

Example: $\dfrac{7}{15} - \dfrac{3}{10} =$ $\dfrac{7 \times 2}{15 \times 2} = \dfrac{14}{30}$ $\dfrac{3 \times 3}{10 \times 3} = \dfrac{9}{30}$ $\dfrac{14}{30} - \dfrac{9}{30} = \dfrac{5}{30} = \dfrac{1}{6}$

REWRITE the fractions with their lowest common denominators. Then WRITE the difference as a fraction in its simplest form.

$\dfrac{1}{2} - \dfrac{2}{5} =$ $\dfrac{1}{10}$

1

$\dfrac{5}{6} - \dfrac{1}{4} =$ $\dfrac{7}{12}$

2

$\dfrac{7}{8} - \dfrac{3}{5} =$ $\dfrac{11}{40}$

3

$\dfrac{3}{4} - \dfrac{7}{12} =$ $\dfrac{1}{6}$

4

$\dfrac{1}{3} - \dfrac{2}{9} =$ $\dfrac{1}{9}$

5

$\dfrac{17}{24} - \dfrac{1}{4} =$ $\dfrac{11}{24}$

6

$\dfrac{5}{3} - \dfrac{1}{6} =$ $1\dfrac{1}{2}$

7

$\dfrac{9}{5} - \dfrac{2}{3} =$ $1\dfrac{2}{15}$

8

$\dfrac{15}{4} - \dfrac{3}{10} =$ $3\dfrac{9}{20}$

9

Subtracting Fractions

Mixed Up

When subtracting mixed numbers, subtract the fractions, then the whole numbers.

$$6\frac{3}{4}$$
$$-\ 3\frac{1}{2}$$

$$6\frac{3}{4}$$
$$-\ 3\frac{2}{4}$$
$$\frac{1}{4}$$

$$6\frac{3}{4}$$
$$-\ 3\frac{2}{4}$$
$$3\frac{1}{4}$$

If the smaller fraction is on top, then regrouping is necessary.

$$7\frac{1}{3}$$
$$-\ 1\frac{1}{2}$$

$$7\frac{2}{6}$$
$$-\ 1\frac{3}{6}$$

$$\overset{6}{\cancel{7}}\frac{8}{6}$$
$$-\ 1\frac{3}{6}$$

$$\overset{6}{\cancel{7}}\frac{8}{6}$$
$$-\ 1\frac{3}{6}$$
$$5\frac{5}{6}$$

$$1 = \frac{6}{6}$$

$$\frac{6}{6} + \frac{2}{6} = \frac{8}{6}$$

WRITE each difference as a fraction in its simplest form.

1.
$$4\frac{4}{7}$$
$$-\ 2\frac{3}{7}$$
$$2\frac{1}{7}$$

2.
$$9\frac{7}{9}$$
$$-\ 2\frac{1}{9}$$
$$7\frac{6}{9}$$

3.
$$6\frac{7}{12}$$
$$-\ 3\frac{1}{12}$$
$$3\frac{6}{12}$$

4.
$$7\frac{9}{10}$$
$$-\ 6\frac{4}{5}$$
$$1\frac{1}{10}$$

5.
$$10\frac{2}{3}$$
$$-\ 1\frac{5}{9}$$
$$9\frac{1}{9}$$

6.
$$8\frac{5}{7}$$
$$-\ 4\frac{1}{2}$$
$$4\frac{3}{14}$$

7.
$$5\frac{1}{4}$$
$$-\ 2\frac{5}{8}$$
$$2\frac{5}{8}$$

8.
$$2\frac{2}{5}$$
$$-\ 1\frac{11}{15}$$
$$\frac{2}{3}$$

9.
$$11\frac{5}{6}$$
$$-\ 5\frac{8}{9}$$
$$5\frac{17}{18}$$

Picture It

When a number is multiplied by a fraction that is less than one, the product will be a smaller number.

Multiplying 8 by $\frac{1}{4}$ is like looking for $\frac{1}{4}$ of 8.

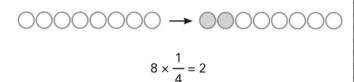

$$8 \times \frac{1}{4} = 2$$

Multiplying $\frac{1}{3}$ by $\frac{1}{2}$ is like looking for $\frac{1}{2}$ of $\frac{1}{3}$.

$$\frac{1}{3} \times \frac{1}{2} = \frac{1}{6}$$

Use the pictures to help you answer the problems. WRITE each product.

1. $7 \times \frac{1}{7} = \dfrac{7}{7}$

2. $10 \times \frac{1}{2} = \dfrac{10}{2}$

3. $9 \times \frac{1}{3} = \dfrac{9}{3}$

4. $1 \times \frac{1}{5} = \dfrac{1}{5}$

5. $\frac{1}{2} \times \frac{1}{4} = \dfrac{1}{8}$

6. $\frac{2}{3} \times \frac{1}{3} = \dfrac{2}{9}$

Multiplying Fractions

Straight Across

To multiply fractions, multiply the numerators, multiply the denominators, and then write the product in its simplest form.

Example: $\dfrac{4}{5} \times \dfrac{1}{2} = \dfrac{4 \times 1}{5 \times 2} = \dfrac{4}{10} = \dfrac{2}{5}$

WRITE each product as a fraction in its simplest form.

$\dfrac{1}{5} \times \dfrac{1}{3} = \dfrac{1}{15}$

1

$\dfrac{2}{5} \times \dfrac{1}{4} = \dfrac{1}{10}$

2

$\dfrac{6}{7} \times \dfrac{1}{3} = \dfrac{2}{7}$

3

$\dfrac{4}{9} \times \dfrac{5}{6} = \dfrac{16}{27}$

4

$\dfrac{3}{8} \times \dfrac{2}{3} = \dfrac{1}{4}$

5

$\dfrac{1}{12} \times \dfrac{3}{5} = \dfrac{1}{20}$

6

$\dfrac{3}{4} \times \dfrac{3}{7} = \dfrac{9}{28}$

7

$\dfrac{5}{7} \times \dfrac{1}{10} = \dfrac{1}{14}$

8

$\dfrac{3}{8} \times \dfrac{5}{10} = \dfrac{3}{16}$

9

Simply Simplify

You can make multiplication easier by first simplifying the fractions.

$\dfrac{3}{7} \times \dfrac{1}{9} = \dfrac{3 \times 1}{7 \times 9} = \dfrac{3}{63}$ $\dfrac{3 \div 3}{63 \div 3} = \dfrac{1}{21}$ You know how to simplify after multiplying.	$\dfrac{3}{7} \times \dfrac{1}{9} =$ To simplify before multiplying, look for common factors in the numerator of one fraction and the denominator of the other. The numerator 3 is a factor of 3 and 9.	$\dfrac{\overset{1}{\cancel{3}}}{7} \times \dfrac{1}{\underset{3}{\cancel{9}}} = \dfrac{1}{21}$ $3 \div 3 = 1$ Cross out 3 and write 1. $9 \div 3 = 3$ Cross out 9 and write 3. Multiply the simplified fractions to find the product.

First, SIMPLIFY the fractions. Then WRITE the product.

$\dfrac{2}{5} \times \dfrac{3}{4} = \dfrac{3}{10}$

1

$\dfrac{3}{7} \times \dfrac{5}{12} = \dfrac{5}{28}$

2

$\dfrac{5}{6} \times \dfrac{6}{11} = \dfrac{5}{11}$

3

$\dfrac{5}{8} \times \dfrac{9}{20} = \dfrac{9}{32}$

4

$\dfrac{9}{4} \times \dfrac{7}{18} = \dfrac{7}{8}$

5

$\dfrac{11}{32} \times \dfrac{8}{9} = \dfrac{11}{36}$

6

$\dfrac{4}{7} \times \dfrac{7}{24} = \dfrac{1}{6}$

7

$\dfrac{9}{10} \times \dfrac{5}{6} = \dfrac{3}{4}$

8

$\dfrac{6}{15} \times \dfrac{5}{9} = \dfrac{2}{9}$

9

Mixed Up

To multiply, change the mixed numbers to improper fractions. Simplify, and then multiply.

Examples:

$$3\frac{1}{5} \times 2\frac{1}{4} =$$

$$3\frac{1}{5} \times 2\frac{1}{4} = \frac{16}{5} \times \frac{9}{4} = \frac{\overset{4}{16}}{5} \times \frac{9}{\underset{1}{4}} = \frac{36}{5} = 7\frac{1}{5}$$

$$4 \times 5\frac{1}{6} = \frac{4}{1} \times \frac{31}{6} = \frac{4}{1} \times \frac{31}{\underset{3}{6}} = \frac{62}{3} = 20\frac{2}{3}$$

WRITE the product as a fraction in its simplest form.

$$1\frac{1}{6} \times 2\frac{2}{3} = \boxed{3\frac{1}{1}}$$

1

$$3\frac{3}{4} \times 4\frac{1}{5} = \boxed{15\frac{3}{4}}$$

2

$$3\frac{3}{5} \times 1\frac{2}{3} = \boxed{6}$$

3

$$6\frac{2}{7} \times 1\frac{1}{6} = \boxed{7\frac{4}{3}}$$

4

$$2\frac{1}{2} \times 3\frac{1}{5} = \boxed{8}$$

5

$$4\frac{2}{5} \times 3\frac{3}{4} = \boxed{15\frac{1}{2}}$$

6

$$3 \times 7\frac{2}{9} = \boxed{21\frac{2}{3}}$$

7

$$5 \times 1\frac{1}{20} = \boxed{5\frac{1}{4}}$$

8

$$10 \times 6\frac{4}{5} = \boxed{68}$$

9

Radical Reciprocals

A **reciprocal** of a fraction is its inverse, which means that the numbers in the numerator and the denominator switch places.

HINT: To find the reciprocal of a fraction, flip it upside down.

Examples: The reciprocal of $\frac{3}{4}$ is $\frac{4}{3}$.   The reciprocal of 5 is $\frac{1}{5}$.

WRITE each reciprocal.

$\frac{5}{6}$ $\frac{6}{5}$

1

$\frac{7}{2}$ $\frac{2}{7}$

2

$\frac{1}{3}$ $\frac{3}{1}$

3

$\frac{9}{10}$ $\frac{10}{9}$

4

$\frac{12}{5}$ $\frac{5}{12}$

5

$\frac{1}{11}$ $\frac{11}{1}$

6

$\frac{8}{5}$ $\frac{5}{8}$

7

8 $\frac{1}{8}$

8

$\frac{4}{13}$ $\frac{13}{4}$

9

$\frac{32}{23}$ $\frac{23}{32}$

10

$\frac{55}{67}$ $\frac{67}{55}$

11

$\frac{99}{100}$ $\frac{100}{99}$

12

The One and Only

The product of a fraction and its reciprocal is always 1.

$$\frac{2}{5} \times \frac{5}{2} = \frac{10}{10} = 1$$

$$\frac{3}{7} \times \frac{7}{3} = \frac{\overset{1}{\cancel{3}}}{\underset{1}{\cancel{7}}} \times \frac{\overset{1}{\cancel{7}}}{\underset{1}{\cancel{3}}} = \frac{1}{1} = 1$$

WRITE each missing factor or product.

$$\frac{6}{7} \times \frac{7}{6} = \boxed{1}$$

1

$$\frac{2}{11} \times \frac{11}{2} = \boxed{1}$$

2

$$3\frac{1}{4} \times \frac{4}{13} = \boxed{1}$$

3

$$\frac{4}{3} \times \boxed{\frac{3}{4}} = 1$$

4

$$\frac{8}{9} \times \boxed{\frac{9}{3}} = 1$$

5

$$3 \times \boxed{\frac{1}{3}} = 1$$

6

$$\boxed{\frac{6}{17}} \times \frac{17}{6} = 1$$

7

$$\boxed{\frac{103}{78}} \times \frac{78}{103} = 1$$

8

$$\boxed{\frac{6}{35}} \times 5\frac{5}{6} = 1$$

9

Picture It

When a number is divided by a fraction that is less than one, the product will be a bigger number.

Dividing 3 by $\frac{1}{8}$ is like looking for the number of eighths in 3.

$\frac{1}{8}$ is found in 3 a total of 24 times. $3 \div \frac{1}{8} = 24$.

Dividing $\frac{1}{2}$ by $\frac{1}{4}$ is like looking for the number of fourths in one half.

$\frac{1}{4}$ is found in $\frac{1}{2}$ a total of 2 times. $\frac{1}{2} \div \frac{1}{4} = 2$

Use the pictures to help you answer the problems. WRITE each quotient.

1.
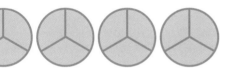

$4 \div \frac{1}{3} = $ 12

2.

$5 \div \frac{1}{2} = $ 10

3.
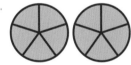

$2 \div \frac{2}{5} = $ 5

4.

$\frac{3}{4} \div \frac{1}{4} = $ 3

5.

$\frac{1}{2} \div \frac{1}{8} = $ 4

6.

$\frac{5}{6} \div \frac{5}{12} = $ 2

Flip and Multiply

To divide fractions, multiply by the reciprocal of the divisor.

$$\frac{6}{7} \div \frac{2}{3} = \frac{6}{7} \times \frac{3}{2} = \frac{\overset{3}{\cancel{6}}}{7} \times \frac{3}{\underset{1}{\cancel{2}}} = \frac{9}{7} = 1\frac{2}{7}$$

WRITE each quotient as a fraction in its simplest form.

$$\frac{3}{4} \div \frac{2}{5} =$$

1

$$\frac{1}{6} \div \frac{2}{3} =$$

2

$$\frac{7}{15} \div \frac{4}{5} =$$

3

$$\frac{7}{8} \div 7 =$$

4

$$\frac{4}{9} \div \frac{1}{15} =$$

5

$$\frac{5}{14} \div \frac{5}{7} =$$

6

$$\frac{9}{32} \div \frac{3}{8} =$$

7

$$\frac{7}{16} \div \frac{3}{40} =$$

8

$$\frac{18}{19} \div \frac{27}{38} =$$

9

Mixed Up

To divide, change the mixed numbers to improper fractions.

Examples: $2\dfrac{4}{7} \div 1\dfrac{1}{5} =$

$2\dfrac{4}{7} \div 1\dfrac{1}{5} = \dfrac{18}{7} \div \dfrac{6}{5} = \dfrac{18}{7} \times \dfrac{5}{6} = \dfrac{\overset{3}{\cancel{18}}}{7} \times \dfrac{5}{\underset{1}{\cancel{6}}} = \dfrac{15}{7} = 2\dfrac{1}{7}$

WRITE each quotient as a fraction in its simplest form.

$3\dfrac{3}{4} \div 2\dfrac{1}{2} =$

1

$1\dfrac{1}{5} \div 5\dfrac{2}{5} =$

2

$2\dfrac{5}{9} \div 2\dfrac{1}{3} =$

3

$1\dfrac{1}{2} \div 3\dfrac{3}{8} =$

4

$4\dfrac{1}{2} \div 4\dfrac{1}{4} =$

5

$5\dfrac{5}{6} \div 10 =$

6

$9 \div 3\dfrac{3}{5} =$

7

$8\dfrac{4}{9} \div 4 =$

8

$2\dfrac{7}{9} \div 15 =$

9

Fraction Action

WRITE the answers.

1. How many $\frac{1}{2}$ miles are in 37 miles? _____

2. How many $\frac{1}{4}$ hours are in 24 hours? _____

3. How many $\frac{1}{12}$ inches are in 10 inches? _____

4. How many $\frac{1}{4}$ pounds are in 90 pounds? _____

5. How many $\frac{1}{2}$ dollars are in 52 dollars? _____

6. How many $\frac{1}{10}$ feet are in 18 feet? _____

7. How many $\frac{1}{3}$ yards are in 123 yards? _____

8. How many $\frac{1}{6}$ dozen are in 15 dozen? _____

Shoes in a Foot

MEASURE the length of each shoe in inches and answer the questions. WRITE the answers as a fraction or mixed number.

HINT: 1 foot (ft) = 12 inches (in.)   1 yard (yd) = 3 ft = 36 in.

_____ in.

1

_____ in.

2

How many of each kind of shoe would fit end to end in one foot?

_____ red shoes   _____ sneakers

3   4

How many of each kind of shoe would fit end to end in one yard?

_____ red shoes   _____ sneakers

5   6

Fitting In

MEASURE the width of the book, DVD, and CD in centimeters and ANSWER the questions. WRITE the answers as decimals.

HINT: 1 meter (m) = 100 centimeters (cm)

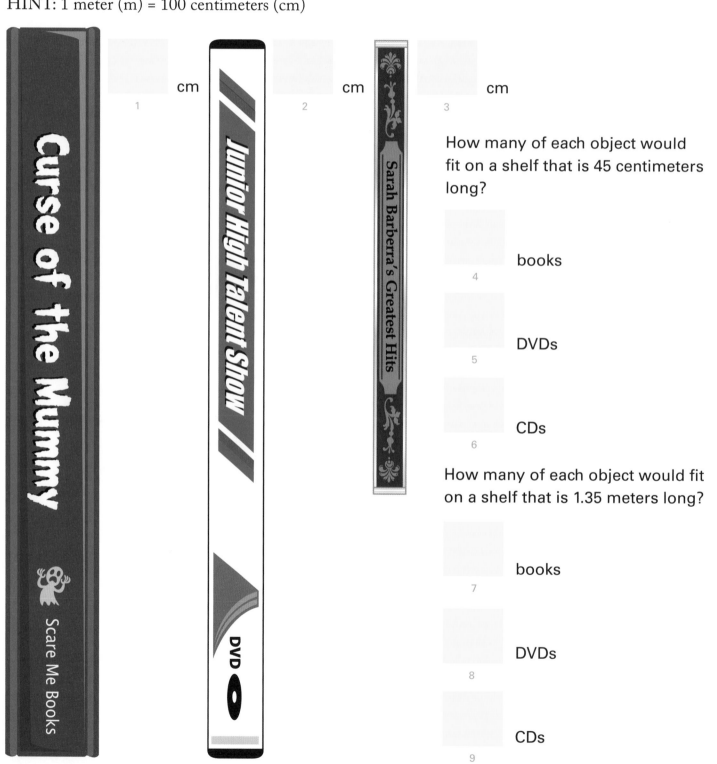

_____ cm

1

_____ cm

2

_____ cm

3

How many of each object would fit on a shelf that is 45 centimeters long?

_____ books

4

_____ DVDs

5

_____ CDs

6

How many of each object would fit on a shelf that is 1.35 meters long?

_____ books

7

_____ DVDs

8

_____ CDs

9

Around We Go

Perimeter is the distance around a two-dimensional shape. To find the perimeter, add the lengths of all of the sides. For shapes with sides that are the same length, multiply the length of one side by the number of sides.

4 in.

7 in.

$7 + 4 + 7 + 4 = 22$
The perimeter of this rectangle is 22 in.

6 cm

$6 \times 3 = 18$
The perimeter of this triangle is 18 cm.

WRITE the perimeter of each shape.

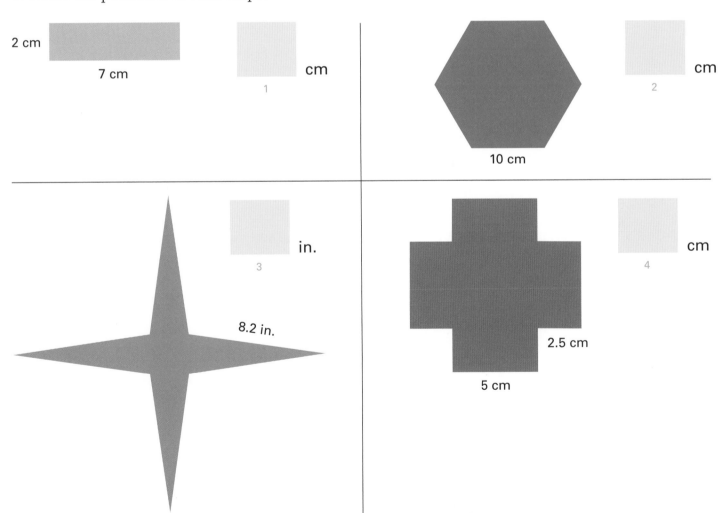

2 cm

7 cm

1 cm

10 cm

2 cm

3 in.

8.2 in.

2.5 cm

5 cm

4 cm

Around the Yard

WRITE the perimeter of the yard and each object in it.

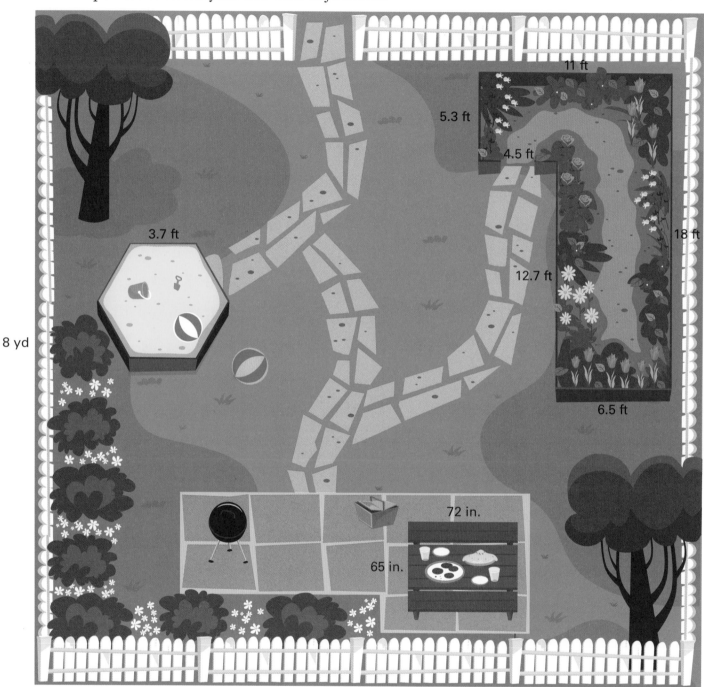

1. Yard: _____ yd

2. Table: _____ in.

3. Garden: _____ ft

4. Sandbox: _____ ft

Angle Untangle

An **angle** is formed when two lines meet, and it is measured in degrees using a protractor. There are three different types of angles: right, acute, and obtuse.

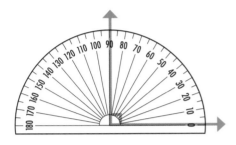 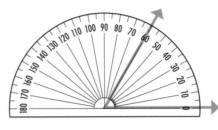 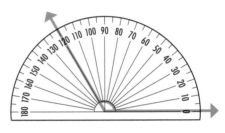

A **right** angle is an angle measuring exactly 90°, indicated by the ⌐ symbol in the corner.

An **acute** angle is any angle measuring less than 90°.

An **obtuse** angle is any angle measuring more than 90°.

WRITE *right*, *acute*, or *obtuse* for each angle.

1. _____

2. _____

3. _____

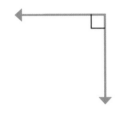

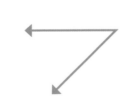

4. _____

5. _____

6. _____

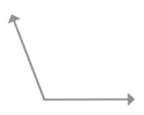

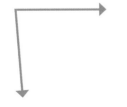

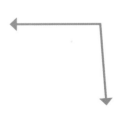

7. _____

8. _____

9. _____

Circle the Same

CIRCLE all of the angles that are in the correct column.

Right	Acute	Obtuse

Hidden Angles

Two sides of a shape meet to form an angle.

Example:

A square has four right angles.

WRITE the number of right, acute, and obtuse angles in each shape.

	Right Angles	Acute Angles	Obtuse Angles

Measure Up

MEASURE each angle using a protractor. WRITE the approximate measurement.

HINT: If you don't have a protractor, cut out the one in the example.

Example:

Line up one side of the angle with the line at the bottom of the protractor. Line up the point where the two lines meet with the circle or hole at the bottom of the protractor. This angle measures 48°.

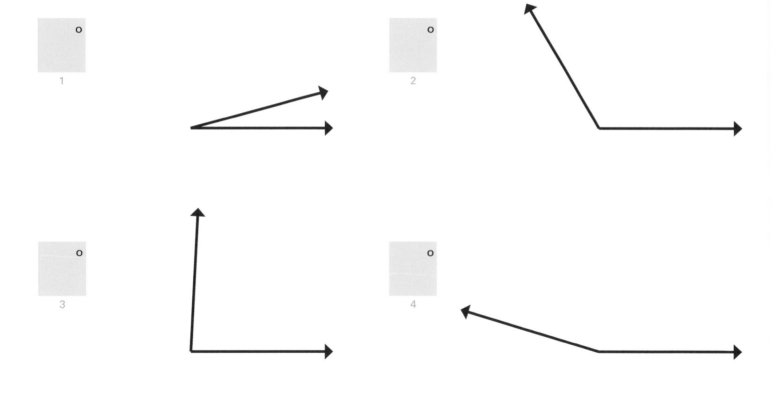

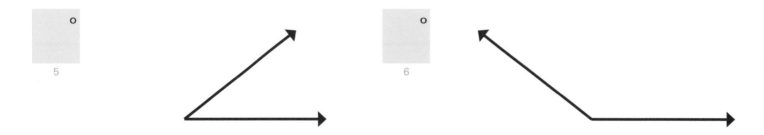

Circle the Same

A **point** marks a place in space, represented by a dot.

A **line** is a straight path that has no end in either direction.

A **line segment** is the part of a line between two points, called **endpoints**.

A **ray** is a line that begins at an endpoint and has no end in the other direction.

CIRCLE the name in each row that matches the picture.

1. line segment   point   ray

2. line   line segment   point

3. ray   point   line

4. line   line segment   ray

5. ray   line   endpoint

What's My Name?

Letters are used to name points, lines, and rays.

A point is named by a single letter: *A*

Two points on a line are used to name the line: $\overleftrightarrow{AB}$ or $\overleftrightarrow{BA}$

The endpoints are used to name a line segment: $\overline{AB}$ or $\overline{BA}$

The endpoint and another point on the line name a ray: $\overrightarrow{AB}$
The endpoint is listed first.

WRITE the name of each point, line, or ray.

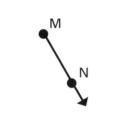

1. _____

2. _____

3. _____

4. _____

5. _____

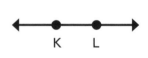

6. _____

7. _____

8. _____

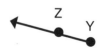

9. _____

Match Up

DRAW a line to connect each name to the correct line, point, or ray.

A

$\overline{AB}$

$\overrightarrow{BA}$

B

$\overrightarrow{AB}$

$\overleftrightarrow{BA}$

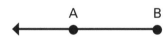

Circle the Same

Intersecting lines are lines that cross one another.

Perpendicular lines intersect to form right angles.

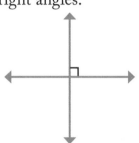

Parallel lines never intersect and are always the same distance apart.

CIRCLE all of the lines that are in the correct column.

Intersecting	Perpendicular	Parallel

Taking Shape

A **polygon** is a closed plane shape that has three or more sides. Polygons are named according to their number of sides.

 A **triangle** has three sides.

 A **heptagon** has seven sides.

 A **quadrilateral** has four sides.

 An **octagon** has eight sides.

 A **pentagon** has five sides.

 A **nonagon** has nine sides.

 A **hexagon** has six sides.

 A **decagon** has ten sides.

WRITE the name of each polygon.

1. _____

2. _____

3. _____

4. _____

5. _____

6. _____

7. _____

8. _____

Taking Shape

A **quadrilateral** is a polygon with four sides, and there are several specific types of quadrilaterals.

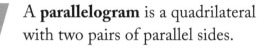

A **rectangle** has four sides and four right angles.

A **parallelogram** is a quadrilateral with two pairs of parallel sides.

A **square** is a rectangle whose sides are all of equal length.

A **rhombus** is a parallelogram whose sides are all of equal length.

A **trapezoid** is a quadrilateral with only one pair of parallel sides.

WRITE the name of each quadrilateral.

HINT: Some will have more than one correct answer.

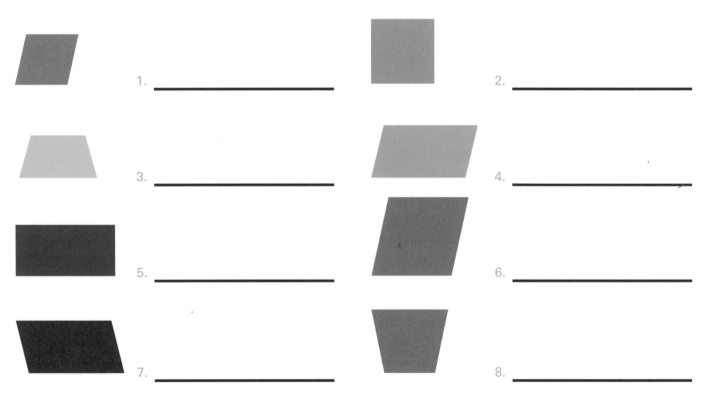

1. _____

2. _____

3. _____

4. _____

5. _____

6. _____

7. _____

8. _____

Shape Up

A **vertex** is the point where two sides meet.

Example:

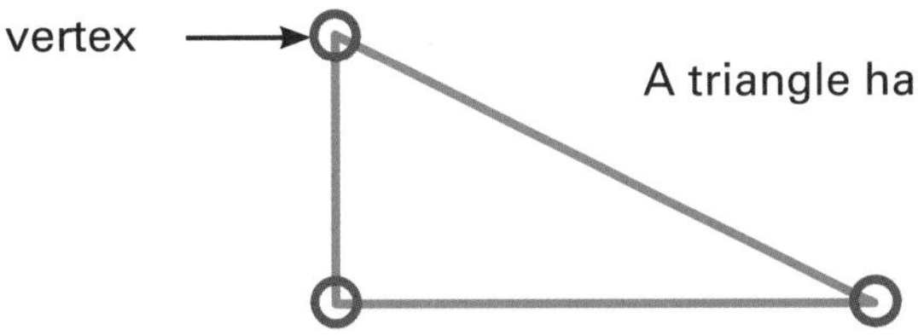

vertex →

A triangle has three vertices.

WRITE the name of each shape and the number of its sides, vertices, and pairs of vertical lines.

	Shape Name	Number of Sides	Number of Vertices	Pairs of Parallel Lines

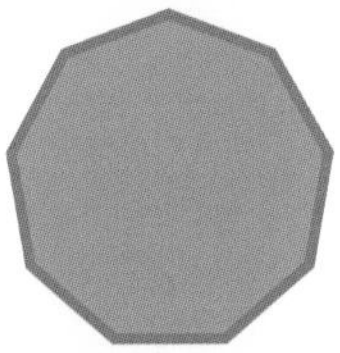				

Circle the Same

A shape is **congruent** to another if it is exactly the same shape and size.

These two shapes are congruent. Even though one is turned, it is still the same size and shape as the other.

These two shapes are not congruent. The second is not exactly the same size and shape as the first.

CIRCLE the shape that is congruent to the first shape.

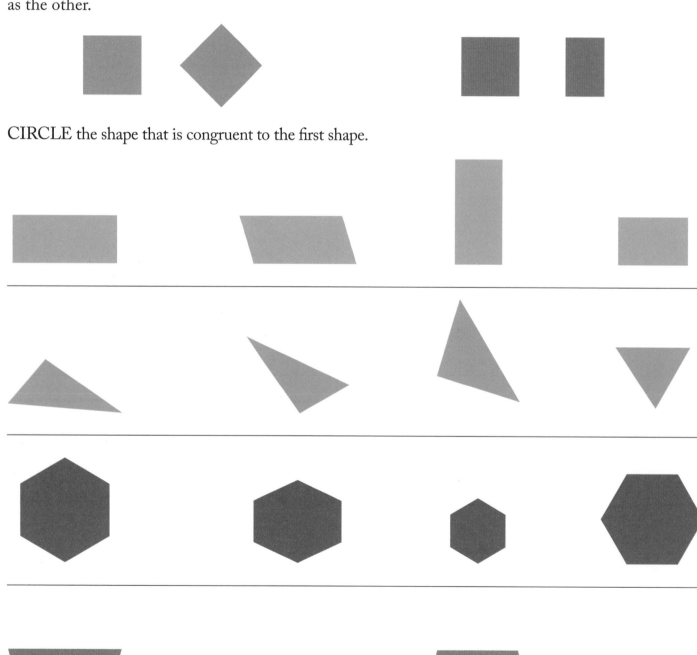

30

Rectangle Range

Area is the size of the surface of a shape, and it is measured in square units. Find the area of a rectangle by multiplying the length by the width.

Example: 2 in.   2 inches × 3 inches = 6 square inches (sq in.)

3 in.

WRITE the area of each rectangle.

7 cm
10 cm

1. _____ sq cm

5 in.

2. _____ sq in.

23 cm
28 cm

3. _____ sq cm

15 in.

32 in.

4. _____ sq in.

$3\frac{3}{4}$ ft

8 ft

5. _____ sq ft

4.8 m

6. _____ sq m

Area

Tricky Triangles

Find the area of a triangle by multiplying $\frac{1}{2}$ times the base of the triangle times the height of the triangle.

Examples:

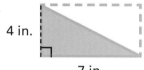

4 in.

7 in.

$$\frac{1}{2} \times 7 \times 4 = \frac{28}{2} = 14$$

Area = 14 sq in.

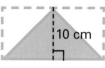

10 cm

16 cm

$$\frac{1}{2} \times 16 \times 10 = \frac{160}{2} = 80$$

Area = 80 sq cm

WRITE the area of each triangle.

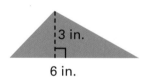

3 in.

6 in.

1. _____ sq in.

8 cm

12 cm

2. _____ sq cm

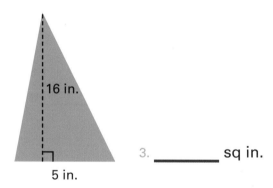

16 in.

5 in.

3. _____ sq in.

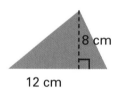

10 cm

21 cm

4. _____ sq cm

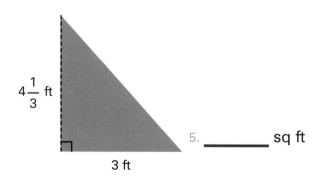

$4\frac{1}{3}$ ft

3 ft

5. _____ sq ft

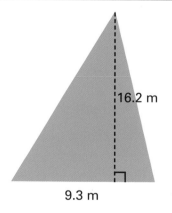

16.2 m

9.3 m

6. _____ sq m

Parallelogram Patch

Find the area of a parallelogram by multiplying the base times the height.

Example:

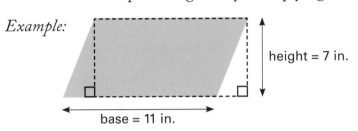

height = 7 in.

base = 11 in.

Area = 11 × 7 = 77 sq in.

The height of a parallelogram is the distance between parallel sides as measured by a perpendicular line.

WRITE the area of each parallelogram.

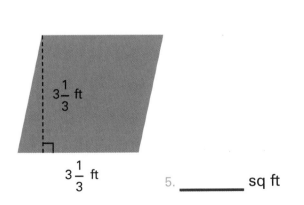

5 in.

3 in.

1. _____ sq in.

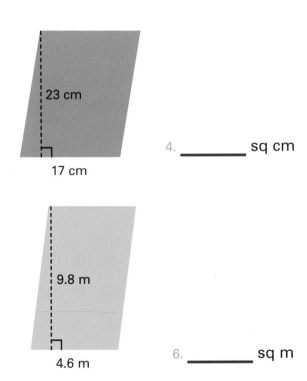

15 in.

8 in.

2. _____ sq in.

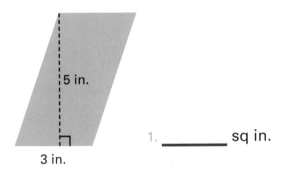

9 cm

9 cm

3. _____ sq cm

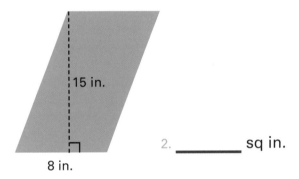

23 cm

17 cm

4. _____ sq cm

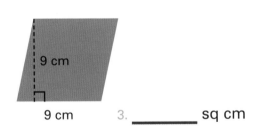

$3\frac{1}{3}$ ft

$3\frac{1}{3}$ ft

5. _____ sq ft

9.8 m

4.6 m

6. _____ sq m

Put It Together

LOOK for the rectangles, triangles, and parallelograms in the shapes. Use the measurements provided, and WRITE the area of each shape.

HINT: Find the area of the individual shapes, then add them together to find the area of the larger shape.

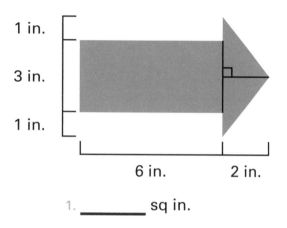

1. _____ sq in.

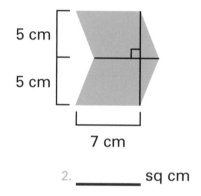

2. _____ sq cm

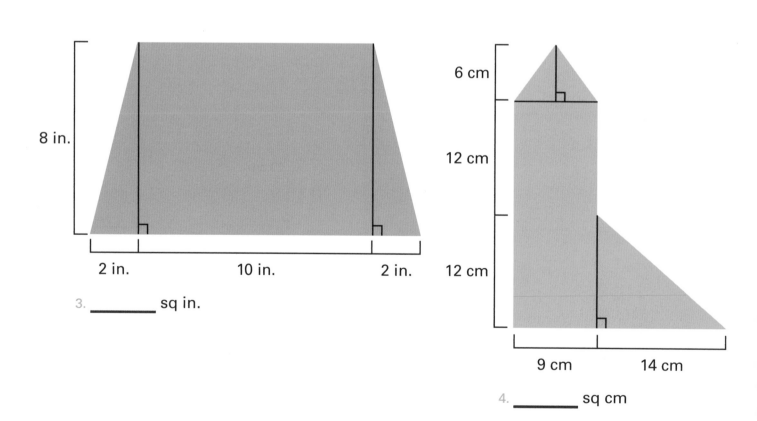

3. _____ sq in.

4. _____ sq cm

31

Taking Shape

Solid shapes are three-dimensional shapes.

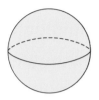 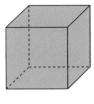 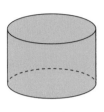 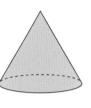 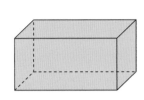 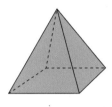

sphere   cube   cylinder   cone   rectangular prism   square pyramid

WRITE the name of each solid shape.

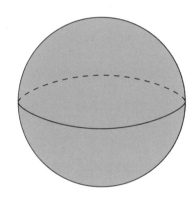 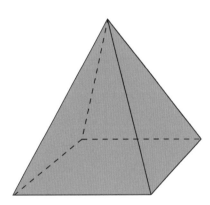 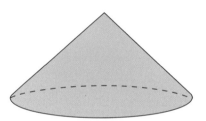

1. _____   2. _____   3. _____

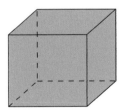 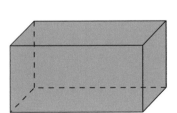 

4. _____   5. _____   6. _____

Shape Up

In a three-dimensional shape, a **vertex** is where three or more edges meet. An **edge** is where two sides meet. A **face** is the shape formed by the edges.

Example:

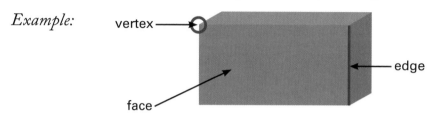

vertex

edge

face

WRITE the name of each shape and the number of its vertices, edges, and faces.

	Shape Name	Number of Vertices	Number of Edges	Number of Faces

Squared Away

Volume is the measure of cubic units that fit inside a space.

Example:

1 cubic unit

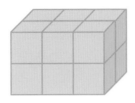

12 cubic units

WRITE the volume of each shape in cubic units.

1. _____ cubic units

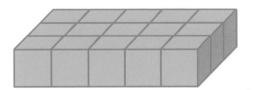

2. _____ cubic units

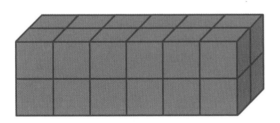

3. _____ cubic units

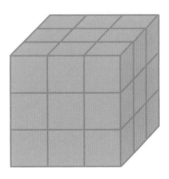

4. _____ cubic units

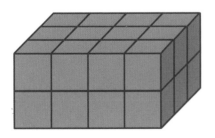

5. _____ cubic units

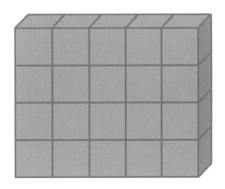

6. _____ cubic units

Speaking Volumes

Find the volume of a rectangular prism by multiplying the length times the width times the height.

Example:

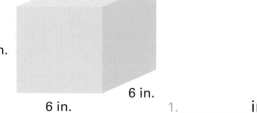

5 cm
10 cm
5 cm

Volume = 10 × 5 × 5
Volume = 250 cubic centimeters = 250 cm³

WRITE the volume of each shape in cubic units.

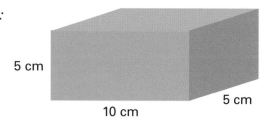

6 in.
6 in.
6 in.

1. _____ in.³

8 cm
10 cm
2 cm

2. _____ cm³

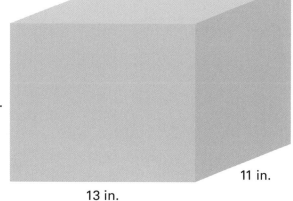

13 in.
13 in.
11 in.

3. _____ in.³

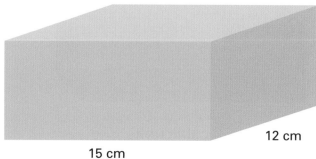

25 cm
15 cm
12 cm

4. _____ cm³

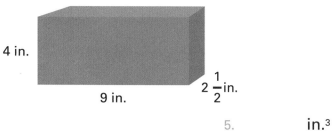

4 in.
9 in.
$2\frac{1}{2}$ in.

5. _____ in.³

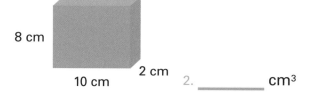

5.2 cm
4.6 cm
7 cm

6. _____ cm³

Maximum Volume

WRITE the volume of each object. Then WRITE the answers to the questions.

5 in.

11 in.

7 in.

1. _____ in.³

10 in.

13 in.

13 in.

2. _____ in.³

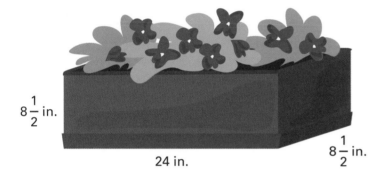

$8\frac{1}{2}$ in.

24 in.

$8\frac{1}{2}$ in.

3. _____ in.³

13 in.

3 in.

$9\frac{1}{2}$ in.

4. _____ in.³

$12\frac{1}{2}$ in.

$17\frac{1}{2}$ in.

4 in.

5. _____ in.³

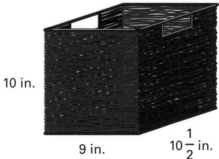

10 in.

9 in.

$10\frac{1}{2}$ in.

6. _____ in.³

7. Which object has the greatest volume? _____

8. Which object has the least volume? _____

Missing Pieces

WRITE the volume of each shape.

HINT: Find the volume as though the shape were a complete rectangular prism, and then subtract the volume of the missing piece.

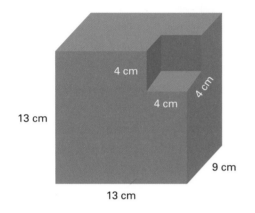

1. _____ cm³

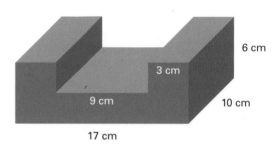

2. _____ cm³

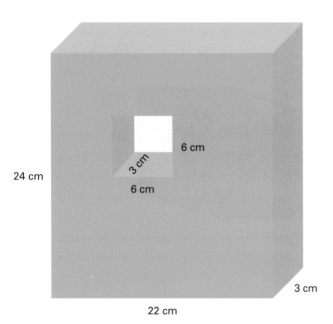

3. _____ cm³

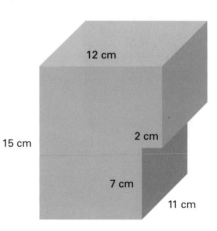

4. _____ cm³

Answers

Page 3
1. 8, 16, 32
2. 6, 12, 24
3. 9, 27, 81
4. 6, 18, 54
5. 5, 25, 125

Page 4
1. 8; 80; 800; 8,000; 80,000; 800,000
2. 42; 420; 4,200; 42,000; 420,000; 4,200,000
3. 6; 60; 600; 6,000; 60,000; 600,000
4. 36; 360; 3,600; 36,000; 360,000; 3,600,000

Page 5
1. 168
2. 455
3. 392

Page 6
1. 135
2. 312
3. 91
4. 296
5. 544
6. 170
7. 1,589
8. 1,178
9. 3,220
10. 2,848
11. 6,965
12. 1,788
13. 6,651
14. 1,518
15. 1,376
16. 3,716
17. 3,420
18. 7,785

Page 7
1. 540
2. 2,112
3. 630
4. 1,568
5. 1,748
6. 1,116
7. 3,384
8. 4,611
9. 1,300
10. 1,716
11. 3,944
12. 306
13. 4,888
14. 2,754
15. 1,125
16. 4,355
17. 5,841
18. 6,552

Page 8
1. 19,825
2. 44,454
3. 54,056
4. 18,705
5. 41,366
6. 49,379
7. 25,970
8. 6,698
9. 73,892
10. 11,165
11. 27,335
12. 55,112
13. 33,024
14. 73,242
15. 13,554
16. 25,002
17. 22,737
18. 57,350

Page 9
1. 129,864
2. 165,105
3. 324,918
4. 434,408
5. 343,542
6. 238,304
7. 168,350
8. 197,802
9. 214,896
10. 303,450
11. 1,394,672
12. 2,564,800
13. 739,383
14. 1,667,624
15. 4,019,089

Page 10
1. 248
2. 308
3. 806
4. 960
5. 1,240
6. 1,350
7. 1,460
8. 5,475
9. 8,760
10. 10,585
11. 13,505
12. 18,250

Page 11
1.
```
    296        300
  ×  24      ×  20
  -------    -------
   7,104      6,000
```
2.
```
    814        800
  ×  96      × 100
  -------    -------
  78,144     80,000
```
3.
```
    571        600
  × 935      × 900
  -------    -------
 533,885    540,000
```

Page 11 (continued)
4.
```
    707        700
  × 682      × 700
  -------    -------
 482,174    490,000
```
5.
```
  4,338      4,000
  ×  472     ×  500
  ---------  ---------
 2,047,536  2,000,000
```
6.
```
  9,566     10,000
  ×  343     ×  300
  ---------  ---------
 3,281,138  3,000,000
```

Page 12

Page 13

Page 14
14: 1, 2, 7, 14
49: 1, 7, 49
Common factors: 1, 7
Greatest common factor: 7

20: 1, 2, 4, 5, 10, 20
32: 1, 2, 4, 8, 16, 32
Common factors: 1, 2, 4
Greatest common factor: 4

24: 1, 2, 3, 4, 6, 8, 12, 24
60: 1, 2, 3, 4, 5, 6, 10, 12, 15, 20, 30, 60
Common factors: 1, 2, 3, 4, 6, 12
Greatest common factor: 12

Page 15
1. 2, 4, 8
2. 7, 14, 28
3. 1, 3, 9
4. 5, 15, 45
5. 5, 25, 125

Page 16
1. 4; 40; 40; 400; 400; 4,000
2. 3; 30; 30; 300; 300; 3,000
3. 2; 20; 20; 200; 200; 2,000
4. 9; 90; 90; 900; 900; 9,000

Page 17
1. 35
2. 59
3. 97
4. 19
5. 560
6. 919
7. 381
8. 754
9. 8,071
10. 7,343
11. 1,648
12. 4,592

Page 18
1. 81 r1
2. 78 r2
3. 58 r1
4. 94 r4
5. 537 r5
6. 343 r3
7. 801 r6
8. 359 r1
9. 9,796 r4
10. 6,415 r3
11. 8,774 r1
12. 1,628 r7

Page 19
1. 44
2. 17
3. 22
4. 39
5. 15 r2
6. 71 r1
7. 21 r8
8. 26 r22
9. 34 r5
10. 14 r4
11. 27 r26
12. 13 r14

Page 20
1. 177
2. 486
3. 113
4. 212
5. 226 r2
6. 304 r5
7. 184 r8
8. 425 r4
9. 326 r3
10. 135 r6
11. 194 r12
12. 367 r11

Page 21
1. 1,281
2. 1,687
3. 2,316
4. 1,263
5. 3,462 r2
6. 1,598 r8
7. 1,029 r23
8. 852 r10
9. 2,398 r7
10. 1,404 r20
11. 1,184 r35
12. 1,436 r13

Page 22
1. 30
2. 44
3. 29
4. 24
5. 52
6. 61
7. 42
8. 56
9. 55
10. 65
11. 58
12. 37

Page 23
1.
```
     19 r2
  5)97
  100 ÷ 5 = 20
```
2.
```
      902 r3
  6)5,415
  5,400 ÷ 6 = 900
```
3.
```
      37 r1
  11)408
  400 ÷ 10 = 40
```
4.
```
      31 r2
  67)2,079
  2,100 ÷ 70 = 30
```
5.
```
      679 r13
  82)55,691
  56,000 ÷ 80 = 700
```
6.
```
      3,141 r12
  29)91,101
  90,000 ÷ 30 = 3,000
```

Page 24

Page 25

Page 26

Page 27
1. 7, 3, 6, 1, 2, 4, 8
2. 9, 4, 8, 2, 1, 5, 6
3. 3, 0, 2, 4, 8, 1, 7
4. 8, 2, 1, 0, 5, 3, 9
5. 4, 1, 9, 4, 6, 8, 2
6. 1, 5, 7, 6, 0, 4, 1

Page 28
1. hundreds
2. tenths
3. thousandths
4. ones
5. thousands
6. hundredths
7. tens
8. tenths
9. hundreds
10. thousandths

Page 29
1. 4.914, 4.952, 5.279, 5.836
2. 7.156, 7.159, 7.671, 8.442
3. 0.482, 0.533, 0.617, 0.694
4. 1.208, 1.228, 1.232, 1.265
5. 4.003, 4.006, 4.014, 4.053
6. 0.239, 0.322, 0.329, 0.932

Answers

Page 30
1. >   2. =   3. >   4. <
5. <   6. >   7. <   8. <
9. >   10. <   11. =   12. >
13. <   14. >   15. >   16. <
17. <   18. >   19. <   20. =

Page 31
1. 1   2. 9   3. 6   4. 4
5. 5   6. 4   7. 5   8. 10
9. 3   10. 9   11. 0   12. 8
13. 6   14. 3   15. 1   16. 7

Page 32
1. 11.79, 12.00
2. 3.12, 3.00
3. 9.85, 10.00
4. 20.28, 20.00
5. 5.41, 5.00
6. 10.50, 11.00

Page 33
1. 2.2   2. 5.7
3. 8.2   4. 1.8
5. 3.3   6. 7.7
7. 4.1   8. 0
9. 9.55   10. 4.48
11. 1.92   12. 4.53
13. 2.38   14. 5.17
15. 3.09   16. 6.90

Page 34

	Nearest One	Nearest Tenth	Nearest Hundredth
25.158	25	25.2	25.16
1.372	1	1.4	1.37
83.614	84	83.6	83.61
390.293	390	390.3	390.29
7.872	8	7.9	7.87
14.426	14	14.4	14.43
5.555	6	5.6	5.56
0.307	0	0.3	0.31

Page 35
1. 9.76   2. 29.55
3. 87.48   4. 58.25
5. 189.87   6. 975.63
7. 5.31   8. 62.23
9. 45.02   10. 24.44
11. 511.90   12. 237.57

Page 36
1. 9.5   2. 11.62
3. 40.84   4. 87.02
5. 108.55   6. 105.387
7. 151.557   8. 675.31
9. 1,366.84   10. 738.362
11. 2,930.382   12. 10,044.42

Page 37
1. 3.4   2. 2.78
3. 58.96   4. 17.931
5. 48.51   6. 535.47
7. 754.37   8. 27.649
9. 471.56   10. 583.248
11. 1,979.78   12. 7,768.15

Page 38
1.
$$\begin{array}{r} 3.42 \\ + 5.6 \\ \hline 9.02 \end{array} \qquad \begin{array}{r} 3 \\ + 6 \\ \hline 9 \end{array}$$
2.
$$\begin{array}{r} 1.84 \\ + 4.95 \\ \hline 6.79 \end{array} \qquad \begin{array}{r} 2 \\ + 5 \\ \hline 7 \end{array}$$
3.
$$\begin{array}{r} 4.068 \\ + 6.75 \\ \hline 10.818 \end{array} \qquad \begin{array}{r} 4 \\ + 7 \\ \hline 11 \end{array}$$
4.
$$\begin{array}{r} 6.17 \\ - 2.9 \\ \hline 3.27 \end{array} \qquad \begin{array}{r} 6 \\ - 3 \\ \hline 3 \end{array}$$
5.
$$\begin{array}{r} 9.81 \\ - 5.66 \\ \hline 4.15 \end{array} \qquad \begin{array}{r} 10 \\ - 6 \\ \hline 4 \end{array}$$
6.
$$\begin{array}{r} 12.691 \\ - 4.32 \\ \hline 8.371 \end{array} \qquad \begin{array}{r} 13 \\ - 4 \\ \hline 9 \end{array}$$

Page 39
1. 13.3   2. 36.5
3. 25.89   4. 124.2
5. 21.12   6. 56.28
7. 19.38   8. 9.75
9. 18.767   10. 0.352
11. 44.064   12. 59.93

Page 40
1. 0.7   2. 0.4
3. 1.67   4. 3.27
5. 2.91   6. 4.32
7. 3.117   8. 0.574
9. 5.86   10. 3.45
11. 0.263   12. 0.174

Page 41
Suggested estimates:
1. $4 \times 7 = 28$
2. $4 \times 4 = 16$
3. $5 \times 8 = 40$
4. $3 \times 40 = 120$
5. $4 \times 11 = 44$
6. $9 \times 9 = 81$
7. $6 \div 6 = 1$
8. $4.8 \div 8 = 0.6$
9. $9.3 \div 3 = 3.1$
10. $1.2 \div 6 = 0.2$
11. $4.5 \div 5 = 0.9$
12. $110 \div 11 = 10$

Page 42
1. 45.1   2. 19.83
3. 724.2   4. 60.3
5. 8,599   6. 4,217
7. 0.36   8. 7.738
9. 9.366   10. 541.03
11. 38.249   12. 0.572

Page 43
1. $\frac{1}{6}$ 2. $\frac{5}{8}$ 3. $\frac{3}{4}$
4. $\frac{2}{5}$ 5. $\frac{7}{8}$ 6. $\frac{3}{7}$
7. $\frac{3}{4}$, $\frac{3}{7}$ 8. $\frac{5}{8}$, $\frac{7}{8}$

Page 44
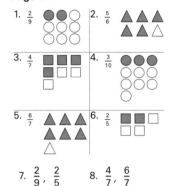

1. $\frac{2}{9}$ 2. $\frac{5}{6}$ 3. $\frac{4}{7}$ 4. $\frac{3}{10}$ 5. $\frac{6}{7}$ 6. $\frac{2}{5}$

7. $\frac{2}{9}$, $\frac{2}{5}$ 8. $\frac{4}{7}$, $\frac{6}{7}$

Page 45
1. $\frac{3}{9}$ 2. $\frac{3}{4}$
3. $\frac{2}{10}$ 4. $\frac{1}{3}$

Page 46
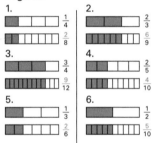

1. $\frac{1}{4}$, $\frac{2}{8}$ 2. $\frac{2}{3}$, $\frac{6}{9}$
3. $\frac{3}{4}$, $\frac{9}{12}$ 4. $\frac{2}{5}$, $\frac{4}{10}$
5. $\frac{1}{3}$, $\frac{2}{6}$ 6. $\frac{1}{2}$, $\frac{5}{10}$

Page 47
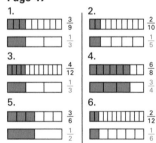

1. $\frac{3}{9}$, $\frac{1}{3}$ 2. $\frac{2}{10}$, $\frac{1}{5}$
3. $\frac{4}{12}$, $\frac{1}{3}$ 4. $\frac{6}{8}$, $\frac{3}{4}$
5. $\frac{3}{6}$, $\frac{1}{2}$ 6. $\frac{2}{12}$, $\frac{1}{6}$

Page 48
1. $\frac{2}{3}$ 2. $\frac{1}{2}$ 3. $\frac{1}{3}$
4. $\frac{1}{4}$ 5. $\frac{2}{5}$ 6. $\frac{3}{4}$
7. $\frac{5}{6}$ 8. $\frac{4}{9}$ 9. $\frac{7}{8}$
10. $\frac{3}{5}$ 11. $\frac{4}{7}$ 12. $\frac{9}{10}$

Page 49
1. $1\frac{6}{7}$ 2. $2\frac{1}{4}$ 3. $1\frac{4}{9}$
4. $2\frac{2}{5}$ 5. $3\frac{1}{2}$ 6. $3\frac{5}{8}$

Page 50
1. $2\frac{3}{4}$ 2. $4\frac{4}{5}$ 3. $6\frac{1}{3}$
4. $4\frac{1}{2}$ 5. $7\frac{3}{7}$ 6. $1\frac{1}{10}$
7. $10\frac{5}{6}$ 8. $5\frac{3}{8}$ 9. $7\frac{2}{3}$
10. $3\frac{4}{9}$ 11. $11\frac{2}{5}$ 12. $3\frac{7}{12}$

Page 51
1. $\frac{17}{2}$ 2. $\frac{13}{6}$ 3. $\frac{31}{4}$
4. $\frac{11}{3}$ 5. $\frac{92}{9}$ 6. $\frac{25}{6}$
7. $\frac{43}{8}$ 8. $\frac{32}{5}$ 9. $\frac{34}{11}$
10. $\frac{37}{4}$ 11. $\frac{44}{10}$ 12. $\frac{79}{9}$

Page 52
1. $1\frac{2}{5}$ 2. $\frac{27}{8}$ 3. $\frac{10}{3}$
4. $2\frac{3}{10}$ 5. $7\frac{3}{7}$ 6. $3\frac{3}{4}$

Page 53
1. $\frac{1}{10}$, 0.1   2. $\frac{4}{10}$, 0.4
3. $\frac{9}{10}$, 0.9   4. $\frac{5}{10}$, 0.5
5. $\frac{7}{10}$, 0.7   6. $\frac{6}{10}$, 0.6

Page 54
1. $\frac{55}{100}$, 0.55   2. $\frac{28}{100}$, 0.28
3. $\frac{96}{100}$, 0.96   4. $\frac{8}{100}$, 0.08

Page 55
1. $\frac{13}{100}$, 13%   2. $\frac{88}{100}$, 88%
3. $\frac{39}{100}$, 39%   4. $\frac{61}{100}$, 61%

Page 56
1. 60%   2. 32%   3. 20%
4. 50%   5. 48%   6. 15%
7. $\frac{7}{50}$ 8. $\frac{2}{5}$ 9. $\frac{9}{25}$
10. $\frac{1}{10}$ 11. $\frac{7}{20}$ 12. $\frac{23}{100}$

Answers

Page 57
1. 20%   2. 45%   3. 99%
4. 13%   5. 51%   6. 88%
7. 27%   8. 6%   9. 39%
10. 21%   11. 72%   12. 63%
13. 0.75 14. 0.46 15. 0.32
16. 0.93 17. 0.08 18. 0.15
19. 0.84 20. 0.01 21. 0.51
22. 0.27 23. 0.68 24. 0.82

Page 58
1. 36   2. 21   3. 13
4. 7.5   5. 5.46   6. 33.6
7. 3.52   8. 35.15 9. 4.35

Page 59
1. 0.45   2. 0.7
3.
4. 100%   5. $\frac{3}{8}$

Page 60
1. =   2. >   3. <   4. >
5. <   6. >   7. <   8. =
9. >   10. =   11. >   12. <
13. <   14. <   15. =   16. <

Page 61
1. $\frac{4}{5}$ 2. $\frac{6}{7}$ 3. $\frac{10}{11}$
4. $\frac{8}{8}$ 5. $\frac{9}{14}$

Page 62
1. $2\frac{2}{3}$ 2. $\frac{1}{2}$ 3. $1\frac{5}{9}$
4. $\frac{5}{6}$ 5. $4\frac{3}{8}$ 6. $\frac{2}{3}$
7. 7   8. $\frac{7}{9}$ 9. $5\frac{1}{4}$
10. $1\frac{3}{5}$

Page 63
1. $1\frac{1}{6}$ 2. $\frac{1}{3}$ 3. $3\frac{1}{8}$
4. $1\frac{3}{20}$ 5. $2\frac{2}{9}$ 6. $1\frac{7}{16}$
7. 2   8. $1\frac{11}{36}$ 9. $2\frac{1}{8}$

Page 64
1. $7\frac{4}{7}$ 2. $6\frac{5}{8}$ 3. $8\frac{14}{15}$
4. $9\frac{8}{9}$ 5. $3\frac{7}{10}$ 6. $6\frac{5}{6}$
7. $8\frac{1}{2}$ 8. $12\frac{3}{8}$ 9. $16\frac{1}{14}$

Page 65
1. $\frac{1}{5}$ 2. $\frac{3}{10}$ 3. $\frac{2}{6}$
4. $\frac{5}{12}$ 5. $\frac{5}{8}$ 6. $\frac{2}{9}$

Page 66
1. $\frac{1}{2}$ 2. $\frac{3}{4}$ 3. $\frac{1}{3}$
4. $\frac{1}{9}$ 5. $\frac{11}{12}$ 6. 1
7. $1\frac{2}{13}$ 8. $3\frac{1}{9}$ 9. $1\frac{1}{5}$
10. $\frac{3}{4}$

Page 67
1. $\frac{1}{10}$ 2. $\frac{7}{12}$ 3. $\frac{11}{40}$
4. $\frac{1}{6}$ 5. $\frac{1}{9}$ 6. $\frac{11}{24}$
7. $1\frac{1}{2}$ 8. $1\frac{2}{15}$ 9. $3\frac{9}{20}$

Page 68
1. $2\frac{1}{7}$ 2. $7\frac{2}{3}$ 3. $3\frac{1}{2}$
4. $1\frac{1}{10}$ 5. $9\frac{1}{9}$ 6. $4\frac{3}{14}$
7. $2\frac{5}{8}$ 8. $\frac{2}{3}$ 9. $5\frac{17}{18}$

Page 69
1. 1   2. 5   3. 3
4. $\frac{1}{5}$ 5. $\frac{1}{8}$ 6. $\frac{2}{9}$

Page 70
1. $\frac{1}{15}$ 2. $\frac{1}{10}$ 3. $\frac{2}{7}$
4. $\frac{10}{27}$ 5. $\frac{1}{4}$ 6. $\frac{1}{20}$
7. $\frac{9}{28}$ 8. $\frac{1}{14}$ 9. $\frac{3}{16}$

Page 71
1. $\frac{3}{10}$ 2. $\frac{5}{28}$ 3. $\frac{5}{11}$
4. $\frac{9}{32}$ 5. $\frac{7}{8}$ 6. $\frac{11}{36}$
7. $\frac{1}{6}$ 8. $\frac{3}{4}$ 9. $\frac{2}{9}$

Page 72
1. $3\frac{1}{9}$ 2. $15\frac{3}{4}$ 3. 6
4. $7\frac{1}{3}$ 5. 8   6. $16\frac{1}{2}$
7. $21\frac{2}{3}$ 8. $5\frac{1}{4}$ 9. 68

Page 73
1. $\frac{6}{5}$ 2. $\frac{2}{7}$ 3. $\frac{3}{1}$
4. $\frac{10}{9}$ 5. $\frac{5}{12}$ 6. $\frac{11}{1}$
7. $\frac{5}{8}$ 8. $\frac{1}{8}$ 9. $\frac{13}{4}$
10. $\frac{23}{32}$ 11. $\frac{67}{55}$ 12. $\frac{100}{99}$

Page 74
1. 1   2. 1   3. 1
4. $\frac{3}{4}$ 5. $\frac{9}{8}$ 6. $\frac{1}{3}$
7. $\frac{6}{17}$ 8. $\frac{103}{78}$ 9. $\frac{6}{35}$

Page 75
1. 12   2. 10   3. 5
4. 3   5. 4   6. 2

Page 76
1. $1\frac{7}{8}$ 2. $\frac{1}{4}$ 3. $\frac{7}{12}$
4. $\frac{1}{8}$ 5. $6\frac{2}{3}$ 6. $\frac{1}{2}$
7. $\frac{3}{4}$ 8. $5\frac{5}{6}$ 9. $1\frac{1}{3}$

Page 77
1. $1\frac{1}{2}$ 2. $\frac{2}{9}$ 3. $1\frac{2}{21}$
4. $\frac{4}{9}$ 5. $1\frac{1}{17}$ 6. $\frac{7}{12}$
7. $2\frac{1}{2}$ 8. $2\frac{1}{9}$ 9. $\frac{5}{27}$

Page 78
1. 74   2. 96   3. 120
4. 360   5. 104   6. 180
7. 369   8. 90

Page 79
1. $4\frac{1}{2}$ 2. $6\frac{3}{4}$ 3. $2\frac{2}{3}$
4. $1\frac{7}{9}$ 5. 8   6. $5\frac{1}{3}$

Page 80
1. 2.5   2. 1.5   3. 0.9
4. 18   5. 30   6. 50
7. 54   8. 90   9. 150

Page 81
1. 18   2. 60
3. 65.6   4. 40

Page 82
1. 36   2. 274
3. 58   4. 22.2

Page 83
1. right   2. obtuse   3. acute
4. obtuse   5. acute   6. right
7. acute   8. obtuse   9. obtuse

Page 84
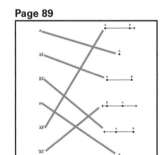

Page 85

Right Angles	Acute Angles	Obtuse Angles
4	0	0
1	2	0
0	2	2
0	0	8
0	2	2
1	1	3

Page 86
1. 15   2. 120   3. 87
4. 163   5. 38   6. 142

Page 87
1. ray
2. line segment
3. point
4. line
5. ray

Page 88
1. *AB*   2. *QR*   3. *F*
4. *MN*   5. *CD*   6. *KL*
7. *X*   8. *GH*   9. *YZ*

Page 89
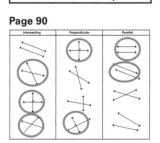

Page 90

Answers

Page 91
1. hexagon
2. quadrilateral
3. decagon
4. heptagon
5. quadrilateral
6. nonagon
7. pentagon
8. octagon

Page 92
1. rhombus, parallelogram
2. square, rectangle
3. trapezoid
4. parallelogram
5. rectangle
6. rhombus, parallelogram
7. parallelogram
8. trapezoid

Page 93

Shape Name	Sides	Vertices	Pairs of Parallel Lines
parallel-ogram	4	4	2
hexagon	6	6	3
nonagon	9	9	0
trapezoid	4	4	1
pentagon	5	5	0

Page 94

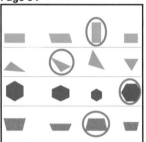

Page 95
1. 70   2. 25   3. 644
4. 480   5. 30   6. 23.04

Page 96
1. 9   2. 48   3. 40
4. 105   5. $6\frac{1}{2}$ 6. 75.33

Page 97
1. 15   2. 120   3. 81
4. 391   5. $11\frac{1}{9}$ 6. 45.08

Page 98
1. 23   2. 70
3. 96   4. 327

Page 99
1. sphere
2. square pyramid
3. cone
4. cube
5. rectangular prism
6. cylinder

Page 100

Shape Name	Vertices	Edges	Faces
rectangular prism	8	12	6
square pyramid	5	8	5
cube	8	12	6

Page 101
1. 4   2. 15   3. 24
4. 27   5. 24   6. 20

Page 102
1. 216   2. 160   3. 1,859
4. 4,500 5. 90   6. 167.44

Page 103
1. 385   2. 1,690
3. 1,734   4. $370\frac{1}{2}$
5. 875   6. 945
7. flower planter
8. cereal box

Page 104
1. 1,457   2. 750
3. 1,476   4. 1,826

5th Grade
Math
Games & Puzzles

Number Factory

WRITE the numbers that will come out of each machine.

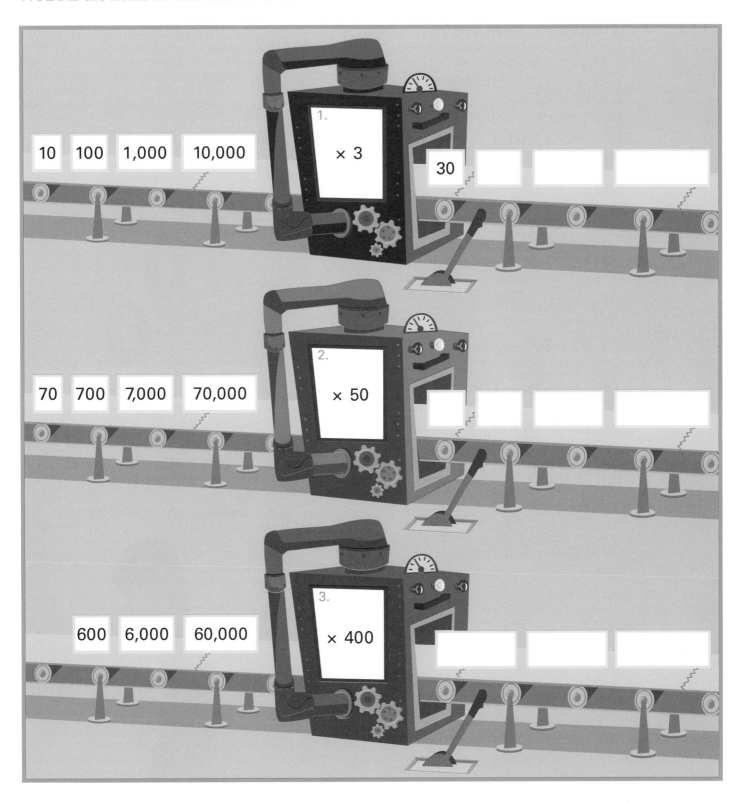

1. × 3

10   100   1,000   10,000

30 ___ ___ ___

2. × 50

70   700   7,000   70,000

___ ___ ___ ___

3. × 400

600   6,000   60,000

___ ___ ___

Zero In

There are 10 zeros missing from the products. WRITE zeros where they belong.

HINT: Not all products are missing zeros.

1. 40 × 80 = 320
2. 200 × 60 = 12000
3. 120 × 3 = 360
4. 5,000 × 400 = 200000
5. 700 × 700 = 49000
6. 100 × 1,000 = 10000
7. 60 × 50 = 300
8. 9,000 × 3,000 = 270000
9. 70 × 800 = 56000
10. 2,000 × 1,500 = 300000
11. 20 × 90 = 180
12. 600 × 800 = 48000

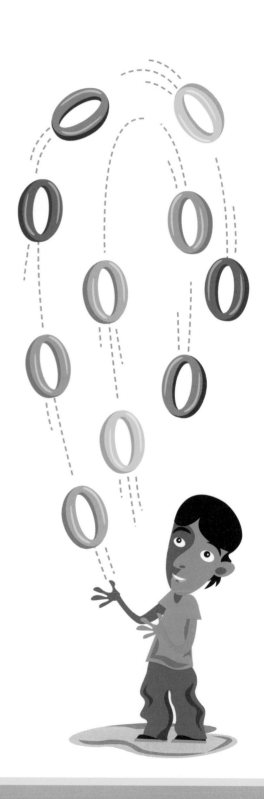

Pipe Down

WRITE the missing number. Then FOLLOW the pipe, and WRITE the same number in the next problem.

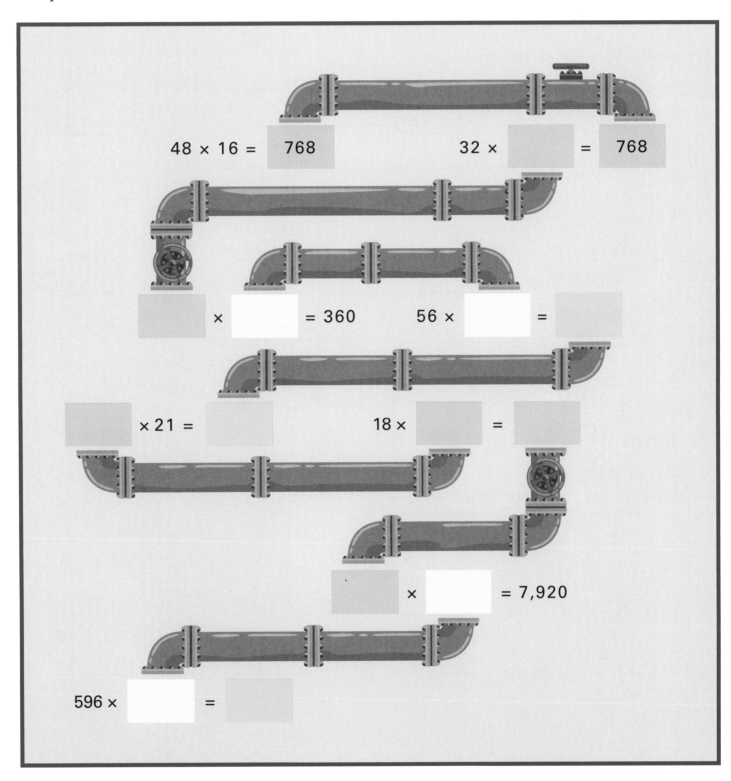

48 × 16 = 768

32 × ___ = 768

___ × ___ = 360

56 × ___ =

___ × 21 =

18 × ___ =

___ × ___ = 7,920

596 × ___ = ___

Multidigit Multiplication

Criss Cross

SOLVE the multiplication problems, and WRITE the products in the puzzle.

ACROSS

1.
   2,901
   × 165

5.
   6,226
   ×   95

7.
   2,468
   × 227

9.
   6,234
   × 103

11.
   802
   × 377

12.
   1,591
   × 282

13.
   4,232
   ×   69

15.
   882
   × 565

DOWN

1.
   1,757
   ×   24

2.
   5,402
   × 125

3.
   1,263
   × 421

4.
   176
   × 614

6.
   3,987
   ×   55

8.
   1,158
   × 533

10.
   2,135
   × 116

14.
   642
   × 362

Secret Meeting

Genius scientist Professor Wormhole wants to meet with you, but you must first decode the secret location. SOLVE each problem by substituting numbers for letters using the code. Then WRITE the answers as letters in the same order to find the secret location.

N	A	H	B	E	I	M	F	T	C
0	1	2	3	4	5	6	7	8	9

1.   E N B
   ×   A M
   _____

2.   B H N C
   ×   H
   _____

3.   A N B
   ×   T
   _____

4.   H A E A
   ×   E
   _____

5.   A H C
   ×   E T
   _____

6.   A H M
   ×   E
   _____

___ ___ ___ ___ ___

___ ___ ___ ___ ___

___ ___ ___ ___ ___ ___

___ ___ ___ ___ ___ ___ ___ .

Just Right

WRITE each number so that it is a factor of the blue number next to it.

HINT: There may be more than one place to put a number, but you need to use every factor.

| 3 | 5 | 6 | 7 | 12 | 15 | 18 | 20 |

35

1

60

2

21

3

28

4

54

5

15

6

42

7

84

8

Gridlock

WRITE factors so that the product of the rows and columns is correct.

Example:

	11	12
6	66	72
3	33	36

11 × 6 = 66

11 × 3 = 33

12 × 6 = 72

12 × 3 = 36

	12	21
	36	63

	30	54
	40	72

	40	60
	80	120

	48	160
	75	250

	60	105
	80	140

	78	117
	150	225

Just Right

WRITE each number so that it is a multiple of the blue number next to it.

HINT: There may be more than one place to put a number, but you need to use every multiple.

| 14 | 49 | 55 | 63 | 88 | 100 | 180 | 72 |

10 _____
1

18 _____
2

5 _____
3

7 _____
4

9 _____
5

25 _____
6

2 _____
7

11 _____
8

Who Am I?

READ the clues, and CIRCLE the mystery number.

HINT: Cross out any number that does not match the clues.

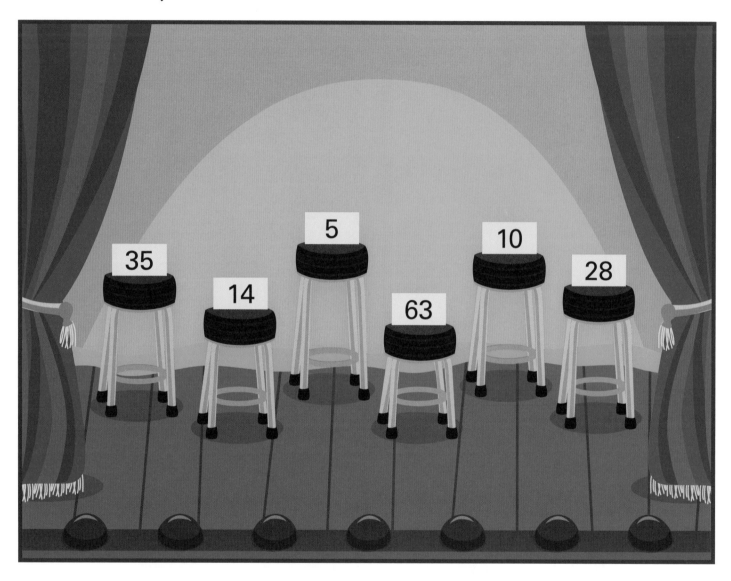

I am a multiple of 7.

I am not a multiple of 4.

I am a factor of 490.

I am the greatest common factor of 35 and 70.

Who am I?

Number Factory

WRITE the numbers that will come out of each machine.

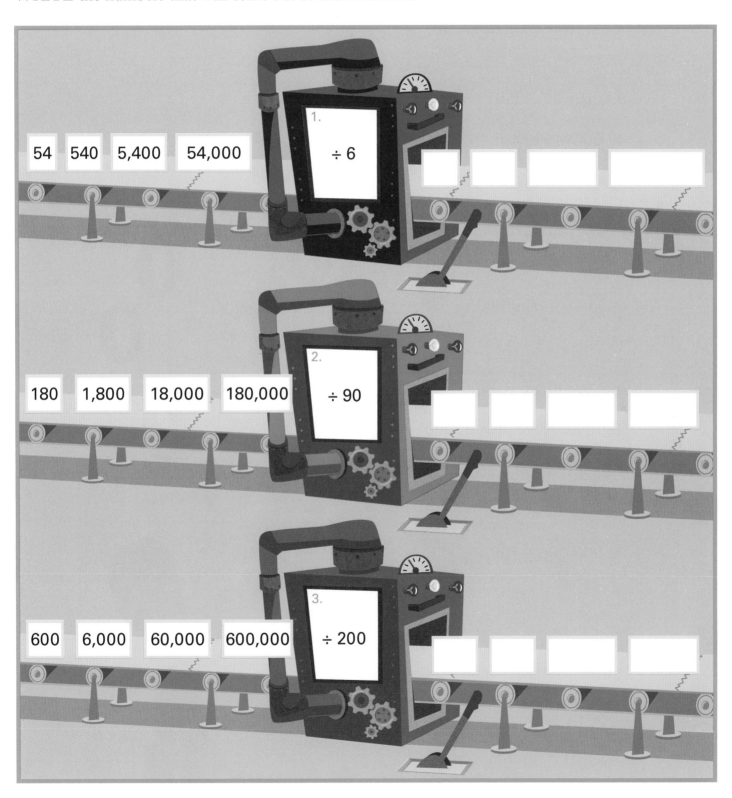

1. 54   540   5,400   54,000   ÷ 6

2. 180   1,800   18,000   180,000   ÷ 90

3. 600   6,000   60,000   600,000   ÷ 200

Division Patterns

Zero In

There are 10 zeros missing from the quotients. WRITE zeros where they belong.

HINT: Not all quotients are missing zeros.

1. 8,000 ÷ 40 = 200

2. 40,000 ÷ 500 = 8

3. 3,000,000 ÷ 600 = 500

4. 50,000 ÷ 25 = 200

5. 36,000,000 ÷ 9,000 = 4000

6. 640,000 ÷ 80 = 800

7. 10,000 ÷ 20 = 50

8. 4,500,000 ÷ 5 = 90000

9. 27,000,000 ÷ 900 = 30000

10. 700,000 ÷ 350 = 200

11. 5,000,000 ÷ 10 = 5000

12. 42,000,000 ÷ 700 = 6000

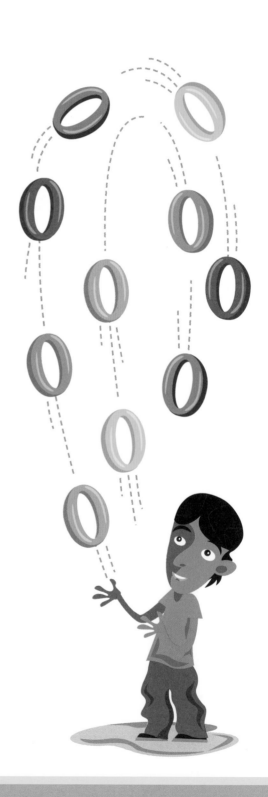

Pipe Down

WRITE the missing number. Then FOLLOW the pipe, and WRITE the same number in the next problem.

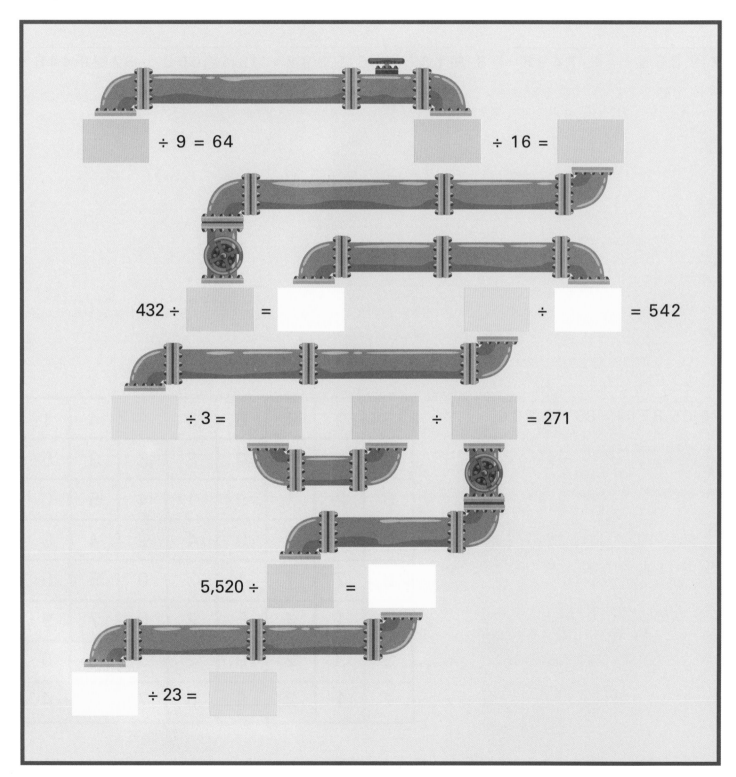

$576 \div 9 = 64$

$576 \div 16 = 36$

$432 \div 36 = 12$

$6{,}504 \div 12 = 542$

$6{,}504 \div 3 = 2{,}168$

$2{,}168 \div 8 = 271$

$5{,}520 \div 8 = 690$

$690 \div 23 = 30$

Number Search

WRITE each quotient. Then CIRCLE it in the puzzle.

HINT: Numbers are across and down only.

1. $7\overline{)8{,}855}$ 2. $4\overline{)7{,}496}$ 3. $3\overline{)9{,}165}$ 4. $6\overline{)5{,}898}$ 5. $15\overline{)12{,}060}$ 6. $32\overline{)20{,}448}$

7. $70\overline{)65{,}870}$ 8. $86\overline{)49{,}536}$

5	2	7	6	3	9	4	1
9	1	5	0	8	8	3	5
8	2	1	9	1	4	5	0
3	5	8	0	4	2	4	8
6	7	7	1	3	0	5	5
0	1	4	5	2	5	7	9
9	3	2	9	2	3	6	0
7	1	2	6	5	7	9	4

Secret Meeting

James Blonde, the super spy, has given you this code to let you know where to find him. SOLVE each problem by substituting numbers for letters using the code. Then WRITE the answers as letters in the same order to find the secret location.

HINT: The last word will be made from the remainders.

U	S	B	T	A	E	L	I	N	R
0	1	2	3	4	5	6	7	8	9

1.
E)TNTB

2.
SS)BNAT

3.
SE)NBAA

4.
EA)BBTUN

5.
NS)TANTI

6.
TR)BBEEU

Super Square

WRITE numbers in the empty squares to finish all of the division problems.

89,376	÷	266	=	**336**
÷		÷		÷
392	÷	**14**	=	**28**
=		=		=
228	÷	19	=	**12**

Prime Path

A **prime number** can only be divided evenly by itself and 1. DRAW a line from the start of the maze through only prime numbers to get to the end.

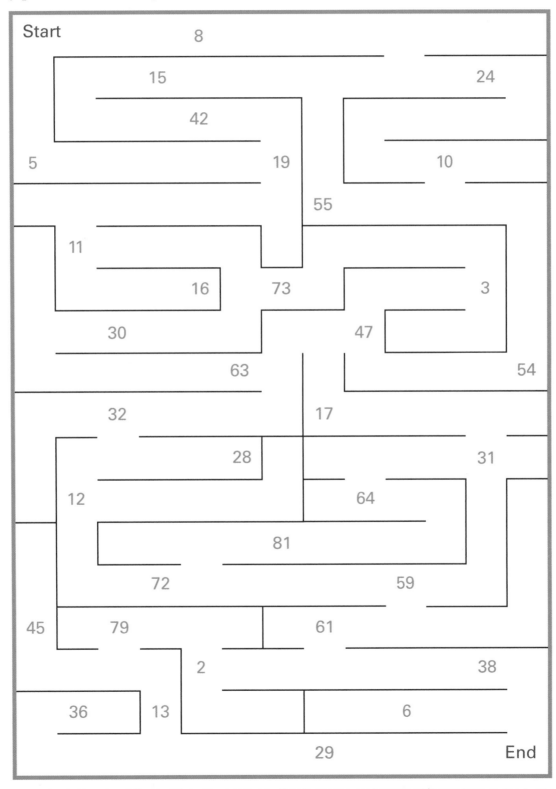

Five of a Kind

A **composite number** has more factors than itself and 1. CIRCLE any five composite numbers in a row.

HINT: Numbers are across and down only.

5	19	12	11	47	65	17	35
10	18	40	54	27	2	48	18
1	77	25	29	6	9	31	46
30	13	8	96	24	61	22	21
4	49	55	67	42	23	3	34
63	71	43	33	16	74	89	53
36	60	32	59	41	79	56	73
20	83	26	99	64	14	40	7

Totally Tangled

Each numbered circle is connected to another numbered circle. FIND the pairs of numbers, and SHADE the circle with the smaller number.

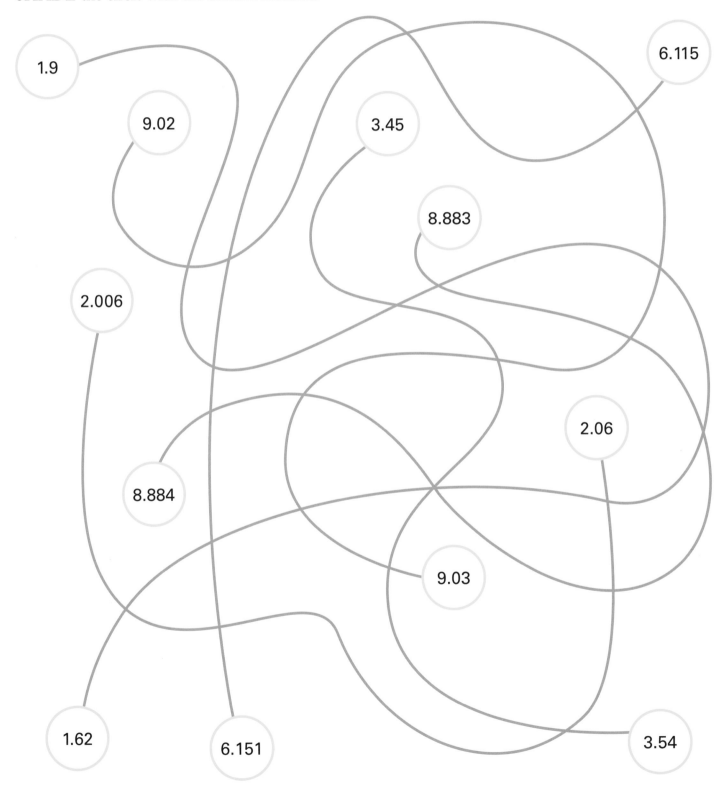

Comparing & Ordering Decimals

Win Big

Wherever two boxes point to one box, WRITE the larger number. START at the sides and work toward the center to see which number will win big.

Totally Tangled

Each numbered circle is connected to another numbered circle. FIND the pairs of numbers, and SHADE any pair that shows a number with that number correctly rounded to the nearest hundredth.

HINT: When the thousandths place has 1 to 4, round down to the nearest hundredth. When the thousandths place has 5 to 9, round up to the nearest hundredth.

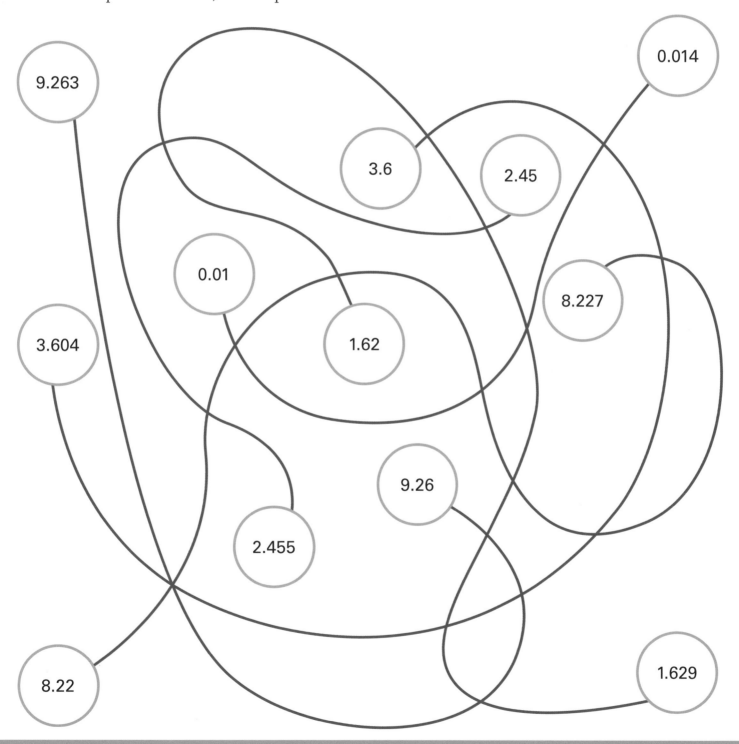

Just Right

WRITE the numbers to correctly complete each sentence.

HINT: There may be more than one place to put a number, but you need to use every number.

| 3.196 | 3.503 | 2.484 | 3.562 | 2.444 | 3.194 | 3.538 | 2.489 | 3.145 |

1. _____ rounded to the nearest one is 4.

2. _____ rounded to the nearest hundredth is 3.19.

3. _____ rounded to the nearest tenth is 2.4.

4. _____ rounded to the nearest one is 3.

5. _____ rounded to the nearest tenth is 3.6.

6. _____ rounded to the nearest hundredth is 2.48.

7. _____ rounded to the nearest tenth is 3.2.

8. _____ rounded to the nearest one is 2.

9. _____ rounded to the nearest hundredth is 3.54.

Crossing Paths

WRITE the missing numbers.

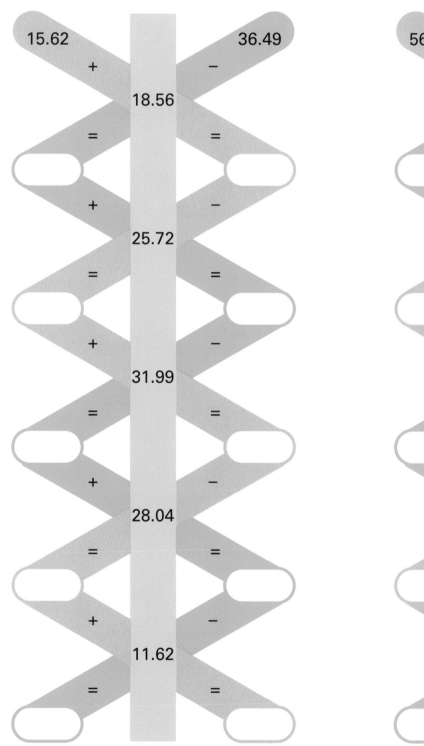

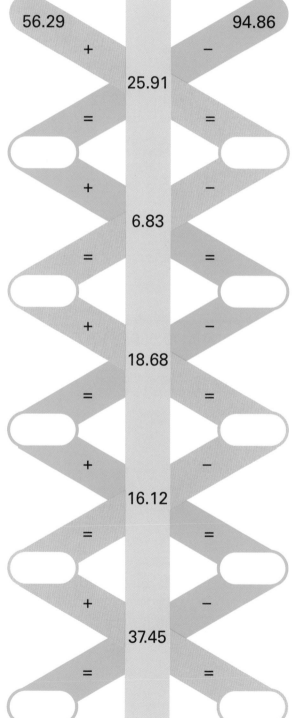

Left puzzle:

15.62   36.49

\+   18.56   −

=   =

( )   ( )

\+   25.72   −

=   =

( )   ( )

\+   31.99   −

=   =

( )   ( )

\+   28.04   −

=   =

( )   ( )

\+   11.62   −

=   =

( )   ( )

Right puzzle:

56.29   94.86

\+   25.91   −

=   =

( )   ( )

\+   6.83   −

=   =

( )   ( )

\+   18.68   −

=   =

( )   ( )

\+   16.12   −

=   =

( )   ( )

\+   37.45   −

=   =

( )   ( )

Number Factory

WRITE the numbers that will come out of each machine.

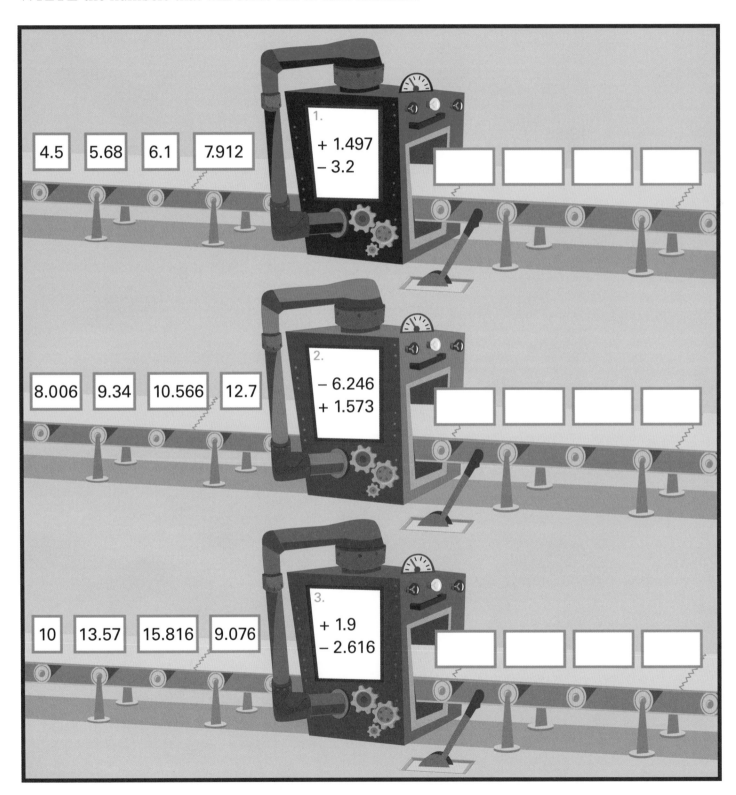

1.
+ 1.497
− 3.2

4.5   5.68   6.1   7.912

2.
− 6.246
+ 1.573

8.006   9.34   10.566   12.7

3.
+ 1.9
− 2.616

10   13.57   15.816   9.076

Totally Tangled

Each problem is connected to a product or quotient. FIND the problem pairs, and SHADE any product or quotient that has the decimal point in the wrong place.

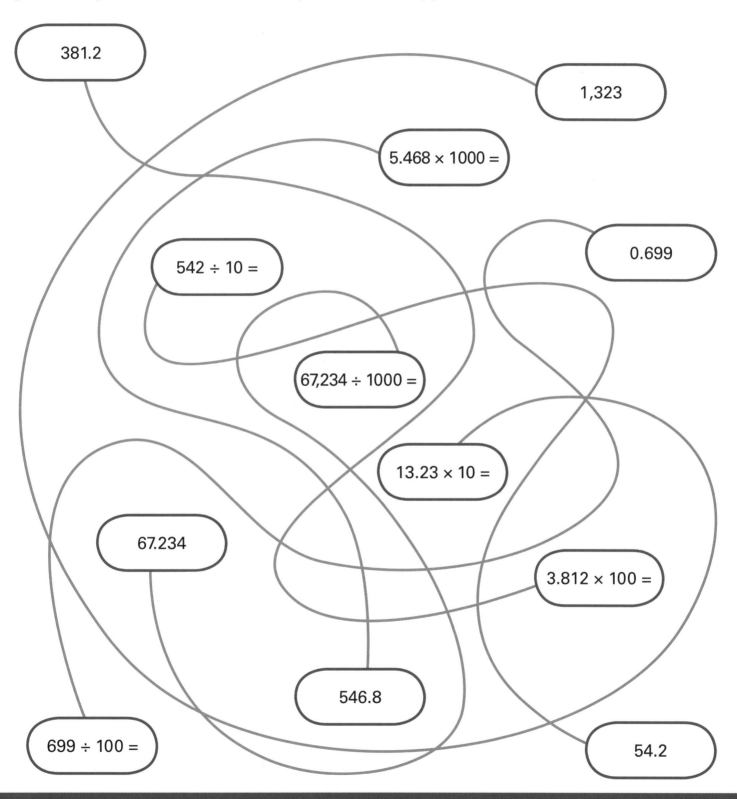

381.2

1,323

5.468 × 1000 =

542 ÷ 10 =

0.699

67,234 ÷ 1000 =

13.23 × 10 =

67.234

3.812 × 100 =

546.8

699 ÷ 100 =

54.2

Pipe Down

WRITE the missing number. Then FOLLOW the pipe, and WRITE the same number in the next problem.

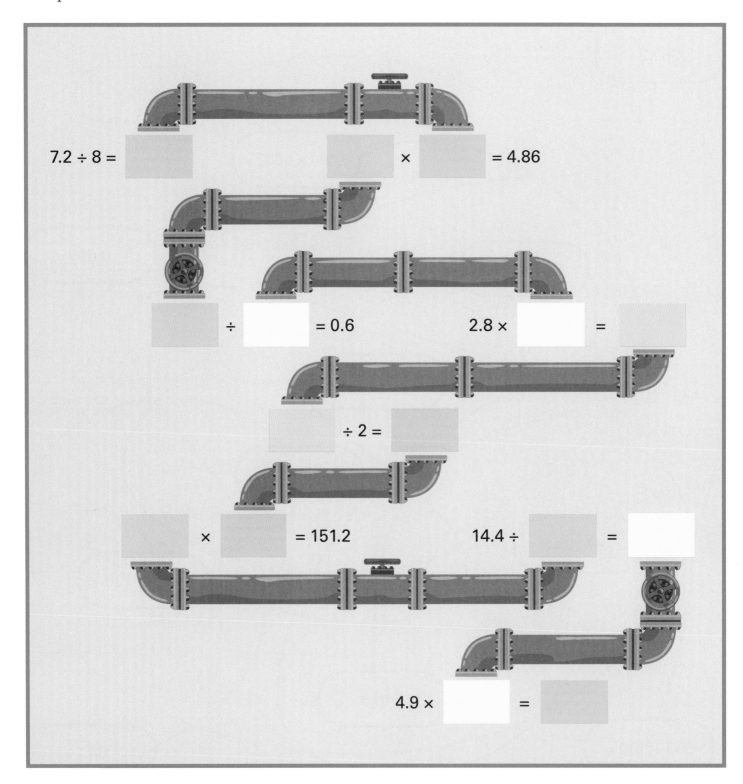

$7.2 \div 8 = $ ☐   ☐ × ☐ = 4.86

☐ ÷ ☐ = 0.6   2.8 × ☐ = ☐

☐ ÷ 2 = ☐

☐ × ☐ = 151.2   14.4 ÷ ☐ = ☐

4.9 × ☐ = ☐

Crossing Paths

WRITE the missing numbers.

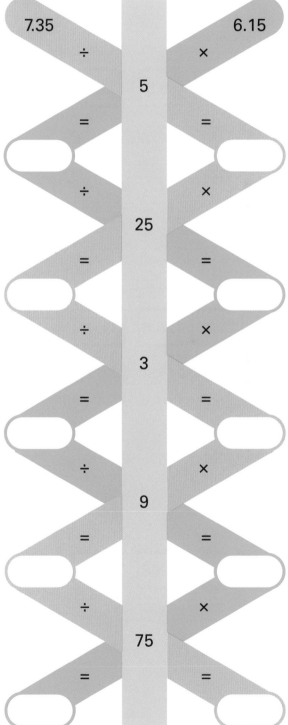

Number Factory

WRITE the numbers that will come out of each machine.

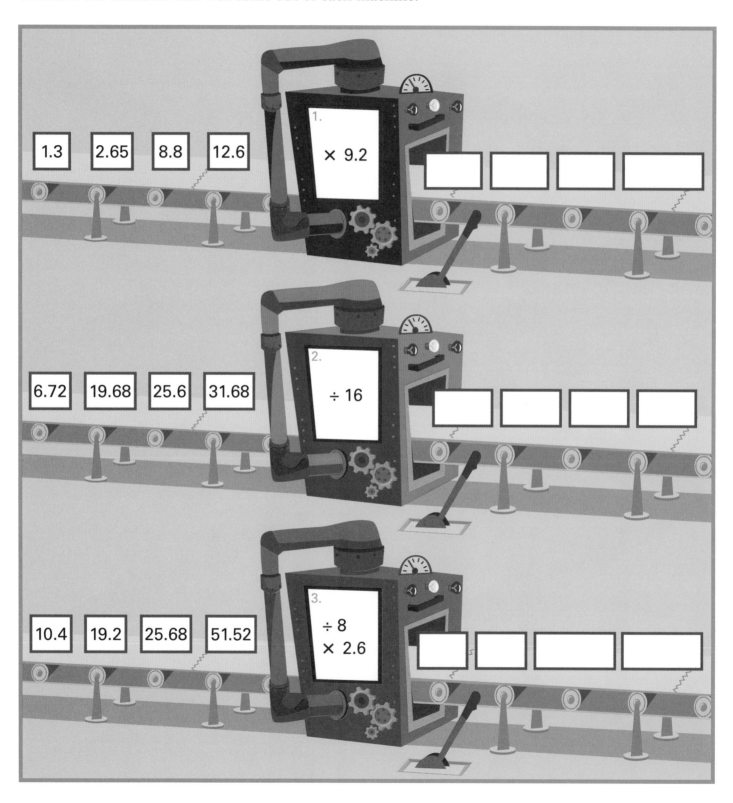

Totally Tangled

Equivalent fractions are fractions that have the same value. FIND the fraction and picture pairs that are connected, and SHADE any fraction that is not equivalent to the picture.

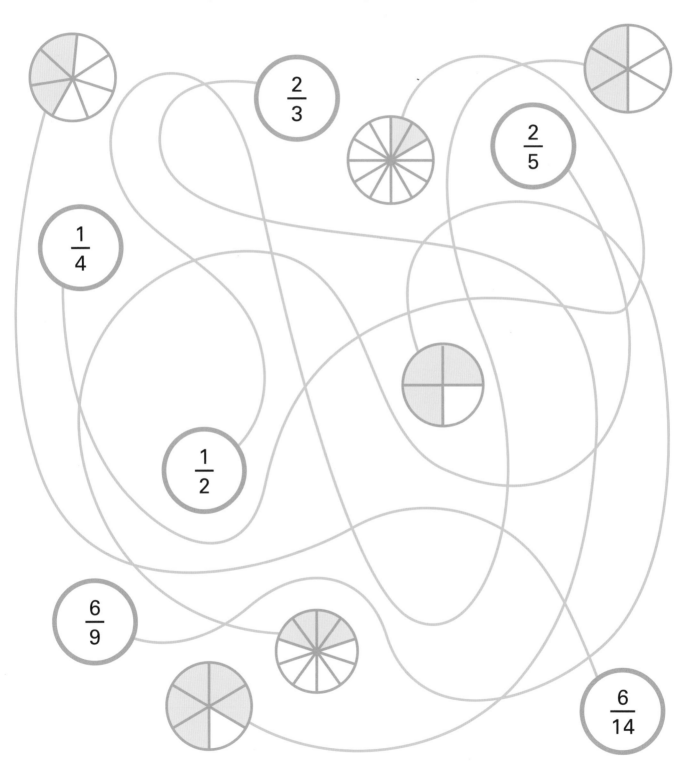

Fraction Flip

Use the orange cards from page 203, and PLACE each card next to an equivalent fraction. (Save the cards to use again.)

1.

$$\frac{2}{5} =$$

2.

$$\frac{3}{4} =$$

3.

$$\frac{5}{8} =$$

4.

$$\frac{1}{3} =$$

5.

$$\frac{1}{2} =$$

6.

$$\frac{3}{7} =$$

7.

$$\frac{2}{3} =$$

8.

$$\frac{5}{6} =$$

Number Factory

Each machine changes fractions into their simplest form. WRITE the fractions that will come out of each machine.

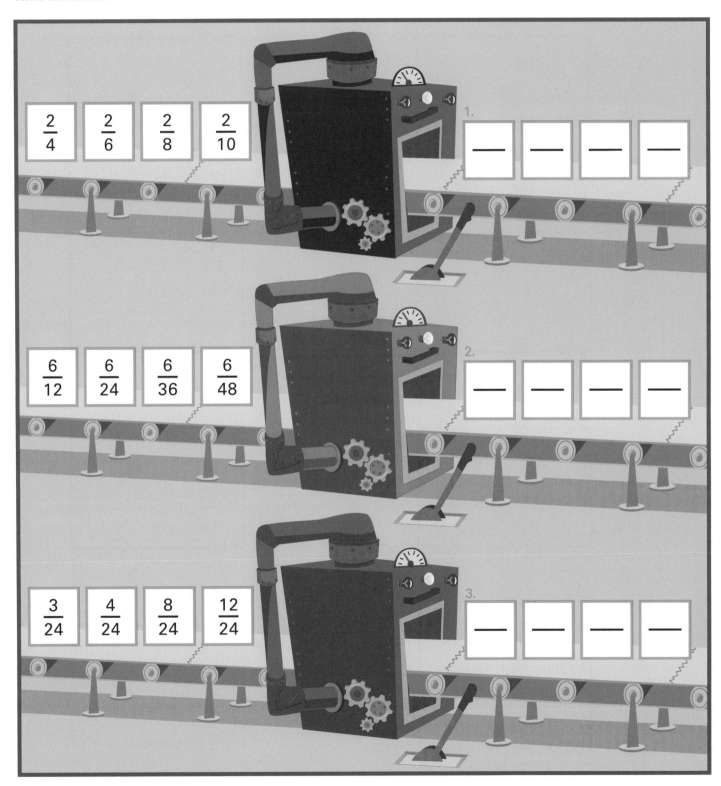

Fraction Flip

Use the blue cards from page 203, and PLACE each card so that it shows the fraction in its simplest form. (Save the cards to use again.)

1. $\dfrac{3}{18}$ =

2. $\dfrac{9}{36}$ =

3. $\dfrac{6}{16}$ =

4. $\dfrac{24}{28}$ =

5. $\dfrac{32}{64}$ =

6. $\dfrac{18}{27}$ =

7. $\dfrac{8}{40}$ =

8. $\dfrac{30}{50}$ =

Totally Tangled

FIND the fraction and mixed number pairs that are connected, and SHADE any fraction that is not equivalent to the mixed number.

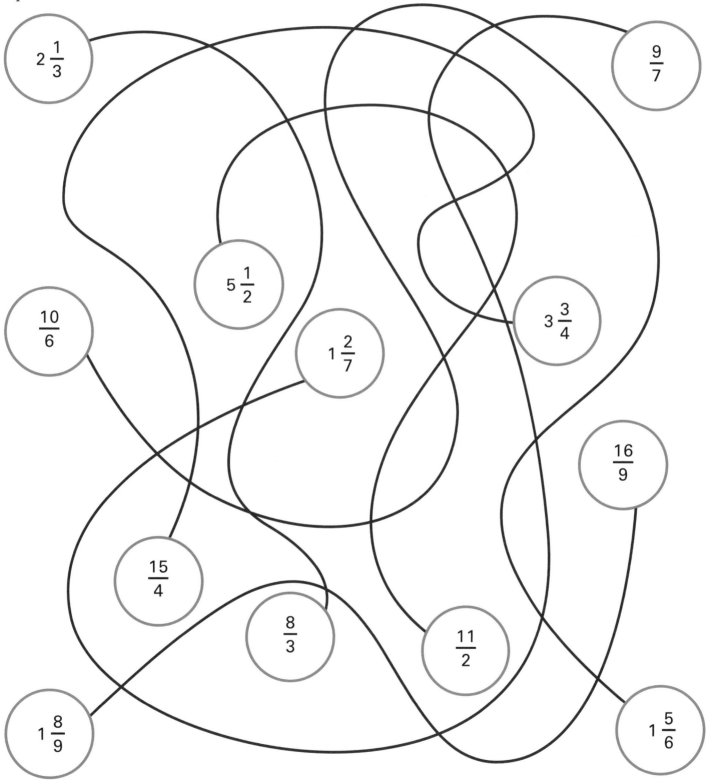

Code Breaker

WRITE each improper fraction as a mixed number. Then WRITE the letter that matches each mixed number to solve the riddle.

$\frac{7}{4}$ = ⬚¹	$\frac{23}{9}$ = ⬚²	$\frac{17}{8}$ = ⬚³	$\frac{11}{3}$ = ⬚⁴	$\frac{9}{2}$ = ⬚⁵
F	Y	O	T	A
$\frac{26}{8}$ = ⬚⁶	$\frac{18}{7}$ = ⬚⁷	$\frac{16}{6}$ = ⬚⁸	$\frac{25}{8}$ = ⬚⁹	$\frac{22}{5}$ = ⬚¹⁰
L	H	R	U	J

Which holiday lasts $7\frac{3}{4}$ days?

___ ___ ___ ___ ___ ___ ___
$4\frac{1}{2}$ $1\frac{3}{4}$ $2\frac{1}{8}$ $3\frac{1}{8}$ $2\frac{2}{3}$ $3\frac{2}{3}$ $2\frac{4}{7}$

___ ___ ___ ___ ___ ___.
$2\frac{1}{8}$ $1\frac{3}{4}$ $4\frac{2}{5}$ $3\frac{1}{8}$ $3\frac{1}{4}$ $2\frac{5}{9}$

Totally Tangled

A **percent** (%) is another way of showing parts of 100. FIND the pairs that are connected, and SHADE any pair that is not equivalent.

Example: $\dfrac{57}{100} = 0.57 = 57\%$

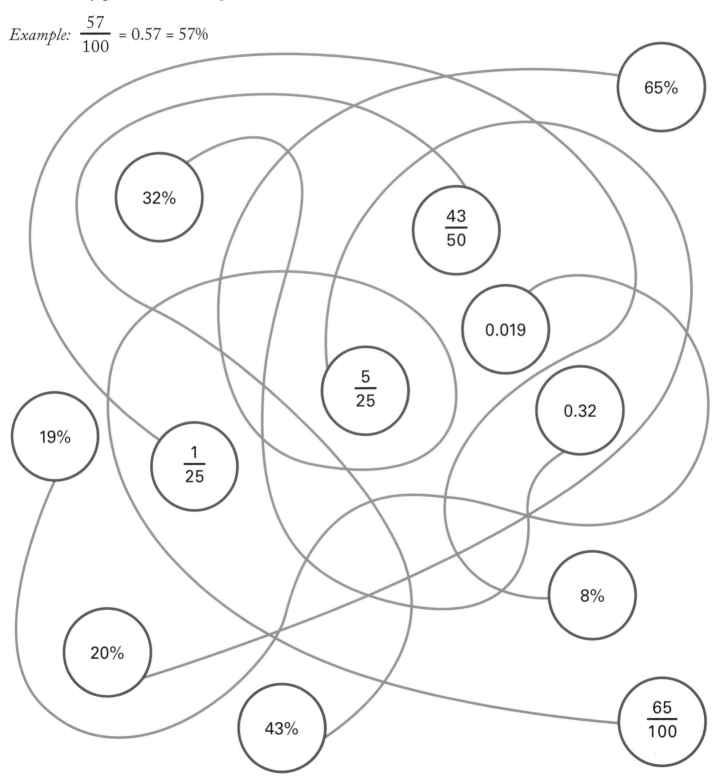

Code Breaker

WRITE the percent of each number. Then WRITE the letter that matches each number to solve the riddle.

HINT: To find the percent of a number, change the percent to a decimal and multiply.

25% of 24 = ¹ Y	10% of 40 = ² P	50% of 34 = ³ C	90% of 50 = ⁴ F
20% of 65 = ⁵ N	40% of 20 = ⁶ E	16% of 75 = ⁷ O	75% of 64 = ⁸ T
12% of 25 = ⁹ R	27% of 100 = ¹⁰ I		

Why did the girl buy a doll with no legs?

It was ___ ___ ___ ___ ___
       45   27   45   48   6

___ ___ ___ ___ ___ ___ ___
4   8   3   17   8   13   48

___ ___ ___ .
12   45   45

Totally Tangled

Each numbered circle is connected to another numbered circle. FIND the pairs of numbers, and SHADE the circle with the smaller amount.

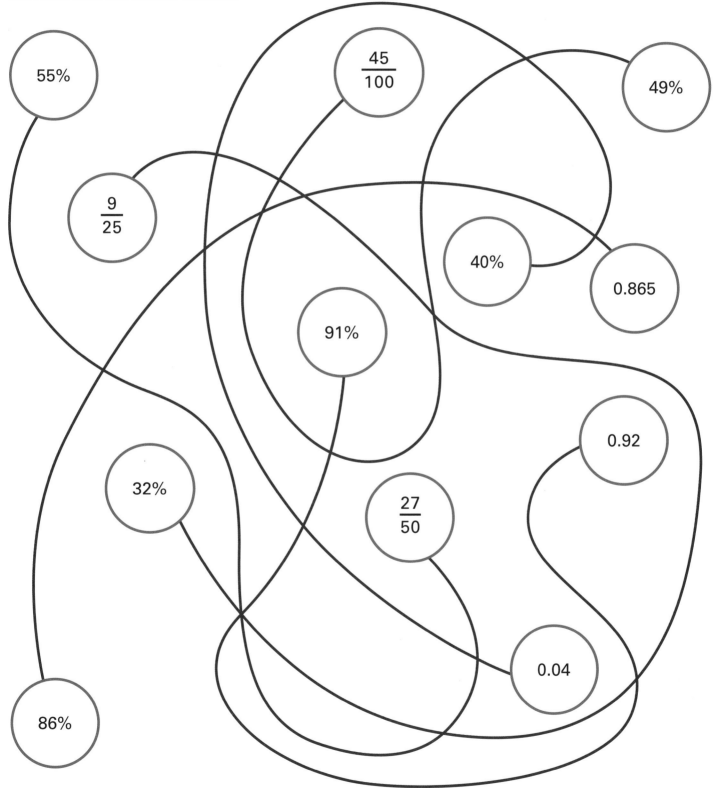

Win Big

Wherever two boxes point to one box, WRITE the larger number. START at the sides and work toward the center to see which number will win big.

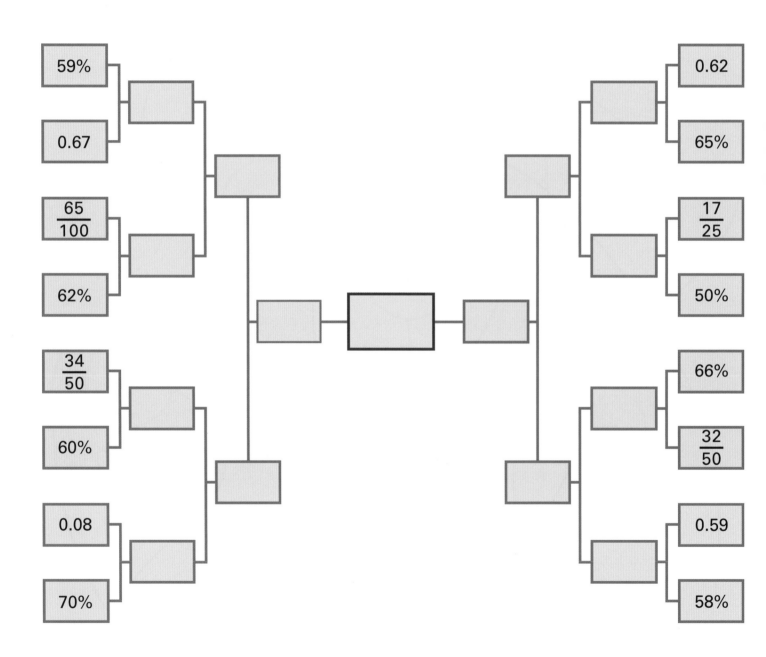

Number Factory

WRITE the fractions that will come out of each machine in their simplest form.

HINT: When adding fractions with different denominators, rewrite the fractions with their lowest common denominators.

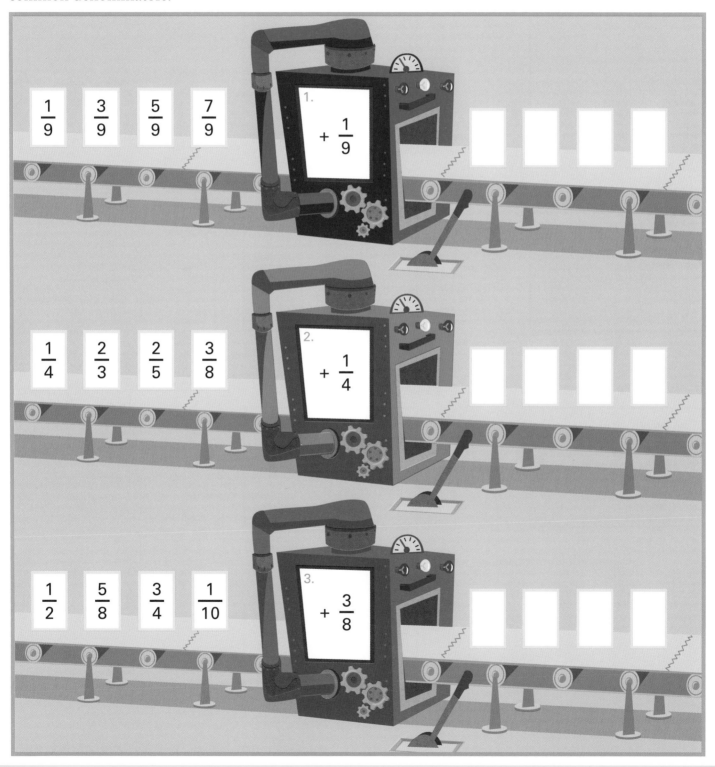

Fraction Flip

Use any of the cards from page 203, and DEAL the cards into the boxes. Then WRITE each sum. (Save the cards to use again.)

 +  = _____

 +  = _____

 +  = _____

 +  = _____

Pipe Down

WRITE the missing fraction or mixed number in its simplest form. Then FOLLOW the pipe, and WRITE the same fraction in the next problem.

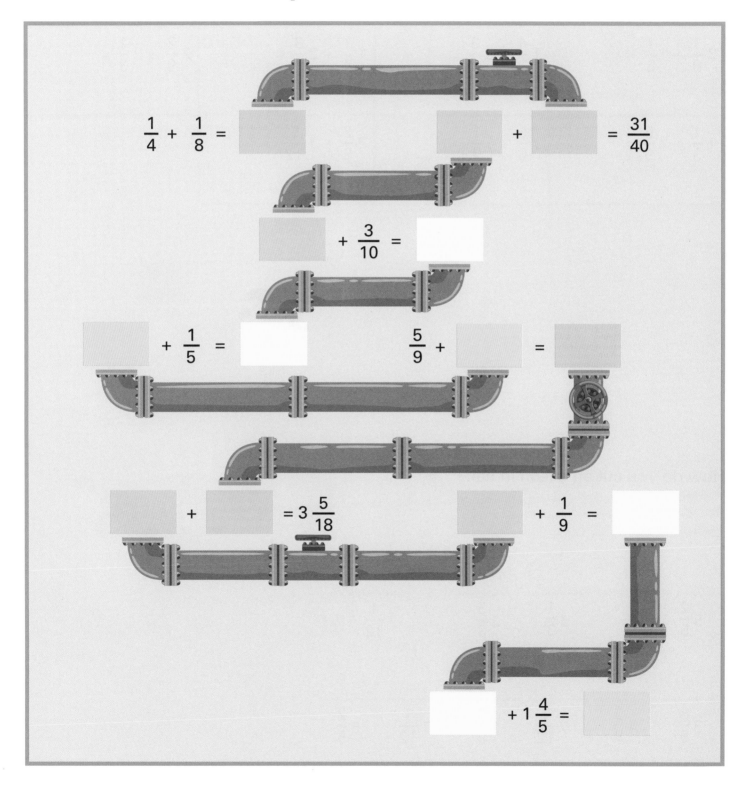

$\dfrac{1}{4} + \dfrac{1}{8} =$ ⬚ ⬚ $+$ ⬚ $= \dfrac{31}{40}$

⬚ $+ \dfrac{3}{10} =$ ⬚

⬚ $+ \dfrac{1}{5} =$ ⬚ $\dfrac{5}{9} +$ ⬚ $=$ ⬚

⬚ $+$ ⬚ $= 3\dfrac{5}{18}$ ⬚ $+ \dfrac{1}{9} =$ ⬚

⬚ $+ 1\dfrac{4}{5} =$ ⬚

Code Breaker

WRITE each sum as a fraction or mixed number in its simplest form. Then WRITE the letter that matches each sum to solve the riddle.

$3\frac{1}{8} + 1\frac{7}{8} =$ [1]	$1\frac{4}{5} + 3\frac{3}{5} =$ [2]	$1\frac{1}{4} + 2\frac{3}{8} =$ [3]	$2\frac{2}{9} + 2\frac{1}{3} =$ [4]
I	W	H	E
$1\frac{1}{3} + 2\frac{5}{9} =$ [5]	$2\frac{5}{6} + 1\frac{1}{2} =$ [6]	$3\frac{2}{3} + 3\frac{5}{12} =$ [7]	
S	T	A	

How do you cut an ocean in half?

$$\overline{\quad}\ \overline{\quad}\ \overline{\quad}\ \overline{\quad}\ \quad \overline{\quad}$$
$$5\frac{2}{5} \qquad 5 \qquad 4\frac{1}{3} \qquad 3\frac{5}{8} \qquad 7\frac{1}{12}$$

$$\overline{\quad}\ \overline{\quad}\ \overline{\quad}\ \overline{\quad}\ \overline{\quad}\ \overline{\quad}.$$
$$3\frac{8}{9} \qquad 4\frac{5}{9} \qquad 7\frac{1}{12} \qquad 3\frac{8}{9} \qquad 7\frac{1}{12} \qquad 5\frac{2}{5}$$

Number Factory

WRITE the fractions that will come out of each machine in their simplest form.

HINT: When subtracting fractions with different denominators, rewrite the fractions with their lowest common denominators.

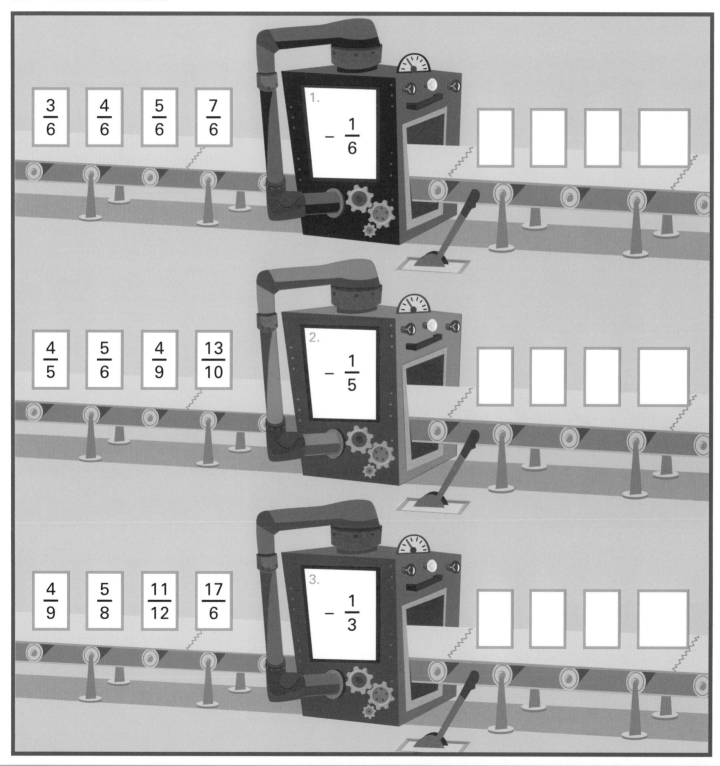

Fraction Flip

Use the green and blue cards from page 203, and DEAL the cards into boxes of the same color. Then WRITE each difference. (Save the cards to use again.)

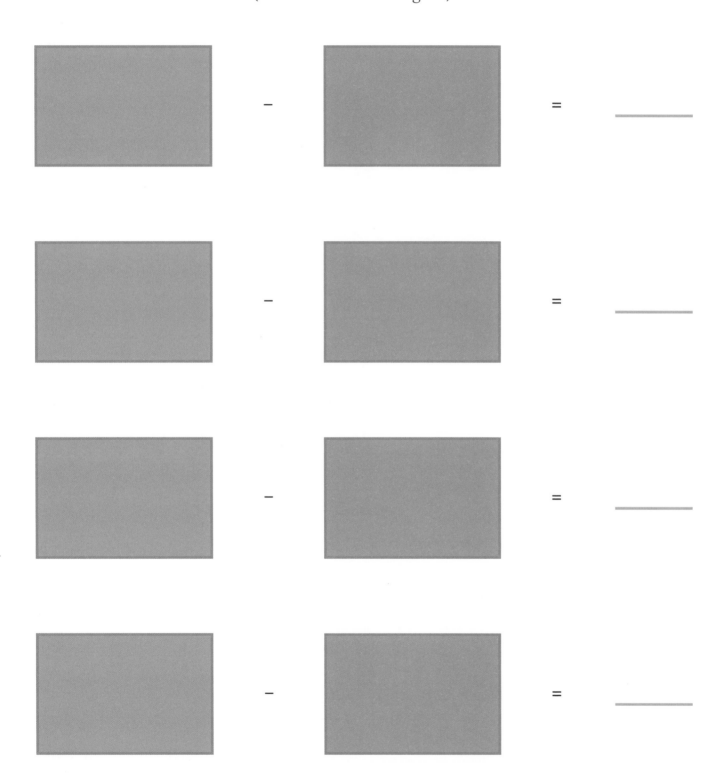

Pipe Down

WRITE the missing fraction or mixed number in its simplest form. Then FOLLOW the pipe, and WRITE the same fraction in the next problem.

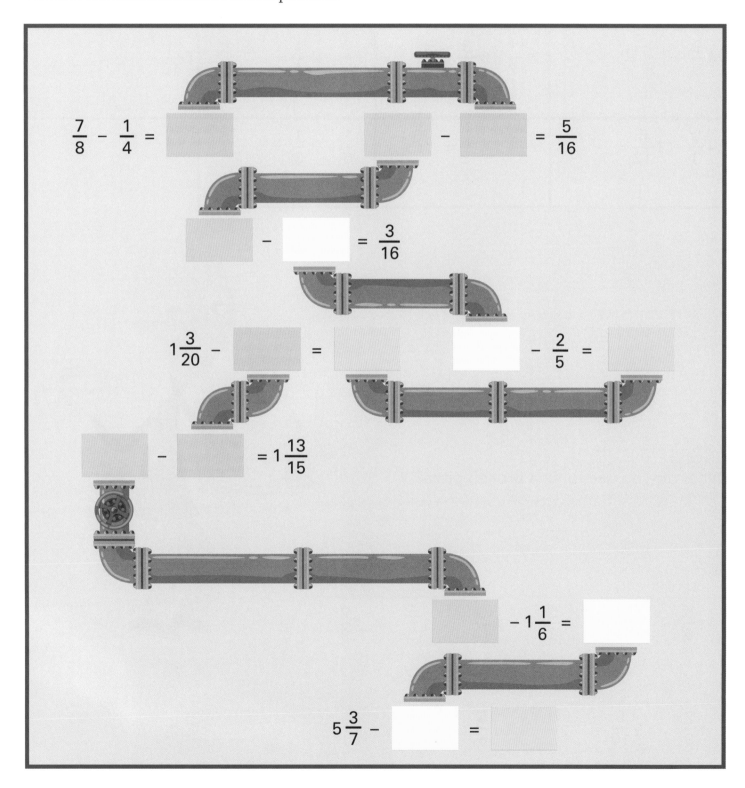

$\dfrac{7}{8} - \dfrac{1}{4} = $ ☐   ☐ $-$ ☐ $= \dfrac{5}{16}$

☐ $-$ ☐ $= \dfrac{3}{16}$

$1\dfrac{3}{20} - $ ☐ $= $ ☐   ☐ $- \dfrac{2}{5} = $ ☐

☐ $-$ ☐ $= 1\dfrac{13}{15}$

☐ $- 1\dfrac{1}{6} = $ ☐

$5\dfrac{3}{7} - $ ☐ $= $ ☐

Code Breaker

WRITE each difference as a fraction or mixed number in its simplest form. Then WRITE the letter that matches each difference to solve the riddle.

$4\frac{3}{9} - 1\frac{1}{9} =$ [1]	$2\frac{11}{12} - 1\frac{3}{12} =$ [2]	$3\frac{7}{8} - 2\frac{1}{4} =$ [3]	$6\frac{1}{10} - 3\frac{1}{5} =$ [4]
O	P	M	A
$4\frac{2}{3} - 1\frac{5}{12} =$ [5]	$6\frac{2}{3} - 4\frac{1}{15} =$ [6]	$5\frac{1}{6} - 3\frac{1}{3} =$ [7]	
E	S	T	

What do you use to fix a broken pizza?

___ ___ ___ ___ ___ ___
$1\frac{5}{6}$ $3\frac{2}{9}$ $1\frac{5}{8}$ $2\frac{9}{10}$ $1\frac{5}{6}$ $3\frac{2}{9}$

___ ___ ___ ___ ___ .
$1\frac{2}{3}$ $2\frac{9}{10}$ $2\frac{3}{5}$ $1\frac{5}{6}$ $3\frac{1}{4}$

Number Factory

WRITE the fractions that will come out of each machine in their simplest form.

HINT: When multiplying fractions, multiply the numerators and then the denominators.

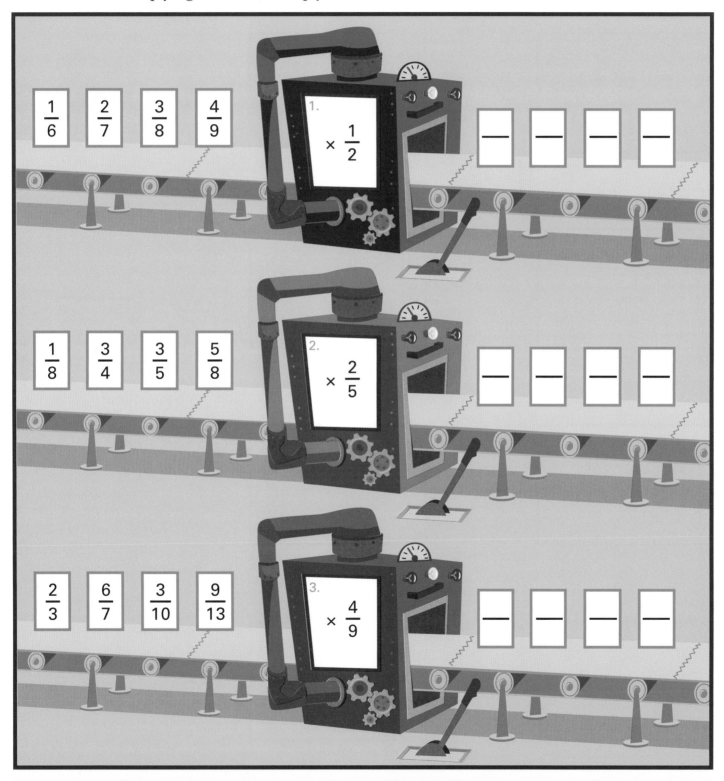

Fraction Flip

Use any of the cards from page 203, and DEAL the cards into the boxes. Then WRITE each product. (Save the cards to use again.)

 ×  = _____

 ×  = _____

 ×  = _____

 ×  = _____

Pipe Down

WRITE the missing fraction or mixed number in its simplest form. Then FOLLOW the pipe, and WRITE the same fraction in the next problem.

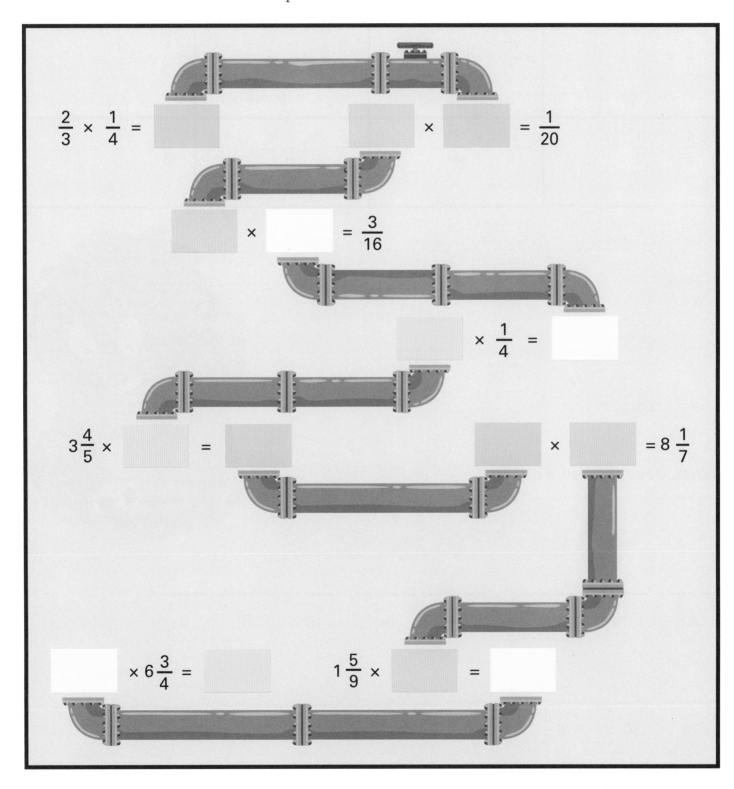

$\frac{2}{3} \times \frac{1}{4} =$ ⬚   ⬚ × ⬚ $= \frac{1}{20}$

⬚ × ⬚ $= \frac{3}{16}$

⬚ × $\frac{1}{4}$ = ⬚

$3\frac{4}{5} \times$ ⬚ $=$ ⬚   ⬚ × ⬚ $= 8\frac{1}{7}$

⬚ $\times 6\frac{3}{4} =$ ⬚ $1\frac{5}{9} \times$ ⬚ $=$ ⬚

Multiplying Fractions

Code Breaker

WRITE each product as a fraction or mixed number in its simplest form. Then WRITE the letter that matches each product in the spaces to solve the riddle.

$1\frac{1}{2} \times 2\frac{2}{9} =$ [1]	$3\frac{6}{7} \times 4\frac{2}{3} =$ [2]	$2\frac{3}{8} \times 1\frac{3}{5} =$ [3]	$3\frac{1}{6} \times 2\frac{4}{7} =$ [4]
R	H	F	T
$6\frac{4}{5} \times 4\frac{1}{2} =$ [5]	$3\frac{1}{10} \times 3\frac{3}{4} =$ [6]	$2\frac{5}{6} \times 2\frac{2}{5} =$ [7]	$4\frac{7}{8} \times 5\frac{1}{3} =$ [8]
A	O	L	E

What looks like half a dog?

$$\overline{\quad} \ \overline{\quad} \ \overline{\quad} \ \overline{\quad} \ \overline{\quad} \ \overline{\quad} \ \overline{\quad} \ \overline{\quad}$$
$8\frac{1}{7} \quad 18 \quad 26 \quad 11\frac{5}{8} \quad 8\frac{1}{7} \quad 18 \quad 26 \quad 3\frac{1}{3}$

$$\overline{\quad} \ \overline{\quad} \ \overline{\quad} \ \overline{\quad} \ .$$
$18 \quad 30\frac{3}{5} \quad 6\frac{4}{5} \quad 3\frac{4}{5}$

Number Factory

WRITE the fractions that will come out of each machine in their simplest form.

HINT: When dividing fractions, multiply by the reciprocal of the divisor.

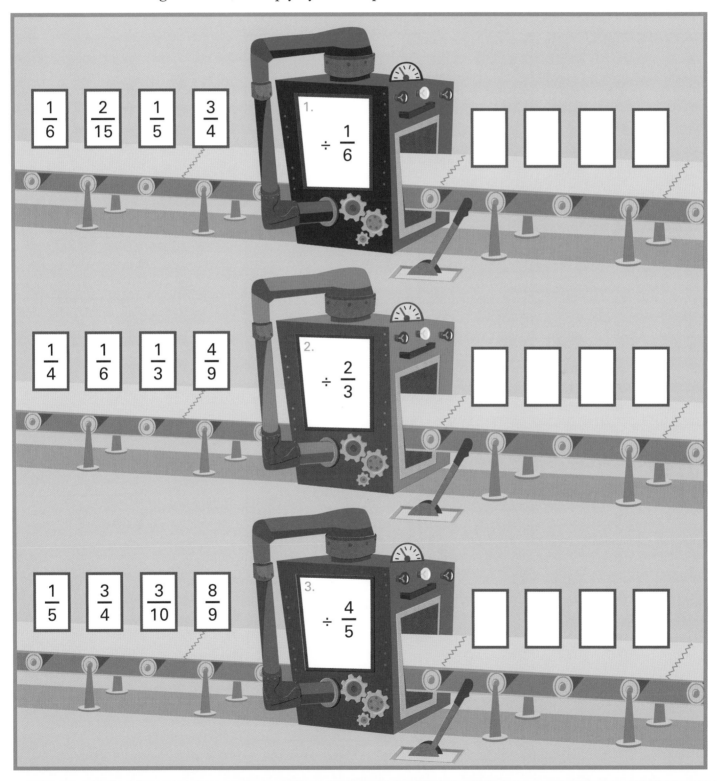

Fraction Flip

Use any of the cards from page 203, and DEAL the cards into the boxes. Then WRITE each quotient.

 ÷  = _____

 ÷  = _____

 ÷  = _____

 ÷  = _____

Pipe Down

WRITE the missing fraction or mixed number in its simplest form. Then FOLLOW the pipe, and WRITE the same fraction in the next problem.

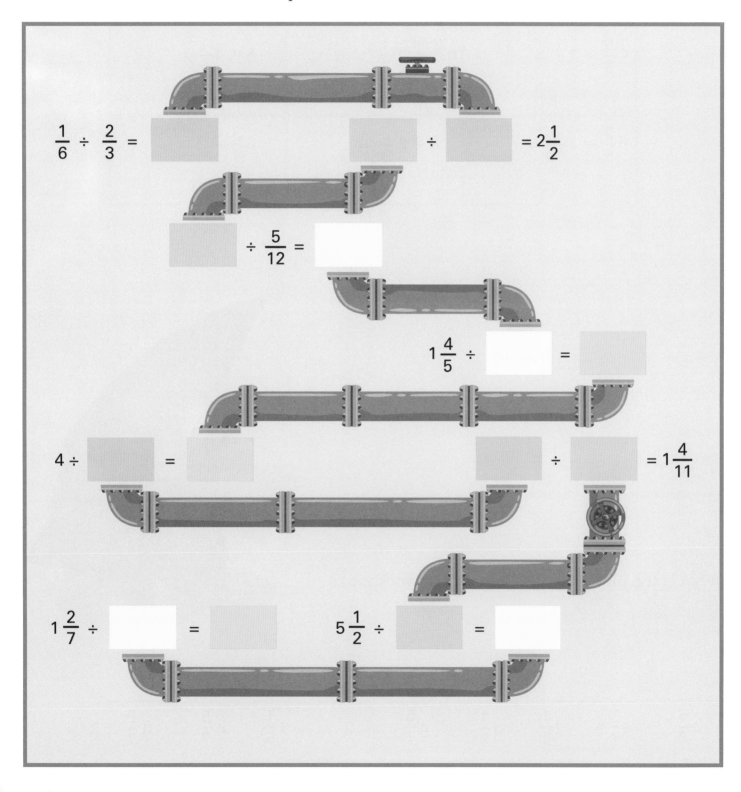

$\dfrac{1}{6} \div \dfrac{2}{3} = \boxed{}$ $\boxed{} \div \boxed{} = 2\dfrac{1}{2}$

$\boxed{} \div \dfrac{5}{12} = \boxed{}$

$1\dfrac{4}{5} \div \boxed{} = \boxed{}$

$4 \div \boxed{} = \boxed{}$ $\boxed{} \div \boxed{} = 1\dfrac{4}{11}$

$1\dfrac{2}{7} \div \boxed{} = \boxed{}$ $5\dfrac{1}{2} \div \boxed{} = \boxed{}$

Code Breaker

WRITE each quotient as a fraction or mixed number in its simplest form. Then WRITE the letter that matches each quotient to solve the riddle.

$4\frac{5}{8} \div 1\frac{1}{8} =$ ☐ [1] M	$6\frac{2}{7} \div 1\frac{1}{3} =$ ☐ [2] E	$5 \div 4\frac{1}{6} =$ ☐ [3] R
$9\frac{3}{5} \div 2\frac{1}{10} =$ ☐ [4] G	$8 \div 2\frac{2}{3} =$ ☐ [5] T	$6\frac{3}{4} \div 3 =$ ☐ [6] O

What is the pine's favorite part of this workbook?

____ ____ ____ ____ ____ ____ ____ ____ ____ .
$4\frac{4}{7}$ $4\frac{5}{7}$ $2\frac{1}{4}$ $4\frac{1}{9}$ $4\frac{5}{7}$ 3 $1\frac{1}{5}$ $4\frac{5}{7}$ $4\frac{5}{7}$

Who Am I?

READ the clues, and CIRCLE the mystery shape.

HINT: Cross out any shape that does not match the clues.

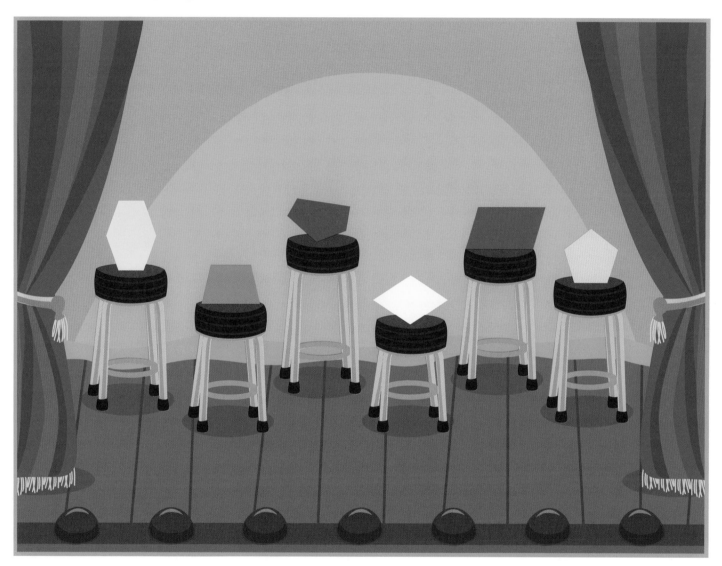

My sides are not all the same length.

I have fewer than six sides.

I am a quadrilateral.

I am not a parallelogram.

Who am I?

Shape Shuffle

If the top picture is flipped horizontally and has its colors reversed, CIRCLE the matching picture.

Perimeter Puzzler

Perimeter is the distance around a two-dimensional shape. One equilateral triangle has the perimeter of 27 inches (in.). WRITE the perimeter of each shape.

27 in.

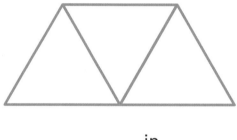

_____ in.
1

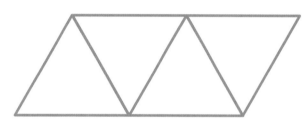

_____ in.
2

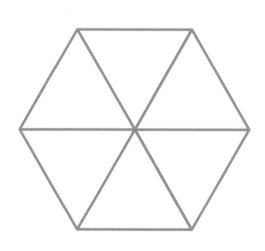

_____ in.
3

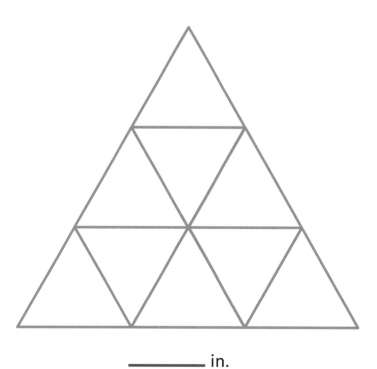

_____ in.
4

Shape Creator

Each neighboring pair of dots is 1 centimeter (cm) apart. DRAW four different shapes that all have a perimeter of 24 centimeters.

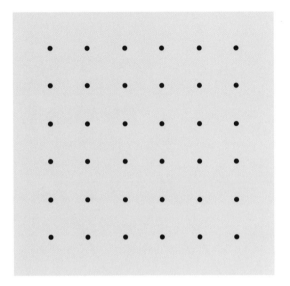

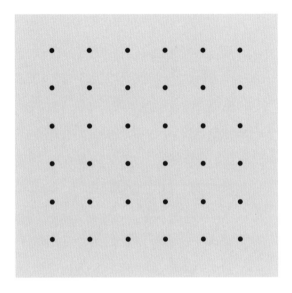

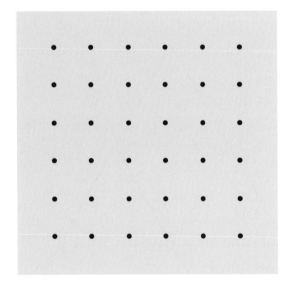

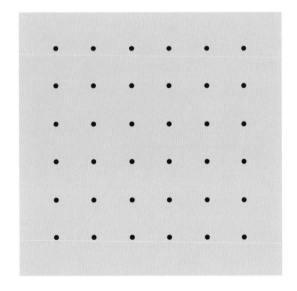

Hidden Shapes

Area is the size of the surface of a shape. FIND each shape hidden in the picture. WRITE the area of each shape.

HINT: You may need to add together line segment lengths when calculating area.

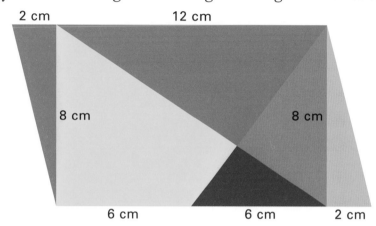

2 cm   12 cm

8 cm   8 cm

6 cm   6 cm   2 cm

For a rectangle or parallelogram,
Area = base × height

For a triangle,
Area = $\frac{1}{2}$ × base × height

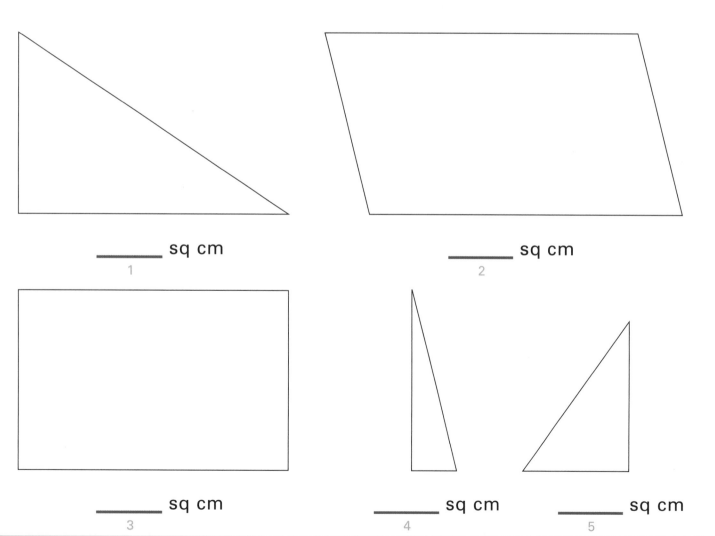

_____ sq cm

1

_____ sq cm

2

_____ sq cm

3

_____ sq cm

4

_____ sq cm

5

Land and Lakes

WRITE the fraction of the area that is land and the fraction of the area that is lake.

HINT: Use the small squares to help you. Look for squares that are the converse of one another.

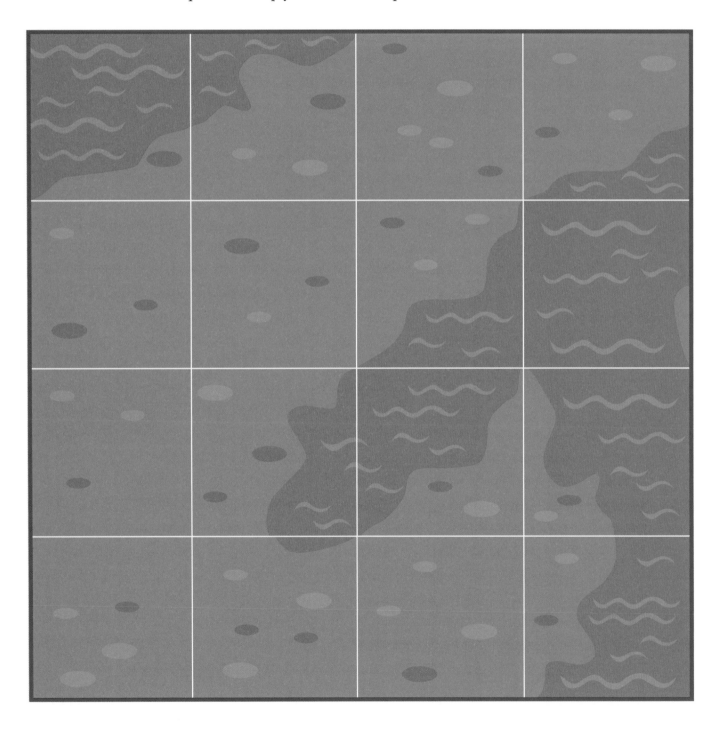

_____ land   _____ lake

Semaphore Signals

Someone is sending you a message in **semaphore**, a system that uses two flags to represent the letters of the alphabet. Use the clues, and CIRCLE the correct picture in each row. Then WRITE the letters to decode the message.

HINT: Look at the angle of the arms.

A   B   E   H   K

L   N   O   P   W

1. acute angle			
2. obtuse angle			
3. straight line			
4. right angle			

Message: _____ _____ _____ _____ !

Code Breaker

MEASURE each angle using a protractor, and WRITE the measurement. Then WRITE the letter that matches each measurement to solve the riddle.

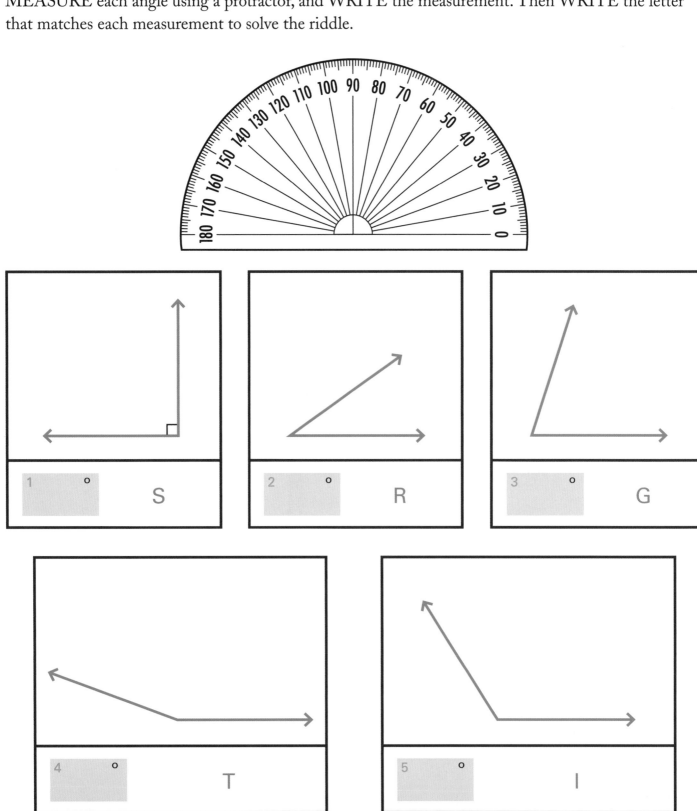

1. _____ °   S

2. _____ °   R

3. _____ °   G

4. _____ °   T

5. _____ °   I

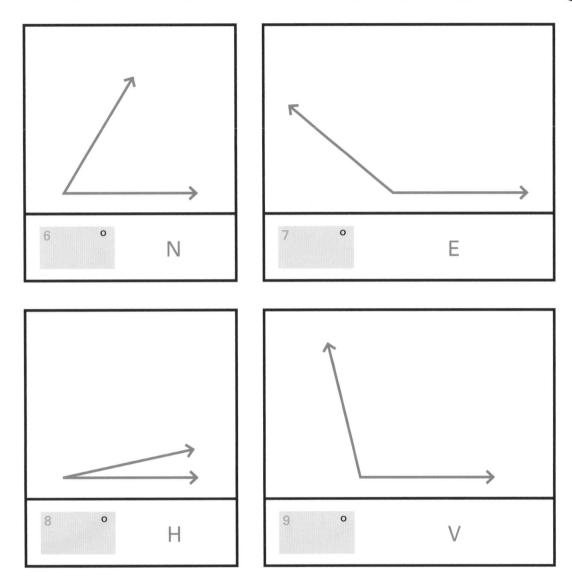

6 [ ] °   N

7 [ ] °   E

8 [ ] °   H

9 [ ] °   V

Why is the obtuse angle always frustrated?

122°	160°	122°	90°	58°	140°	103°	140°	35°

35°	122°	72°	12°	160°
.

Secret Meeting

Professor Wormhole wants to have another meeting. She left a note saying to meet at the clock tower, but the time is in code. WRITE the time of the meeting.

Meet me at the clock tower at 100°.

Signed,

Professor Wormhole

_____ : _____

Code Breaker

WRITE the name of each point, line, or ray. Then WRITE the letter that matches each name to solve the riddle.

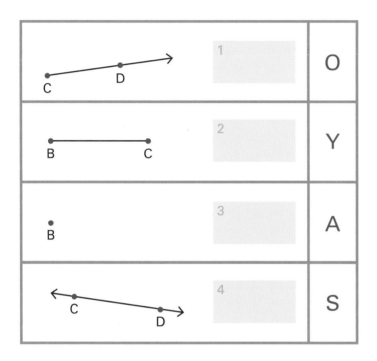

1	O
2	Y
3	A
4	S

5	E
6	N
7	R
8	T

Why couldn't the two rays walk down the street together?

It was

$\underline{}$ $\underline{}$ $\underline{}$ $\underline{}$ $\underline{}$ $\underline{}$ $\underline{}$
  B $\overrightarrow{CD}$ C $\overline{AB}$ $\overleftrightarrow{AB}$ B $\overline{BC}$

$\underline{}$ $\underline{}$ $\underline{}$ $\underline{}$ $\underline{}$ $\underline{}$.
  $\overleftrightarrow{CD}$ $\overrightarrow{CB}$ $\overrightarrow{AB}$ $\overline{AB}$ $\overline{AB}$ $\overrightarrow{CB}$

Secret Meeting

Super Spy James Blonde would like to meet with you again. DRAW the line segments to figure out where to find him.

$\overline{CP}$ $\overline{JK}$ $\overline{AM}$ $\overline{GH}$ $\overline{IQ}$ $\overline{EF}$ $\overline{BL}$ $\overline{EQ}$ $\overline{MN}$ $\overline{BO}$ $\overline{DI}$ $\overline{QR}$

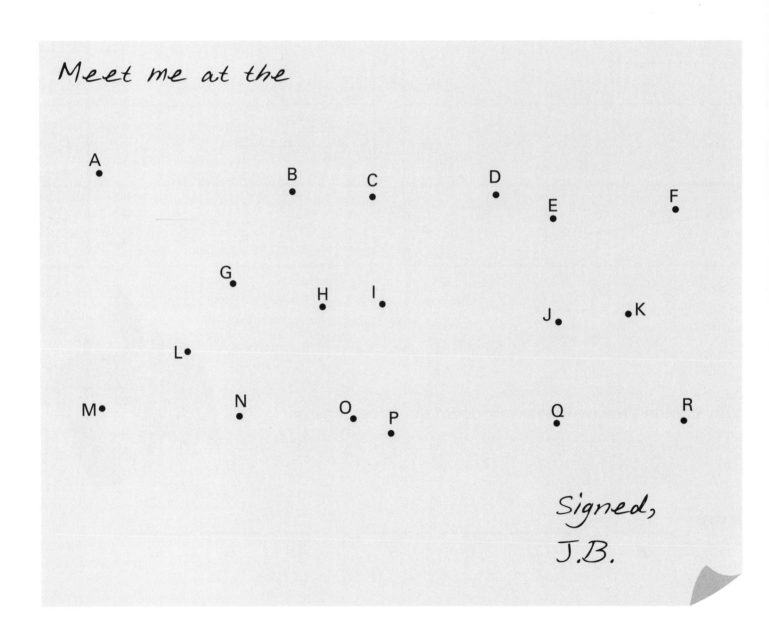

Meet me at the

Signed,
J.B.

Who Am I?

READ the clues, and CIRCLE the mystery shape.

HINT: Cross out any shape that does not match the clues.

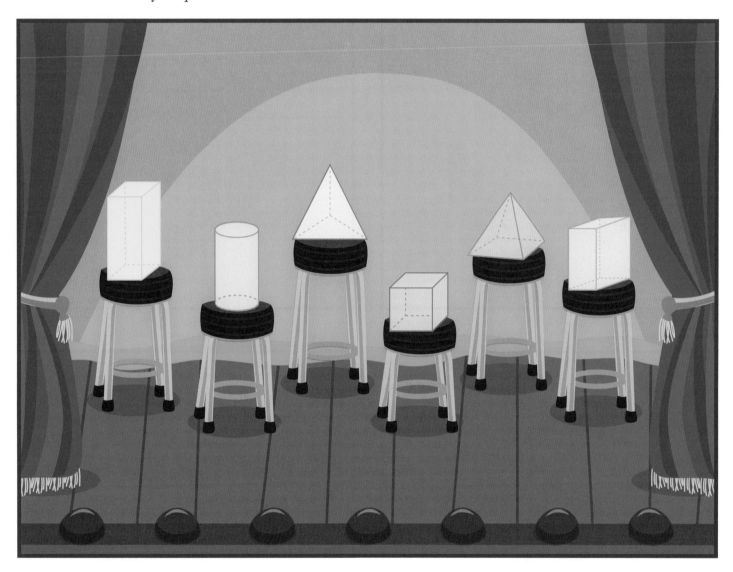

I'm not round.

I have at least one square face.

I have more than five vertices.

All of my edges are the same length.

Who am I?

Complete the Cube

These parts can be combined to make four cubes. WRITE the letter pairs of the parts that go together.

A

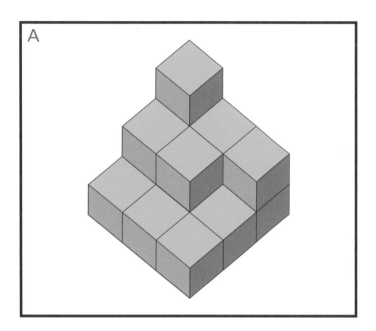

B

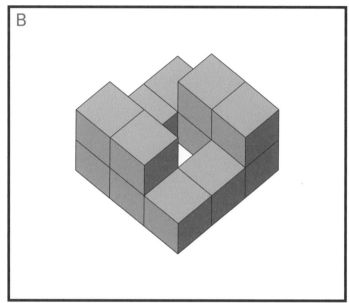

C

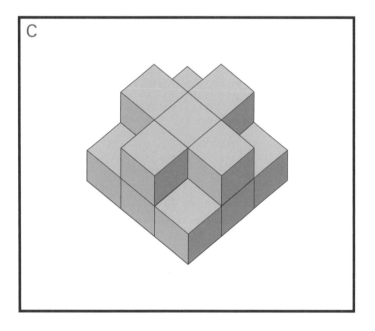

D

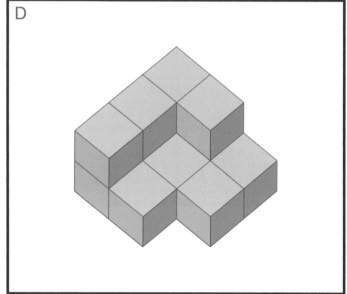

E

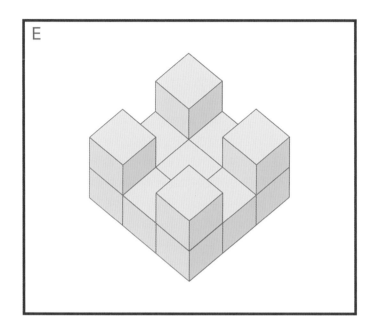

F

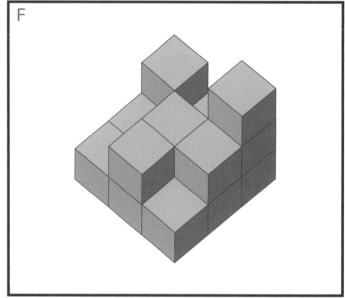

G

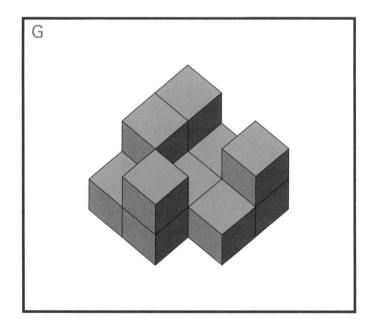

H

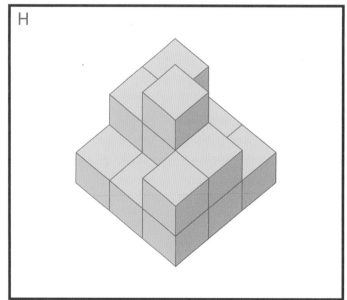

Cube 1: _____, _____   Cube 2: _____, _____

Cube 3: _____, _____   Cube 4: _____, _____

Shape Builders

Use the shapes from pages 205 and 207. LOOK at the shapes, and WRITE the answers to the questions. (Save these shapes to use again.)

This shape is called an **octahedron**.

This shape is called a **dodecahedron**.

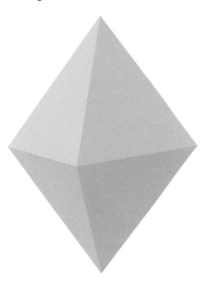

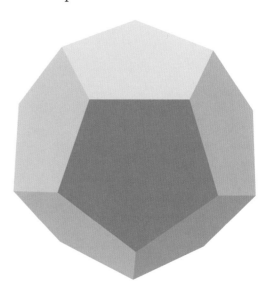

1. How many faces does the octahedron have? _____

2. How many faces does the dodecahedron have? _____

3. What is the shape of each face on the octahedron? _____

4. What is the shape of each face on the dodecahedron? _____

5. How many vertices does the octahedron have? _____

6. How many vertices does the dodecahedron have? _____

7. How many edges does the octahedron have? _____

8. How many edges does the dodecahedron have? _____

Code Breaker

WRITE the volume of each shape in cubic centimeters. Then WRITE the letter that matches each volume to solve the riddle.

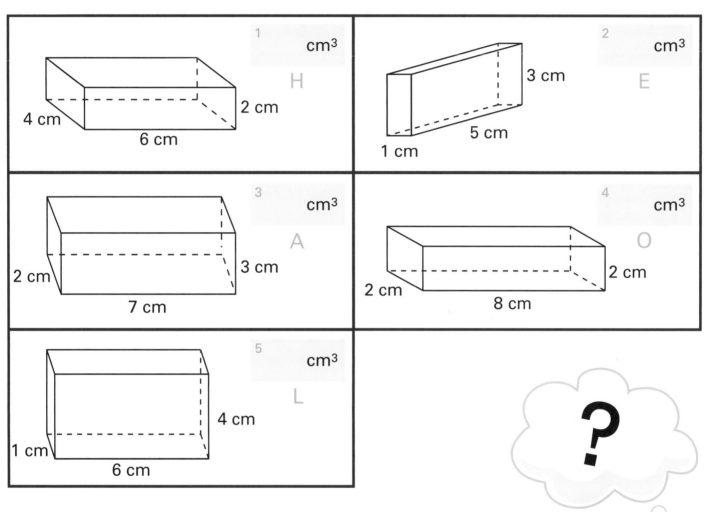

1 ___ cm³ H

4 cm · 6 cm · 2 cm

2 ___ cm³ E

3 cm · 5 cm · 1 cm

3 ___ cm³ A

2 cm · 7 cm · 3 cm

4 ___ cm³ O

2 cm · 8 cm · 2 cm

5 ___ cm³ L

1 cm · 6 cm · 4 cm

What gets bigger the more you take away from it?

___   ___ ___ ___ ___ .
42   48   32   24   15

Just Right

A measurement is missing from each shape. WRITE each of these measurements so that the volume for each shape is correct.

| 3.1 | 2.9 | 5.2 | 4.1 | 4.9 | 5.6 | 3.8 | 4 | 3.3 |

Volume = 141.44 cm³

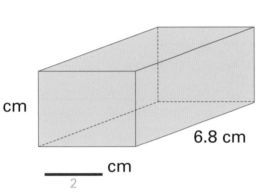

_____ cm (1)

_____ cm (2)

6.8 cm

Volume = 73.5 cm³

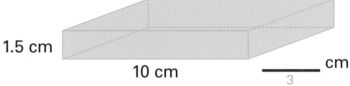

1.5 cm

10 cm

_____ cm (3)

Volume = 47.74 cm³

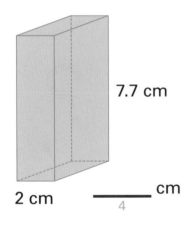

7.7 cm

2 cm

_____ cm (4)

Volume = 191.52 cm³

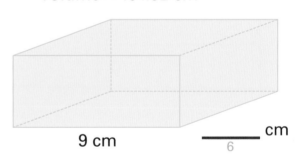

_____ cm (5)

9 cm

_____ cm (6)

Volume = 76.56 cm³

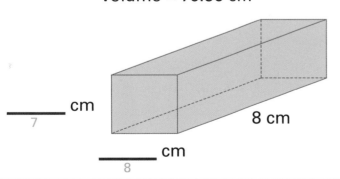

_____ cm (7)

8 cm

_____ cm (8)

Volume = 121.36 cm³

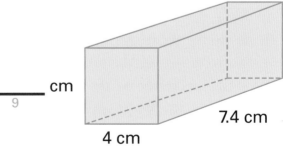

_____ cm (9)

4 cm

7.4 cm

Custom Cars

READ the paragraph, and WRITE the answer.

Color Choices

EXTERIOR

INTERIOR

A new sports car can be customized right down to its audio system. You can choose a hardtop or a convertible. There are eight different colors for the exterior and four different colors for the interior. Then you can choose from two kinds of audio systems: one with a CD player and one with satellite radio. How many different cars can you make from these choices?

_____ cars

Awesome Avatars

READ the paragraph, and WRITE the answer.

A new video game lets you design your character before you start playing. First you can choose to be a boy or a girl. Then you get a choice of four different skin colors, three different hairstyles, five different outfits, and two different pairs of shoes. How many different characters can be made from these choices?

_____ characters

Ferris Wheel

READ the clues. WRITE the name of the person who is in each Ferris wheel car.

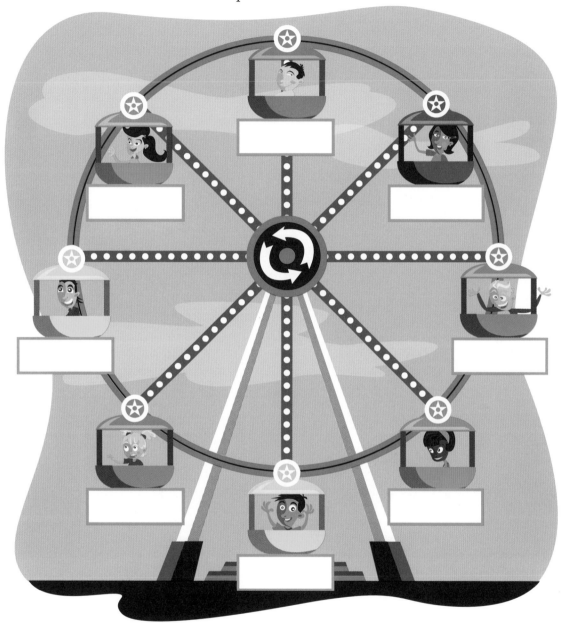

The cars alternate girls and boys.

Tom is at the bottom.

Brooke got on right after Jimmy.

When Tyler reaches the bottom, Aiden will be on top.

Tyler is riding between Haley and Alyssa.

When Alyssa reaches the bottom, Sierra will be on top.

Parking Lot

One car in the parking lot needs to change to make all of the clues true. READ the clues, and DRAW an X on the car that should change to blue.

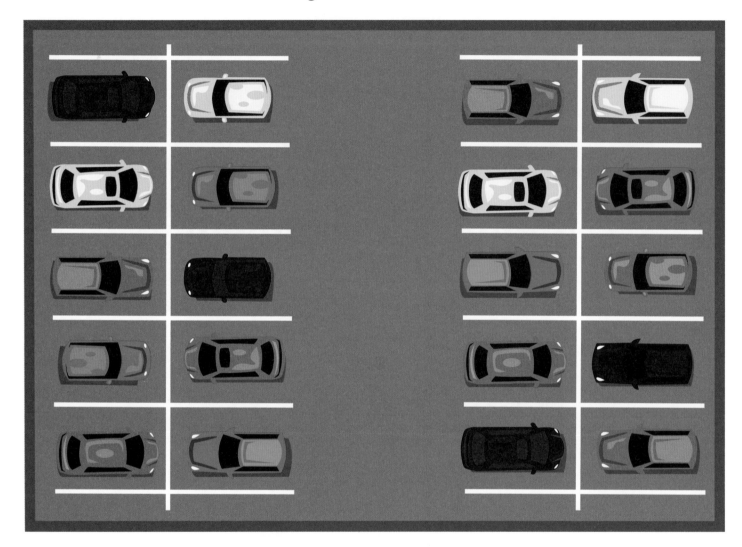

Twenty percent of the cars are black.

There are twice as many blue cars as black cars.

There are the same number of silver and red cars.

No cars that are the same color are parked right next to each other.

Distant Places

DRAW lines between the three pairs of town that have a 20-mile stretch of road between them.

HINT: Use the map key to help you.

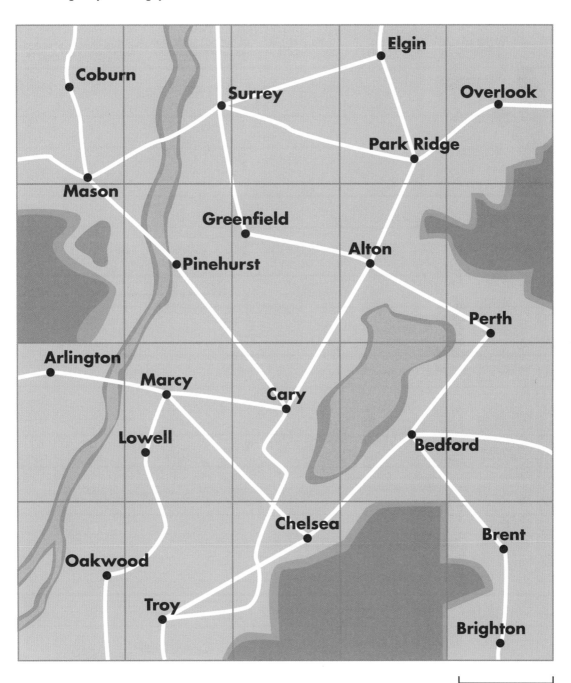

1 inch = 12 miles

Secret Location

FIND the points on the map, and WRITE the name of the country at those coordinates. Then UNSCRAMBLE the letters in yellow to find the secret location on the map.

HINT: Find the first number along the bottom, and the second number along the side. Then find the point where the two lines meet.

1. | 7, 14

2. | 11, 15

3. | 2, 15

4. | 16, 6

5. | 10, 19

6. | 18, 5

7. | 16, 13

8. | 5, 13

Secret location:

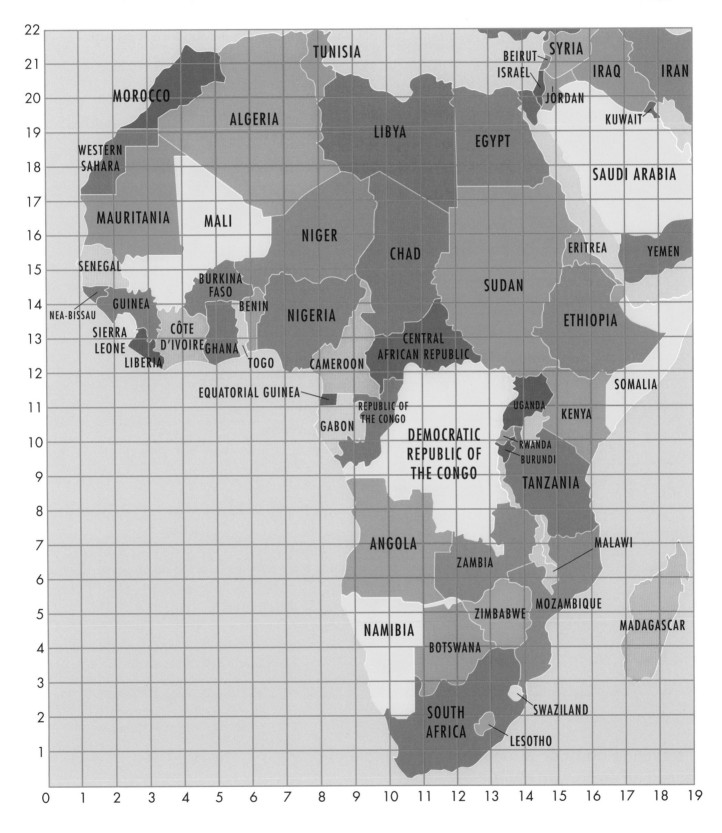

Where Am I?

READ the clues, and DRAW an X to mark the person's approximate location on the map.

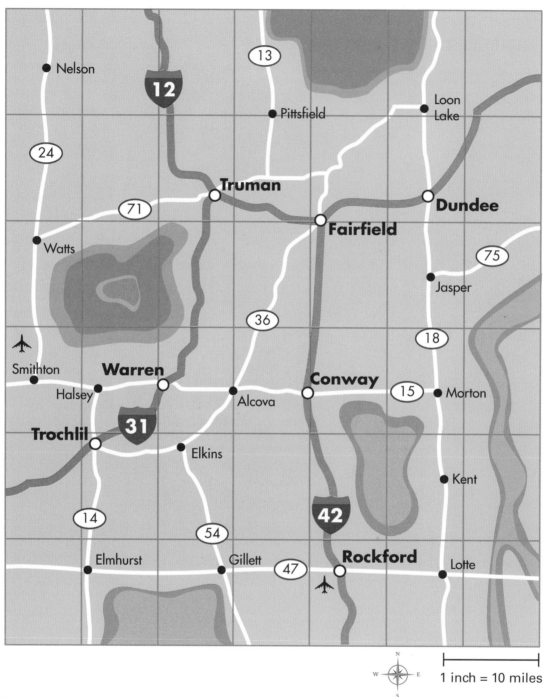

1 inch = 10 miles

I'm traveling north on a road that's a multiple of 6.
I passed an airport on my drive.
I'm driving 60 miles per hour, so I should reach Fairfield in about 15 minutes.

Where am I?

Shape Roll

Probability is used to describe the chance of something happening. A probability of 0% means that something is impossible, and a probability of 100% means that something is certain.

Example: The probability that you will grow to be 30 feet tall is 0%.
The probability that the sun will rise tomorrow morning is 100%.
The probability of getting heads on a coin flip is 50%

To see how probability works, try playing this game. Use the shapes from pages 205 and 207, and roll both shapes. WRITE the numbers facing up on each shape and the total of the two numbers. Repeat this for 10 turns. Then ANSWER the questions as percents.

Turn			Total
1			
2			
3			
4			
5			
6			
7			
8			
9			
10			

1. What is the probability of rolling an even number on the orange shape? _____

2. What is the probability of rolling an odd number on the blue shape? _____

3. What is the probability of a turn totaling 21? _____

4. What is the probability of a turn totaling between 3 and 20? _____

5. What is the probability of a turn totaling an odd number? _____

6. What is the probability of rolling a 5 on both shapes in the same turn? _____

Bag of Beans

CUT OUT the jellybean pieces from the opposite page, and PUT them in a bag. READ the rules. PLAY the game. Then ANSWER the questions.

HINT: Think about the percent of each color of jellybean to the total number of jellybeans.

Rules: Two players
 1. Take turns picking cards out of the bag.
 2. Keep picking until all three of the black jellybeans have been found.

The player with the most black jellybeans wins!

There are three black, two yellow, five red, six green, four orange, and five purple jellybeans.

1. What is the probability that you will pull a black jellybean out of the bag on the first turn? _____

2. What is the probability that you will pull a green jellybean out of the bag on the first turn? _____

3. What color jellybean has a 16% chance of being pulled on the first turn? _____

4. What color is less likely than black to be pulled from the bag? _____

5. If five turns have passed and the jellybeans found are purple, orange, red, red, and black, what is the probability that you will get a black jellybean on the next turn? _____

6. How likely is it that three black jellybeans will be pulled out of the bag before the game ends? _____

7. What is the probability that the game will end in a tie? _____

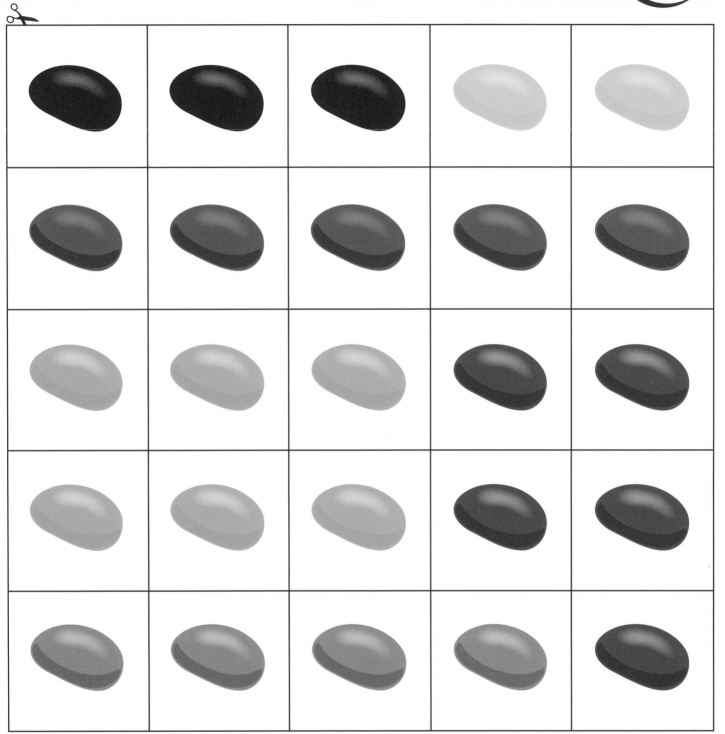

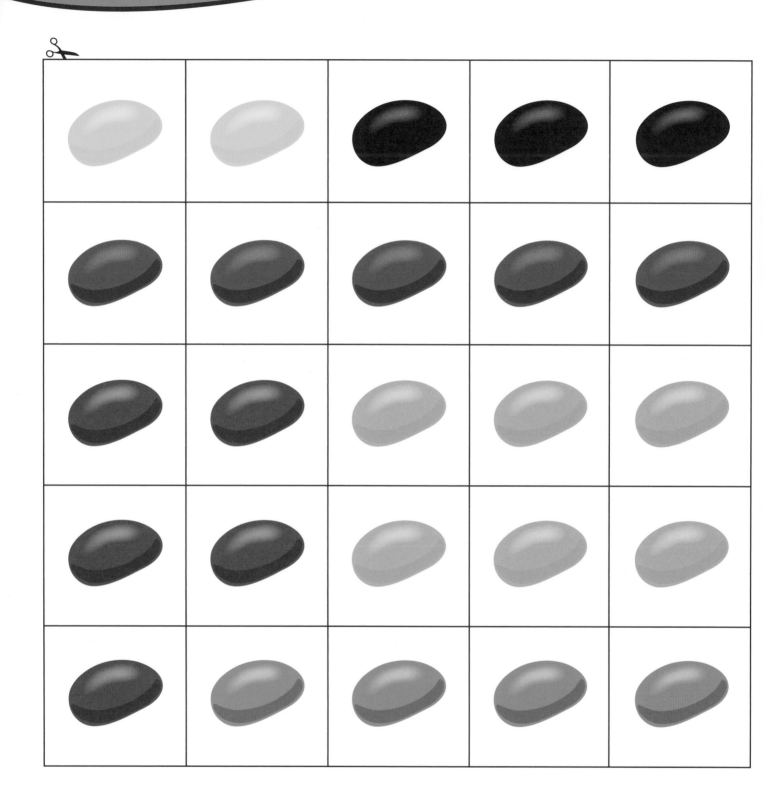

Code Breaker

ANSWER each question. Then WRITE the letter that matches each answer to solve the riddle.

2 hours, 53 minutes – 1 hour, 6 minutes =	1	minutes	A
1 hour, 13 minutes – 25 minutes =	2	minutes	L
3 hours, 39 minutes – 1 hour, 40 minutes =	3	minutes	O
8 hours, 4 minutes – 3 hours, 36 minutes =	4	minutes	R
5 hours, 20 minutes – 2 hours, 18 minutes =	5	minutes	C
7 hours, 31 minutes – 6 hours, 55 minutes =	6	minutes	H
6 hours, 46 minutes – 1 hour, 19 minutes =	7	minutes	K

What kind of bug knows how to tell time?

__107__

____	____	____	____	____	____	____	____	____	____ |.
182	48	119	182	327	268	119	107	182	36

Time and Place

At precisely the same moment, clocks around the world show different times. That's because different places are in different time zones. The clocks on the opposite page show the time across many different time zones. USE the clocks, and WRITE the day and time.

Example:

Hong Kong	London	If it is Monday at 6:30 a.m. in Hong Kong, it is Sunday at 11:30 p.m. in London.
Monday, 6:30 a.m.	<u>Sunday</u> , <u>11:30 p.m.</u>	

1. New York
   Friday, 3:15 a.m.

   New Delhi
   _____ , _____

2. Vancouver
   Tuesday, 11:00 a.m.

   Rio de Janeiro
   _____ , _____

3. Chicago
   Thursday, 10:45 p.m.

   Hong Kong
   _____ , _____

4. Tokyo
   Wednesday, 1:38 p.m.

   Vancouver
   _____ , _____

5. Sydney
   Sunday, 2:10 a.m.

   New York
   _____ , _____

6. New Delhi
   Tuesday, 9:52 p.m.

   Chicago
   _____ , _____

7. Rio de Janeiro
   Saturday, 8:24 a.m.

   Tokyo
   _____ , _____

8. London
   Wednesday, 5:08 p.m.

   Sydney
   _____ , _____

New York	Tokyo	Vancouver

Thursday 6:15 p.m.	Friday 8:15 a.m.	Thursday 3:15 p.m.

London	Hong Kong	Rio de Janeiro

Friday 12:15 a.m.	Friday 7:15 a.m.	Thursday 8:15 p.m.

Chicago	Sydney	New Delhi

Thursday 5:15 p.m.	Friday 9:15 a.m.	Friday 4:15 a.m.

Island Trip

A ferry goes back and forth between Port Henry and Olive Island. READ the clues. Then WRITE the time of the ferries each person took both directions, and CIRCLE the person who was on the island the longest.

Leaving Port Henry	Arriving Olive Island
7:10 a.m.	8:06 a.m.
9:36 a.m.	10:32 a.m.
12:02 p.m.	12:59 p.m.
2:31 p.m.	3:24 p.m.
4:54 p.m.	5:50 p.m.
7:20 p.m.	8:14 p.m.

Leaving Olive Island	Arriving Port Henry
8:23 a.m.	9:19 a.m.
10:49 a.m.	11:45 a.m.
1:16 p.m.	2:13 p.m.
3:41 p.m.	4:37 p.m.
6:07 p.m.	7:03 p.m.
8:31 p.m.	9:24 p.m.

1. The surf is best earliest in the day, and I want to spend as much time as I can surfing before I have to be back for my dentist appointment in Port Henry at 2:30.

   I left Port Henry at _____ : _____ _____.

   I left Olive Island at _____ : _____ _____.

2. There are two ferries, one in each direction, that are faster than all the others, and those are the two I take.

   I left Port Henry at _____ : _____ _____.

   I left Olive Island at _____ : _____ _____.

3. I missed the ferry that I wanted to take, so I was a couple of minutes late for my 1:00 lunch date on Olive Island. I left to be sure I was home to walk my dog by 5:00.

   I left Port Henry at _____ : _____ _____.

   I left Olive Island at _____ : _____ _____.

What's in My Hand?

READ the clues, and WRITE how many of each coin and bill are hidden in the hand.

I'm holding seven paper bills and nine coins.
The money in my hand totals $83.06.
My coins total more than one dollar.
What's in my hand?

1. _____	2. _____
3. _____	4. _____
5. _____	6. _____
7. _____	8. _____

Big Spender

Sonia and Eric went to buy sports equipment together, and Eric spent twice as much as Sonia. DRAW a circle around the things that Eric bought and a square around the things that Sonia bought.

$62.44

$29.97

$58.25

$3.99

$48.13

$32.81

$18.15

Stamp Collector

DRAW lines to mark where you would tear the sheet of stamps to create three sheets of stamps of equal value.

HINT: The three sets do not need to contain the same number of stamps.

Big Spender

Ralph and Jacob bought snacks for themselves and some friends. Ralph spent three times as much as Jacob. DRAW a circle around the things that Ralph bought and a square around the things that Jacob bought.

$1.46

$3.78

$2.58

$3.75

$1.43

$2.60

$0.99

$4.25

Fraction Cards

CUT OUT the cards.

These cards are for use with pages 140, 142, 150, 154, 158, and 162.

$\dfrac{3}{6}$	$\dfrac{6}{15}$	$\dfrac{4}{12}$	$\dfrac{15}{18}$
$\dfrac{14}{21}$	$\dfrac{9}{12}$	$\dfrac{10}{16}$	$\dfrac{12}{28}$
$\dfrac{1}{2}$	$\dfrac{2}{3}$	$\dfrac{1}{4}$	$\dfrac{1}{5}$
$\dfrac{3}{5}$	$\dfrac{1}{6}$	$\dfrac{6}{7}$	$\dfrac{3}{8}$
$1\dfrac{1}{2}$	$1\dfrac{3}{8}$	$2\dfrac{5}{9}$	$2\dfrac{1}{4}$
$3\dfrac{3}{5}$	$3\dfrac{1}{7}$	$4\dfrac{2}{3}$	$4\dfrac{1}{10}$

Numbered Shapes

CUT OUT the shape. FOLD on the dotted lines, and GLUE the tabs to construct the shape.

This shape is for use with pages 180 and 191.

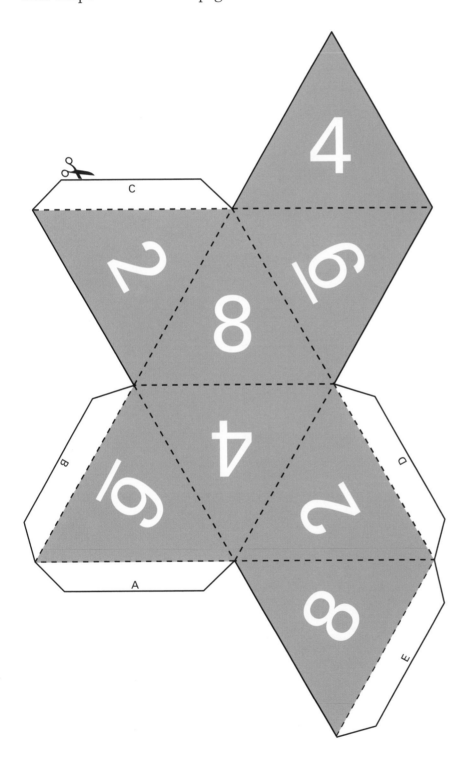

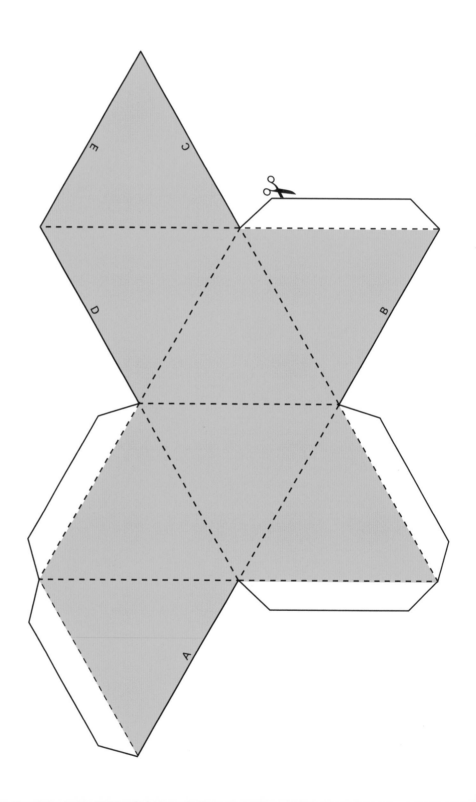

Numbered Shapes

CUT OUT the shape. Be sure to cut along all solid lines. FOLD on the dotted lines, and GLUE the tabs to construct the shape.

This shape is for use with pages 180 and 191.

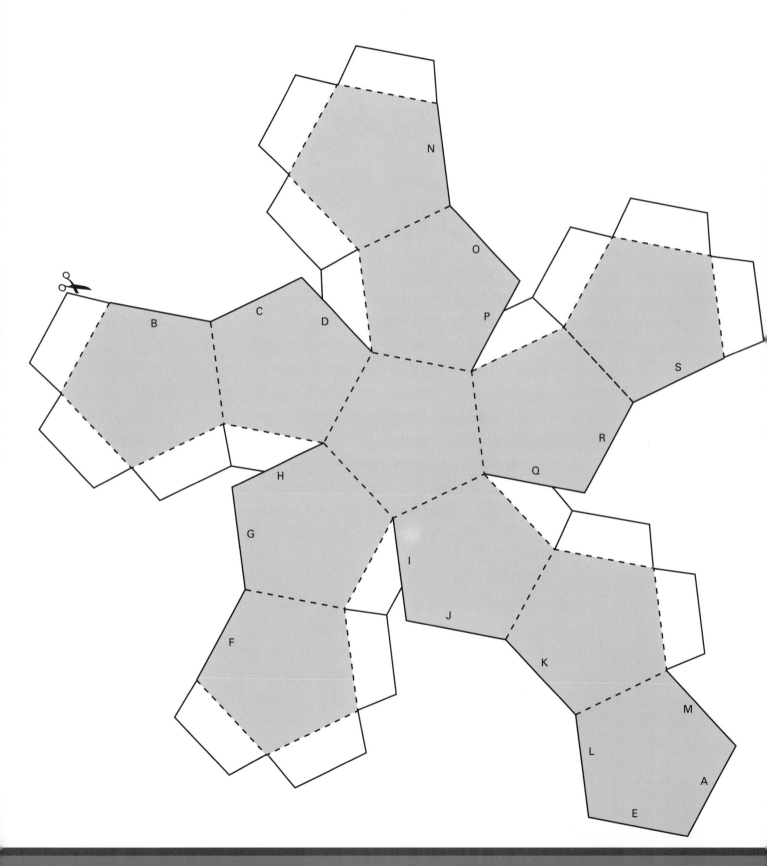

Page 111
1. 30; 300; 3,000; 30,000
2. 3,500; 35,000; 350,000; 3,500,000
3. 240,000; 2,400,000; 24,000,000

Page 112
1. 3,200
2. 12,000
3. 360
4. 2,000,000
5. 490,000
6. 100,000
7. 3,000
8. 27,000,000
9. 56,000
10. 3,000,000
11. 1,800
12. 480,000

Page 113

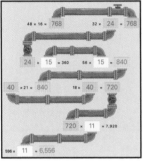

Pages 114–115

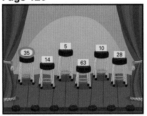

Page 116
1. 6,448 (MEET)
2. 6,418 (MEAT)
3. 824 (THE)
4. 8,564 (TIME)
5. 6,192 (MACH)
6. 504 (INE)
MEET ME AT THE TIME MACHINE.

Page 117
1. 5
2. 20
3. 3
4. 7
5. 18
6. 15
7. 6
8. 12

Page 118
Suggestion:

	4	7
3	12	21
9	36	63

	10	18
3	30	54
4	40	72

	40	60
1	40	60
2	80	120

	3	10
16	48	160
25	75	250

	20	35
3	60	105
4	80	140

	6	9
13	78	117
25	150	225

Page 119
1. 180
2. 72
3. 55
4. 49
5. 63
6. 100
7. 14
8. 88

Page 120

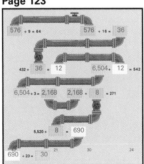

Page 121
1. 9, 90, 900, 9,000
2. 2, 20, 200, 2,000
3. 3, 30, 300, 3,000

Page 122
1. 200
2. 80
3. 5,000
4. 2,000
5. 4,000
6. 8,000
7. 500
8. 900,000
9. 30,000
10. 2,000
11. 500,000
12. 60,000

Page 123

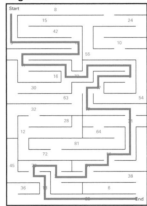

Page 124
1. 1,265
2. 1,874
3. 3,055
4. 983
5. 804
6. 639
7. 941
8. 576

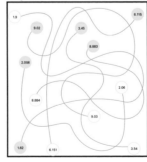

Page 125
1. 766 r2 (ILL rB)
2. 258 r5 (BEN rE)
3. 549 r9 (EAR rR)
4. 413 r6 (AST rL)
5. 430 r7 (ATU rI)
6. 578 r8 (EIN rN)
I'LL BE NEAR A STATUE IN BERLIN.

Pages 126

89,376	÷	266	=	336
÷		÷		÷
392	÷	14	=	28
=		=		=
228	÷	19	=	12

Page 127

Page 128

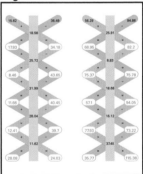

Page 129

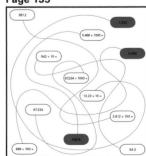

Page 130

Page 131

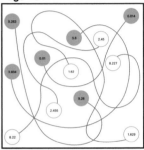

Page 132
1. 3,503
2. 3.194
3. 2.444
4. 3.145
5. 3.562
6. 2.484
7. 3.196
8. 2.489
9. 3.538

Page 133

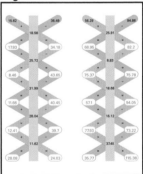

Page 134
1. 2.797, 3.977, 4.397, 6.209
2. 3.333, 4.667, 5.893, 8.027
3. 9.284, 12.854, 15.1, 8.36

Page 135

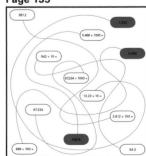

Answers

Page 136

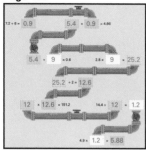

7.2 ÷ 8 = 0.9   5.4 ÷ 0.9 = 4.86
5.4 ÷ 9 = 0.6   2.8 × 9 = 25.2
25.2 ÷ 2 = 12.6
12 × 12.6 = 151.2   14.4 ÷ 12 = 1.2
4.9 × 1.2 = 5.88

Page 137

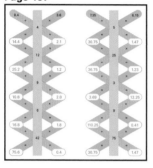

Page 138

1. 11.96, 24.38, 80.96, 115.92
2. 0.42, 1.23, 1.6, 1.98
3. 3.38, 6.24, 8.346, 16.744

Page 139

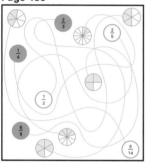

Page 140

1. $\frac{6}{15}$ 2. $\frac{9}{12}$ 3. $\frac{10}{16}$

4. $\frac{4}{12}$ 5. $\frac{3}{6}$ 6. $\frac{12}{28}$

7. $\frac{14}{21}$ 8. $\frac{15}{18}$

Page 141

1. $\frac{1}{2}, \frac{1}{3}, \frac{1}{4}, \frac{1}{5}$

2. $\frac{1}{2}, \frac{1}{4}, \frac{1}{6}, \frac{1}{8}$

3. $\frac{1}{8}, \frac{1}{6}, \frac{1}{3}, \frac{1}{2}$

Page 142

1. $\frac{1}{6}$ 2. $\frac{1}{4}$

3. $\frac{3}{8}$ 4. $\frac{6}{7}$

5. $\frac{1}{2}$ 6. $\frac{2}{3}$

7. $\frac{1}{5}$ 8. $\frac{3}{5}$

Page 143

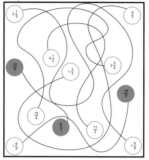

Page 144

1. $1\frac{3}{4}$ 2. $2\frac{5}{9}$ 3. $2\frac{1}{8}$

4. $3\frac{2}{3}$ 5. $4\frac{1}{2}$ 6. $3\frac{1}{4}$

7. $2\frac{4}{7}$ 8. $2\frac{2}{3}$ 9. $3\frac{1}{8}$

10. $4\frac{2}{5}$

A FOURTH OF JULY.

Page 145

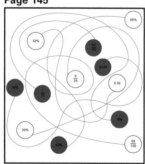

Page 146

1. 6   2. 4   3. 17
4. 45   5. 13   6. 8
7. 12   8. 48   9. 3
10. 27

It was FIFTY PERCENT OFF.

Page 147

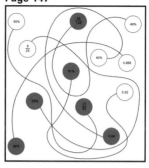

Page 148

Page 149

1. $\frac{2}{9}, \frac{4}{9}, \frac{2}{3}, \frac{8}{9}$

2. $\frac{1}{2}, \frac{11}{12}, \frac{13}{20}, \frac{5}{8}$

3. $\frac{7}{8}, 1, 1\frac{1}{8}, \frac{19}{40}$

Page 150

Have someone check
your answers.

Page 151

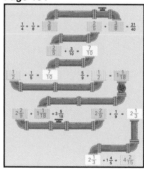

Page 152

1. 5   2. $5\frac{2}{5}$

3. $3\frac{5}{8}$ 4. $4\frac{5}{9}$

5. $3\frac{8}{9}$ 6. $4\frac{1}{3}$

7. $7\frac{1}{12}$

WITH A SEASAW.

Page 153

1. $\frac{1}{3}, \frac{1}{2}, \frac{2}{3}, 1$

2. $\frac{3}{5}, \frac{19}{30}, \frac{11}{45}, 1\frac{1}{10}$

3. $\frac{1}{9}, \frac{7}{24}, \frac{7}{12}, 2\frac{1}{2}$

Page 154

Have someone check
your answers.

Page 155

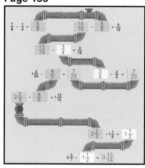

Page 156

1. $3\frac{2}{9}$ 2. $1\frac{2}{3}$

3. $1\frac{5}{8}$ 4. $2\frac{9}{10}$

5. $3\frac{1}{4}$ 6. $2\frac{3}{5}$

7. $1\frac{5}{6}$

TOMATO PASTE.

Page 157

1. $\frac{1}{12}, \frac{1}{7}, \frac{3}{16}, \frac{2}{9}$

2. $\frac{3}{20}, \frac{3}{10}, \frac{6}{25}, \frac{1}{4}$

3. $\frac{8}{27}, \frac{8}{21}, \frac{4}{15}, \frac{4}{13}$

Page 158

Have someone check
your answers.

Page 159

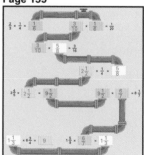

Answers

Page 160
1. $3\frac{1}{3}$ 2. 18
3. $3\frac{4}{5}$ 4. $8\frac{1}{7}$
5. $30\frac{3}{5}$ 6. $11\frac{5}{8}$
7. $6\frac{4}{5}$ 8. 26
THE OTHER HALF.

Page 161
1. $1, \frac{4}{5}, 1\frac{1}{5}, 4\frac{1}{2}$
2. $\frac{3}{8}, \frac{1}{4}, \frac{1}{2}, \frac{2}{3}$
3. $\frac{1}{4}, \frac{15}{16}, \frac{3}{8}, 1\frac{1}{9}$

Page 162
Have someone check
your answers.

Page 163
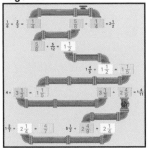

Page 164
1. $4\frac{1}{9}$ 2. $4\frac{5}{7}$
3. $1\frac{1}{5}$ 4. $4\frac{4}{7}$
5. 3 6. $2\frac{1}{4}$
GEOMETREE.

Page 165

Page 166
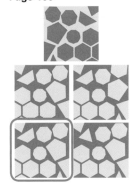

Page 167
1. 45 2. 54
3. 54 4. 81

Page 168
Have someone check
your answers.

Page 169
1. 48 2. 112 3. 96
4. 8 5. 24

Page 170
$\frac{11}{16}, \frac{5}{16}$

Page 171
1.   2. 3. 4.
H E L P
HELP!

Pages 172–173
1. 90 2. 35 3. 72
4. 160 5. 122 6. 58
7. 140 8. 12 9. 103
IT IS NEVER RIGHT.

Page 174
6:15

Page 175
1. $\overrightarrow{CD}$ 2. $\overline{BC}$
3. B 4. $\overleftrightarrow{CD}$
5. $\overline{AB}$ 6. C
7. $\overrightarrow{AB}$ 8. $\overrightarrow{CB}$
It was A ONE RAY STREET.

Page 176

Meet me at the LAKE.

Page 177
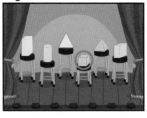

Pages 178–179
A, D
B, H
C, E
F, G

Page 180
1. 8 2. 12
3. triangle 4. pentagon
5. 6 6. 20
7. 12 8. 30

Page 181
1. 48 2. 15
3. 42 4. 32
5. 24
A HOLE.

Page 182
1. 4 2. 5.2
3. 4.9 4. 3.1
5. 3.8 6. 5.6
7. 2.9 8. 3.3
9. 4.1

Page 183
128

Page 184
240

Page 185
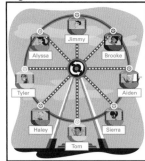

Page 186
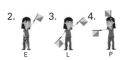

Page 187
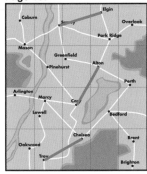

Pages 188–189
1. NIGERIA
2. CHAD
3. SENEGAL
4. MOZAMBIQUE
5. LIBYA
6. MADAGASCAR
7. ETHIOPIA
8. GHANA
TANZANIA

Page 190

Page 191
1. 100% 2. 50%
3. 0% 4. 100%
5. 50% 6. 0%

Page 192
1. 12%
2. 24%
3. orange
4. yellow
5. 10%
6. 100%
7. 0%

Page 195
1. 107 2. 48
3. 119 4. 268
5. 182 6. 36
7. 327
A CLOCKROACH.

Pages 196–197
1. Friday, 1:15 p.m.
2. Tuesday, 4:00 p.m.
3. Friday, 12:45 p.m.
4. Tuesday, 8:38 p.m.
5. Saturday, 11:10 a.m.
6. Tuesday, 10:52 a.m.
7. Saturday, 8:24 p.m.
8. Thursday, 2:08 a.m.

Answers

Page 198
1. 7:10 a.m., 1:16 p.m.
2. 2:31 p.m., 8:31 p.m.
3. 12:02 p.m., 3:41 p.m.

Page 199
Suggestion:
1. 3   2. 2
3. 2   4. 5
5. 0   6. 1
7. 2   8. 1

Page 200

Page 201
Suggestion:

Page 202

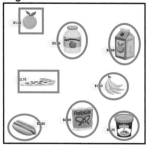

5th Grade
Math in Action

High Score

These four kids are all trying to get the high score in a video game where they earn points by collecting gems. MULTIPLY the gems by the correct number of points. Then ADD the scores, and CIRCLE the person with the highest score.

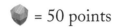 = 50 points   ● = 500 points   ◈ = 5,000 points

Player 1	
800 × ●	
70 × ●	
4 × ◈	
Total Score	

Player 2	
1,000 × ●	
200 × ●	
1 × ◈	
Total Score	

Player 3	
90 × ●	
30 × ●	
20 × ◈	
Total Score	

Player 4	
2,000 × ●	
11 × ●	
9 × ◈	
Total Score	

Multiplication Patterns

Spread the Word

Each person has received some important news to tell a few people. When those people hear the news, they're supposed to tell more people, and so on to spread the word. If everyone tells the news to the same number of people, WRITE the number of people who will have heard the news at each point in the chain.

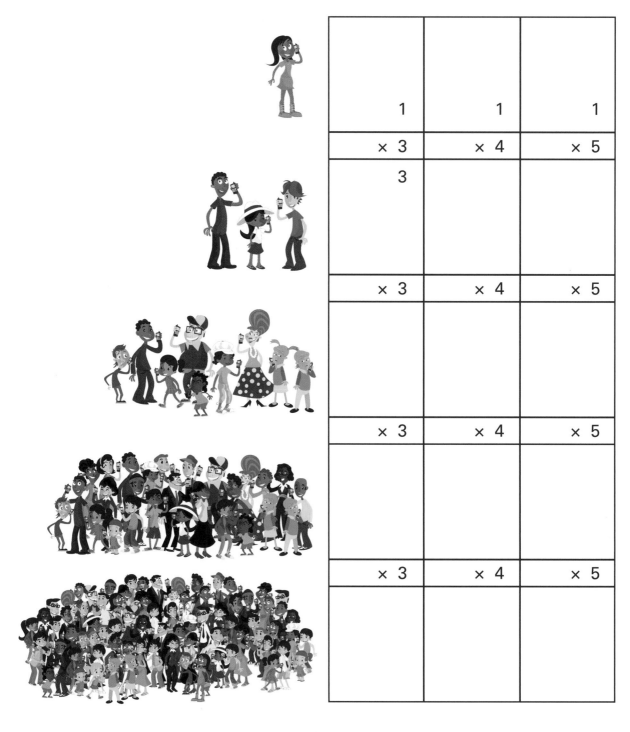

1	1	1
× 3	× 4	× 5
3		
× 3	× 4	× 5
× 3	× 4	× 5
× 3	× 4	× 5

Excellent Exercise

Four friends have been working out together all week. WRITE the number of times each person did each exercise.

 Maria did 25 sets of 15 jumping jacks, 18 sets of 20 sit-ups, 21 sets of 12 push-ups, and 16 sets of 10 pull-ups.

 Al did 22 sets of 15 jumping jacks, 24 sets of 20 sit-ups, 16 sets of 12 push-ups, and 22 sets of 10 pull-ups.

How many times did Maria do each exercise?

_____ jumping jacks   _____ sit-ups
   1   2

_____ push-ups   _____ pull-ups
   3   4

How many times did Al do each exercise?

_____ jumping jacks   _____ sit-ups
   5   6

_____ push-ups   _____ pull-ups
   7   8

 Hannah did 32 sets of 15 jumping jacks, 17 sets of 20 sit-ups, 15 sets of 12 push-ups, and 19 sets of 10 pull-ups.

Jorge did 15 sets of 15 jumping jacks, 26 sets of 20 sit-ups, 26 sets of 12 push-ups, and 20 sets of 10 pull-ups.

How many times did Hannah do each exercise?

_____ jumping jacks   _____ sit-ups
   9   10

_____ push-ups   _____ pull-ups
   11   12

How many times did Jorge do each exercise?

_____ jumping jacks   _____ sit-ups
   13   14

_____ push-ups   _____ pull-ups
   15   16

Time Travelers

Todd and Tamara are time travelers. The trouble is their time machine can only be set to travel in days and months, not weeks and years. WRITE the number of days or months they should use for each time.

1. 11 weeks = _____ days

2. 10 years = _____ months

3. 16 weeks = _____ days

4. 12 years = _____ months

5. 25 weeks = _____ days

6. 31 years = _____ months

7. 46 weeks = _____ days

8. 59 years = _____ months

9. 63 weeks = _____ days

10. 74 years = _____ months

11. 88 weeks = _____ days

12. 97 years = _____ months

Shipping Room

At the factory, action figures get packed in large boxes. There are 24 Electrogirl action figures in a box, 36 Owlboy action figures in a box, 18 Rob Roboto action figures in a box, and 45 Super Chicken action figures in a box. WRITE the number of action figures each store has ordered.

1. Comet Comics ordered 20 boxes of Electrogirl, 35 boxes of Owlboy, 24 boxes of Rob Roboto, and 13 boxes of Super Chicken.

_____ Electrogirl action figures

_____ Owlboy action figures

_____ Rob Roboto action figures

_____ Super Chicken action figures

2. Action Figure Central ordered 17 boxes of Electrogirl, 23 boxes of Owlboy, 46 boxes of Rob Roboto, and 30 boxes of Super Chicken.

_____ Electrogirl action figures

_____ Owlboy action figures

_____ Rob Roboto action figures

_____ Super Chicken action figures

3. Lights, Camera, Action Figures! ordered 25 boxes of Electrogirl, 25 boxes of Owlboy, 25 boxes of Rob Roboto, and 25 boxes of Super Chicken.

_____ Electrogirl action figures

_____ Owlboy action figures

_____ Rob Roboto action figures

_____ Super Chicken action figures

4. Waldo's Wonderworld ordered 52 boxes of Electrogirl, 38 boxes of Owlboy, 65 boxes of Rob Roboto, and 42 boxes of Super Chicken.

_____ Electrogirl action figures

_____ Owlboy action figures

_____ Rob Roboto action figures

_____ Super Chicken action figures

Amusement Adventures

Awesome Adventure Amusement Park is collecting information about the sales of different packs of ride tickets. WRITE the total number of tickets sold.

1. 789 people each bought a 15-ticket pack. _____ tickets

2. 513 people each bought a 20-ticket pack. _____ tickets

3. 794 people each bought a 25-ticket pack. _____ tickets

4. 603 people each bought a 30-ticket pack. _____ tickets

5. 582 people each bought a 35-ticket pack. _____ tickets

6. 441 people each bought a 40-ticket pack. _____ tickets

7. 328 people each bought a 45-ticket pack. _____ tickets

8. 725 people each bought a 50-ticket pack. _____ tickets

9. 196 people each bought a 75-ticket pack. _____ tickets

10. 56 people each bought a 100-ticket pack. _____ tickets

World Tour

Sara Starlight is on a world tour performing sold-out shows in 12 different cities. ESTIMATE the number of tickets sold in each city by rounding the number of tickets to the nearest thousand.

1. In Tokyo, 4,887 tickets were sold for each of Sara Starlight's four shows.

   20,000

2. In Moscow, 3,426 tickets were sold for each of Sara Starlight's three shows.

   _____

3. In Berlin, 6,518 tickets were sold for each of Sara Starlight's six shows.

   _____

4. In Copenhagen, 4,034 tickets were sold for each of Sara Starlight's four shows.

   _____

5. In Madrid, 3,482 tickets were sold for each of Sara Starlight's five shows.

   _____

6. In London, 7,245 tickets were sold for each of Sara Starlight's seven shows.

   _____

7. In Rome, 2,377 tickets were sold for both of Sara Starlight's two shows.

   _____

8. In Atlanta, 5,319 tickets were sold for each of Sara Starlight's three shows.

   _____

9. In New York, 6,348 tickets were sold for each of Sara Starlight's six shows.

   _____

10. In Chicago, 5,599 tickets were sold for each of Sara Starlight's five shows.

   _____

11. In Toronto, 3,692 tickets were sold for each of Sara Starlight's three shows.

   _____

12. In San Francisco, 7,863 tickets were sold for both of Sara Starlight's two shows.

   _____

Calculator Catch

Calculators can be a great help in solving problems if you push the right buttons. ESTIMATE each product by rounding to the nearest hundred, and CIRCLE the calculators showing the wrong answers.

1.
$$\begin{array}{r} 404 \\ \times\ 192 \\ \hline \end{array}$$

↓

$$\begin{array}{r} 400 \\ \times\ 200 \\ \hline 80{,}000 \end{array}$$

2.
$$\begin{array}{r} 769 \\ \times\ 329 \\ \hline \end{array}$$

↓

$$\times \underline{\qquad\qquad}$$

3.
$$\begin{array}{r} 957 \\ \times\ 521 \\ \hline \end{array}$$

↓

$$\times \underline{\qquad\qquad}$$

4.
$$\begin{array}{r} 345 \\ \times\ 466 \\ \hline \end{array}$$

↓

$$\times \underline{\qquad\qquad}$$

5.
$$\begin{array}{r} 2{,}879 \\ \times\ 289 \\ \hline \end{array}$$

↓

$$\times \underline{\qquad\qquad}$$

6.
$$\begin{array}{r} 1{,}664 \\ \times\ 743 \\ \hline \end{array}$$

↓

$$\times \underline{\qquad\qquad}$$

Assigned Seats

Martha has a strange way of seating guests at her parties. She gives each person a number, and each person has to find a table number that is a factor of the number. WRITE each number and name at the correct table.

1. _____

_____

_____

_____

2. _____

_____

_____

_____

3. _____

_____

_____

_____

Victoria: 42   Cassandra: 45   Joseph: 10

Alyssa: 15   Kenneth: 8   Courtney: 16

Hunter: 54   Faith: 66   Diana: 28

Isaac: 25   Aaron: 32   Alejandro: 18

Candy Packages

Stella's Sweet Shoppe is packing up batches of candy. Stella would like to use the largest box that can fit all of the candy with no leftovers. CIRCLE the box she should use for the batches.

HINT: Find the greatest common factor to determine how many pieces should fit in a box.

1. 64 Cinnaswirl Candies
   72 Chewy Chocolate Candies

2. 24 Nougat Nectar Candies
   42 Peanut Blast Candies

3. 35 Yummo Gummo Candies
   90 Lemon Twister Candies

4. 48 Fudgy Nut Candies
   60 Marshmallow Middles Candies

Buy in Bulk

Stores buy a large number of items at one time because they can usually get each item at a better price. WRITE the cost per item.

1. 10 video games for $600 $_____ per game

    100 video games for $5,000 $_____ per game

    1,000 video games for $40,000 $_____ per game

2. 6 purses for $1,800 $_____ per purse

    60 purses for $12,000 $_____ per purse

    600 purses for $60,000 $_____ per purse

3. 10 skateboards for $2,500 $_____ per skateboard

    200 skateboards for $40,000 $_____ per skateboard

    300 skateboards for $45,000 $_____ per skateboard

4. 4 computers for $16,000 $_____ per computer

    100 computers for $350,000 $_____ per computer

    500 computers for $1,000,000 $_____ per computer

Assembly Line

Each person in the assembly line divides batches of cookies into smaller and smaller groups until the cookies are ready to be put in small packages. WRITE the number of cookies there will be in each group in the assembly line.

324	512	3,750
÷ 3	÷ 4	÷ 5
÷ 3	÷ 4	÷ 5
÷ 3	÷ 4	÷ 5
÷ 3	÷ 4	÷ 5

Cool Collections

Four kids have four cool collections, and now they're trying to organize their collections into albums. WRITE the number of album pages needed to hold each collection.

Billy has a collection of 567 baseball cards.
Each album page holds 9 baseball cards.

1. How many album pages will Billy need? _____

Trisha has a collection of 784 photographs.
Each album page holds 4 photographs.

2. How many album pages will Trisha need? _____

Max has a collection of 2,230 stamps.
Each album page holds 10 stamps.

3. How many album pages will Max need? _____

Jin has a collection of 5,048 stickers.
Each album page holds 8 stickers.

4. How many album pages will Jin need? _____

Walking Workout

Ten friends decided to see who could walk the most in a week. Everyone wore a pedometer, a device that tracks the number of steps taken. They checked in with each other at the end of seven days. WRITE the number of steps each person walked per day.

1. Elsa walked 66,045 steps. _____ steps per day

2. Martin walked 56,896 steps. _____ steps per day

3. Sonja walked 81,144 steps. _____ steps per day

4. David walked 74,641 steps. _____ steps per day

5. Brianna walked 63,056 steps. _____ steps per day

6. Isaiah walked 55,650 steps. _____ steps per day

7. Taylor walked 95,368 steps. _____ steps per day

8. Garrett walked 74,956 steps. _____ steps per day

9. Kiara walked 60,984 steps. _____ steps per day

10. Omar walked 87,906 steps. _____ steps per day

Family Vacation

Several families have hit the road for a driving vacation. If each family didn't vary its speed for the whole trip, WRITE the number of hours each family drove.

1. Peter's family drove 420 miles going 60 miles per hour. _____ hours

2. Sandy's family drove 210 miles going 35 miles per hour. _____ hours

3. Dane's family drove 405 miles going 45 miles per hour. _____ hours

4. Ella's family drove 550 miles going 50 miles per hour. _____ hours

5. Ricardo's family drove 624 miles going 48 miles per hour. _____ hours

6. Maya's family drove 456 miles going 57 miles per hour. _____ hours

7. Chen's family drove 160 miles going 32 miles per hour. _____ hours

8. Justine's family drove 522 miles going 29 miles per hour. _____ hours

9. Hurley's family drove 236 miles going 59 miles per hour. _____ hours

10. Claire's family drove 378 miles going 42 miles per hour. _____ hours

11. Austin's family drove 636 miles going 53 miles per hour. _____ hours

12. Karen's family drove 616 going 44 miles per hour. _____ hours

Avid Readers

WRITE the number of days it will take these friends to read each of their books, and the number of pages that will be left to read on the last day.

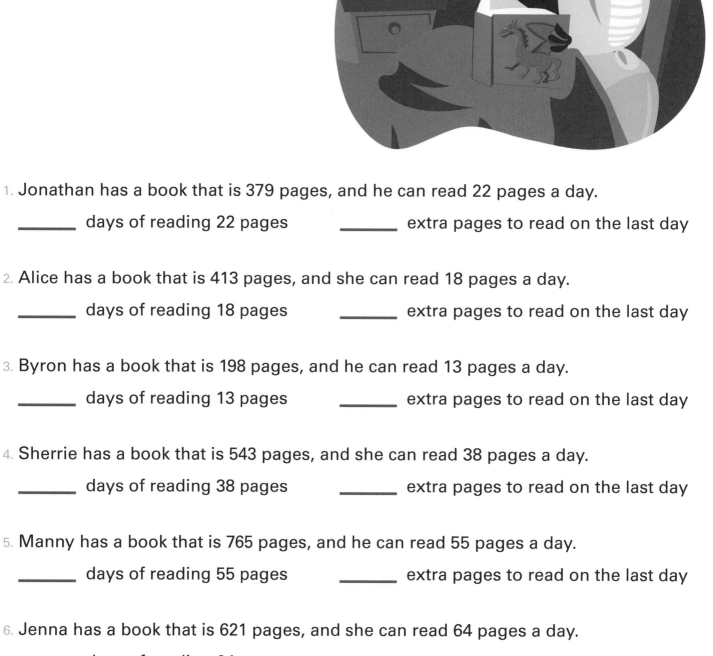

1. Jonathan has a book that is 379 pages, and he can read 22 pages a day.

   _____ days of reading 22 pages   _____ extra pages to read on the last day

2. Alice has a book that is 413 pages, and she can read 18 pages a day.

   _____ days of reading 18 pages   _____ extra pages to read on the last day

3. Byron has a book that is 198 pages, and he can read 13 pages a day.

   _____ days of reading 13 pages   _____ extra pages to read on the last day

4. Sherrie has a book that is 543 pages, and she can read 38 pages a day.

   _____ days of reading 38 pages   _____ extra pages to read on the last day

5. Manny has a book that is 765 pages, and he can read 55 pages a day.

   _____ days of reading 55 pages   _____ extra pages to read on the last day

6. Jenna has a book that is 621 pages, and she can read 64 pages a day.

   _____ days of reading 64 pages   _____ extra pages to read on the last day

Car Share

Different groups of people are talking about buying a car that they could all share. ESTIMATE the cost per person by rounding the cost of the car to the nearest thousand.

1. Six people are talking about splitting
   the cost of a compact car priced at $18,376. $ _____ per person

2. Four people are thinking about splitting
   the cost of a used car priced at $7,823. $ _____ per person

3. Eight people are talking about buying
   a $71,671 SUV. $ _____ per person

4. Five people are talking about buying
   a hybrid car for $25,469. $ _____ per person

5. Seven people are thinking about buying
   a $27,544 minivan. $ _____ per person

6. Three people are going to buy a
   convertible sports car for $104,762. $ _____ per person

Estimating Quotients

Calculator Catch

Calculators can be a great help in solving problems if you push the right buttons. ESTIMATE each quotient by rounding the dividend to the nearest thousand, and CIRCLE the calculators showing the wrong answers.

1. $9\overline{)36,423}$

2. $15\overline{)44,835}$

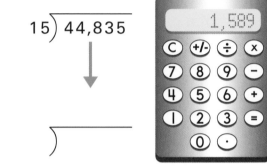

3. $3\overline{)65,763}$

4. $4\overline{)20,328}$

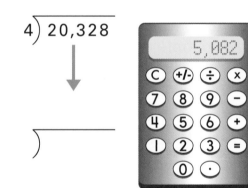

5. $24\overline{)48,144}$

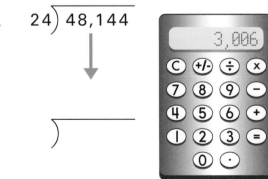

6. $70\overline{)69,580}$

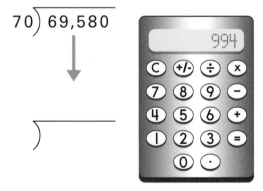

Factor Families

A **prime number** can only be divided evenly by itself and 1. A **composite number** has more factors than itself and 1. WRITE the missing numbers in each factor family.

Example:

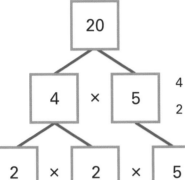

4 and 20 are composite numbers.

2 and 5 are prime numbers.

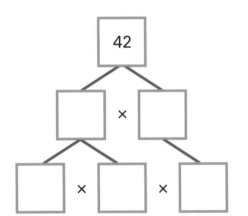

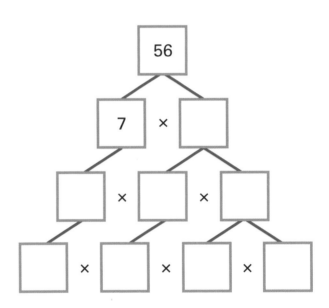

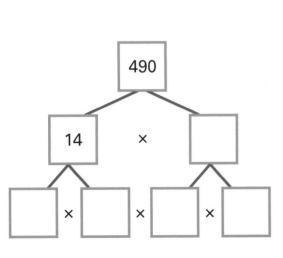

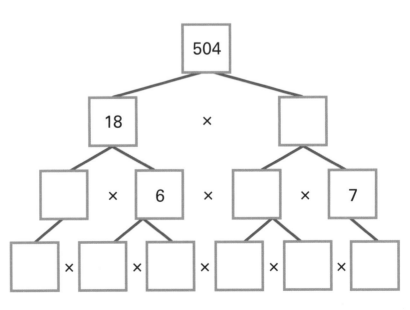

Prime Find

Mikey is trying to find all of the prime numbers between 1 and 100. CIRCLE each prime number.

1	2	3	4	5	6	7	8	9	10
11	12	13	14	15	16	17	18	19	20
21	22	23	24	25	26	27	28	29	30
31	32	33	34	35	36	37	38	39	40
41	42	43	44	45	46	47	48	49	50
51	52	53	54	55	56	57	58	59	60
61	62	63	64	65	66	67	68	69	70
71	72	73	74	75	76	77	78	79	80
81	82	83	84	85	86	87	88	89	90
91	92	93	94	95	96	97	98	99	100

Best Price

CIRCLE the item with the lowest price.

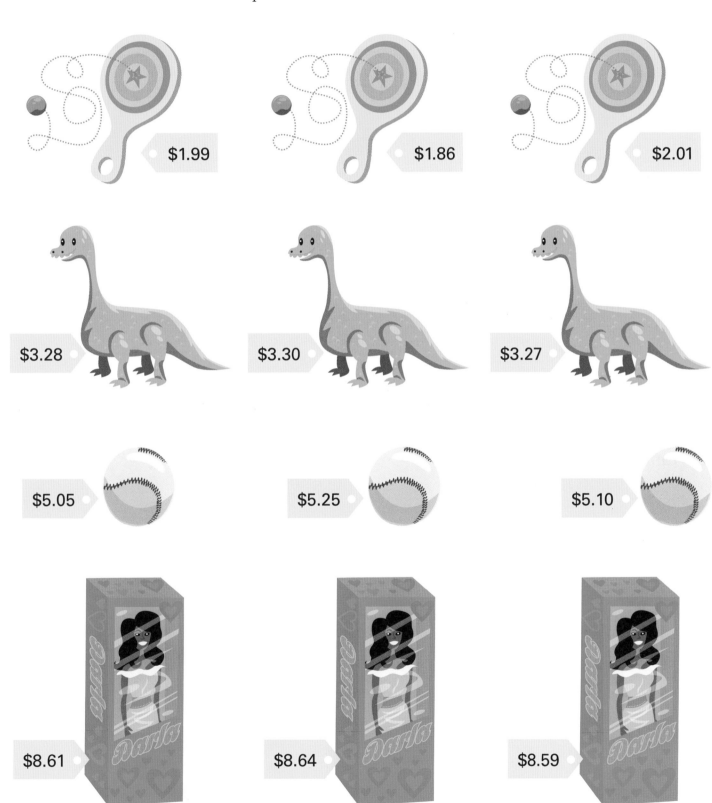

$1.99 $1.86 $2.01

$3.28 $3.30 $3.27

$5.05 $5.25 $5.10

$8.61 $8.64 $8.59

Batter Up

In baseball, the batting average is a number that shows the number of hits a batter got versus the number of times the batter was at bat. The higher the number, the better the batting average. WRITE the numbers 1 through 10 so that 1 is the best batting average and 10 is the worst batting average.

	Player	Batting Average	Rank
1.	Sly Young	.251	_____
2.	Larry Bonds	.278	_____
3.	Josephine Jackson	.349	_____
4.	Willie Frays	.318	_____
5.	Melanie Ott	.185	_____
6.	Ruth Babe	.272	_____
7.	Ned Williams	.367	_____
8.	Jill Hamilton	.299	_____
9.	Frank Aaron	.205	_____
10.	Peg Maddux	.218	_____

Piggy Bank

ROUND the amount of money in each piggy bank to the nearest dollar.

HINT: When rounding, look at the digit to the right of the place you're rounding to. If that digit is less than 5, round down. If it is 5 or greater, round up.

$18.23

$ _____
1

$52.97

$ _____
2

$21.72

$ _____
3

$68.31

$ _____
4

$0.64

$ _____
5

$75.18

$ _____
6

$41.49

$ _____
7

$99.52

$ _____
8

Track and Field

Athletes have come from all over the country to participate in the country's track-and-field events, including shot put, long jump, and the 100-meter hurdles.

ROUND each shot-put score to the nearest meter.

1. **17.43 m** _____ m

2. **22.81 m** _____ m

3. **21.33 m** _____ m

4. **18.62 m** _____ m

5. **20.49 m** _____ m

6. **21.55 m** _____ m

ROUND each long-jump score to the nearest tenth of a meter.

7. **7.21 m** _____ m

8. **5.87 m** _____ m

9. **6.55 m** _____ m

10. **5.98 m** _____ m

11. **6.74 m** _____ m

12. **7.42 m** _____ m

ROUND each hurdle score to the nearest hundredth of a second.

13. **12.932 sec** _____ sec

14. **13.048 sec** _____ sec

15. **12.876 sec** _____ sec

16. **14.215 sec** _____ sec

17. **13.494 sec** _____ sec

18. **12.723 sec** _____ sec

Plus Tax

WRITE the total cost of each item when sales tax is added.

1.

Price	$84.50
Tax	$ 5.49
Total	$

2.

Price	$5.47
Tax	$0.36
Total	$

3.

Price	$159.97
Tax	$ 10.40
Total	$

4.

Price	$575.65
Tax	$ 37.42
Total	$

5.

Price	$27.68
Tax	$ 1.80
Total	$

6.

Price	$229.99
Tax	$ 14.95
Total	$

That Does Not Compute!

The Great Roboto is on the fritz and is spitting out some math problems with wrong answers. CIRCLE the incorrect differences.

$$\begin{array}{r} 7.04 \\ -\ 3.9 \\ \hline 3.14 \end{array}$$

$$\begin{array}{r} 78.131 \\ -\ 4.226 \\ \hline 73.905 \end{array}$$

$$\begin{array}{r} 913.568 \\ -834.92 \\ \hline 78.648 \end{array}$$

$$\begin{array}{r} 15.26 \\ -\ 9.87 \\ \hline 6.39 \end{array}$$

$$\begin{array}{r} 20.8 \\ -16.16 \\ \hline 4.62 \end{array}$$

$$\begin{array}{r} 201.55 \\ -166.65 \\ \hline 34.95 \end{array}$$

$$\begin{array}{r} 0.12 \\ -0.108 \\ \hline 0.012 \end{array}$$

$$\begin{array}{r} 99.9 \\ -88.88 \\ \hline 11.11 \end{array}$$

$$\begin{array}{r} 425.2 \\ -\ 58.29 \\ \hline 366.91 \end{array}$$

$$\begin{array}{r} 300.03 \\ -\ 30.003 \\ \hline 270.27 \end{array}$$

$$\begin{array}{r} 27.51 \\ -15.72 \\ \hline 12.79 \end{array}$$

$$\begin{array}{r} 9.6 \\ -2.007 \\ \hline 7.593 \end{array}$$

Copy Shop

Coco's Copy Shop has different prices for copies depending on how many copies you make. The chart shows the price per copy. WRITE the cost of each copy order.

Number of Copies	Black-and-White Copies	Color Copies
0–25	$0.10	$0.28
26–50	$0.08	$0.25
51–100	$0.06	$0.21
101–500	$0.05	$0.18
501–1,000	$0.04	$0.12

1. Suzie needs to make 20 color copies of her garage-sale sign.

   $_____

2. Brad needs to make 6 black-and-white copies of his latest short story.

   $_____

3. Alison needs to make 80 black-and-white copies of the program for the school play.

   $_____

4. Brent wants to make 33 color copies of a vacation photograph he took.

   $_____

5. Margaret needs to make 175 black-and-white copies of a flyer to sell her bike.

   $_____

6. Kevin wants to make copies of the comic strip he drew. He'll need a total of 375 color copies.

   $_____

7. Adina wants to make 642 black-and-white copies of a poem she wrote.

   $_____

8. Dan needs to make 558 color copies of the flyer for his band's show next week.

   $_____

Everyday Electricity

The electric company charges $0.092 for every kilowatt hour (kWh) of use. One kilowatt hour lights a 100-watt light bulb for about 10 hours. WRITE the cost of the electrical use for each month, rounding to the nearest penny where necessary.

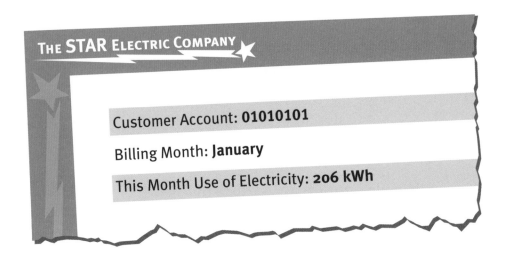

THE **STAR** ELECTRIC COMPANY

Customer Account: **01010101**

Billing Month: **January**

This Month Use of Electricity: **206 kWh**

1. January: 206 kWh $_____
2. February: 275 kWh $_____
3. March: 284 kWh $_____
4. April: 320 kWh $_____
5. May: 349 kWh $_____
6. June: 513 kWh $_____
7. July: 684 kWh $_____
8. August: 736 kWh $_____
9. September: 415 kWh $_____
10. October: 302 kWh $_____
11. November: 266 kWh $_____
12. December: 199 kWh $_____

Snack Bar

Groups of friends are chipping in to buy snacks at the snack bar. WRITE the cost for each person.

1. Four friends are chipping in for nachos that cost $5.48.

   Each person will pay $ _____

2. Two friends are splitting a milkshake and a bag of pretzels for $6.72.

   Each person will pay $ _____

3. Six friends are chipping in for three hot dogs and three lemonades for a total of $11.04.

   Each person will pay $ _____

4. Five friends are splitting two orders of cheeseburgers with fries that have a total cost of $12.45.

   Each person will pay $ _____

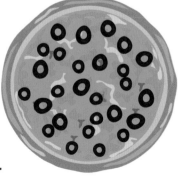

5. Eight friends are chipping in for a pizza that costs $15.92.

   Each person will pay $ _____

6. Seven friends are sharing a bag of popcorn that costs $2.03.

   Each person will pay $ _____

That Does Not Compute!

The Great Roboto is on the fritz and is spitting out some math problems with wrong answers.
CIRCLE the incorrect quotients.

$9 \overline{)3.6}$ = 0.4

$12 \overline{)1.44}$ = 0.14

$8 \overline{)5.6}$ = 0.6

$4 \overline{)4.32}$ = 1.08

$7 \overline{)97.3}$ = 1.39

$5 \overline{)12.5}$ = 2.5

$3 \overline{)5.676}$ = 1.892

$10 \overline{)0.45}$ = 4.5

$15 \overline{)123.45}$ = 8.23

$23 \overline{)0.644}$ = 0.28

$17 \overline{)23.953}$ = 1.49

$40 \overline{)147.2}$ = 3.68

Delicious Duos

Equivalent fractions are fractions that have the same value. CIRCLE the two foods in each row that have the equivalent fraction of food.

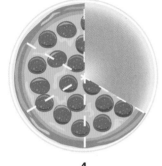  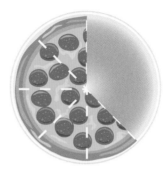 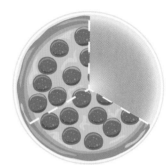

$$\frac{4}{6} \qquad\qquad \frac{3}{4} \qquad\qquad \frac{5}{8} \qquad\qquad \frac{2}{3}$$

$$\frac{9}{12} \qquad\qquad \frac{5}{8} \qquad\qquad \frac{3}{4} \qquad\qquad \frac{7}{9}$$

$$\frac{5}{9} \qquad\qquad \frac{1}{2} \qquad\qquad \frac{5}{6} \qquad\qquad \frac{4}{8}$$

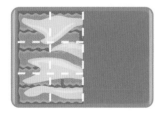  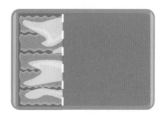 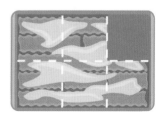

$$\frac{6}{12} \qquad\qquad \frac{3}{9} \qquad\qquad \frac{1}{3} \qquad\qquad \frac{5}{6}$$

Equivalent Fractions

Kate's Kitchen

Today in Kate's Kitchen, Kate is showing how to make measurements when you don't have the right size measuring cup. WRITE the equivalent measurement.

HINT: Fractions that have the same number in the numerator and the denominator are equivalent to 1.

1. $1 \text{ cup} = \dfrac{2}{2} \text{ cup}$ 2. $1 \text{ cup} = \dfrac{}{8} \text{ cup}$

3. $1 \text{ cup} = \dfrac{}{4} \text{ cup}$ 4. $\dfrac{3}{4} \text{ cup} = \dfrac{}{8} \text{ cup}$

5. $1 \text{ cup} = \dfrac{}{3} \text{ cup}$ 6. $\dfrac{1}{2} \text{ cup} = \dfrac{}{4} \text{ cup}$

7. $\dfrac{2}{3} \text{ cup} = \dfrac{}{6} \text{ cup}$ 8. $\dfrac{1}{4} \text{ cup} = \dfrac{}{8} \text{ cup}$

At the Fair

A fraction is in its simplest form if the only common factor of the numerator and the denominator is 1. WRITE each fraction in the paragraph as a fraction in its simplest form.

Ethan and his family head to the county fair, one of Ethan's favorite

places. When they arrive, $\frac{6}{8}$ of the parking lots are already full, so

1. $\dfrac{3}{4}$

they park in lot 7. Ethan's parents buy 12 game tickets for the kids,

and give $\frac{8}{12}$ of the tickets to Ethan and $\frac{4}{12}$ of the tickets to his little

2. —— 3. ——

sister, Nora. Ethan uses $\frac{6}{8}$ of his tickets to play the ring toss. He

4. ——

uses the other $\frac{2}{8}$ of his tickets trying to knock down bottles with a

5. ——

baseball. The most he knocks down is $\frac{3}{9}$ of the bottles. Ethan and

6. ——

Nora split a bag of six pretzel twists. They each take $\frac{3}{6}$ of the bag.

7. ——

Before it's time to go home, Ethan and his family sit down to enjoy a

show with 10 different acts. Ethan likes the $\frac{4}{10}$ of the show in which

8. ——

people tell jokes, but Nora likes the $\frac{6}{10}$ of the show that features

9. ——

musical acts. After a great day at the fair, it's time to go home.

Amusement Adventures

The people at Rocket Launch Amusement Park want to make some changes, so they asked visitors what they thought about the amusement park. WRITE each fraction in its simplest form.

1. **What is your favorite ride?**
Survey of 24 people

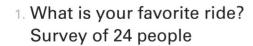 $\frac{12}{24}$ of the people said Rocket Blast

 $\frac{8}{24}$ of the people said Octorama

 $\frac{4}{24}$ of the people said Super Spinner

2. **What is your favorite food?**
Survey of 18 people

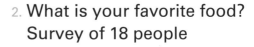 $\frac{2}{18}$ of the people said Blast-off Burger

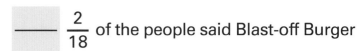 $\frac{4}{18}$ of the people said Saturn Shake

 $\frac{12}{18}$ of the people said Launch Fries

3. **How many tickets did you buy?**
Survey of 30 people

$\frac{10}{30}$ of the people said 15 tickets

$\frac{5}{30}$ of the people said 20 tickets

$\frac{15}{30}$ of the people said 25 tickets

4. **What is the longest you waited for a ride?**
Survey of 36 people

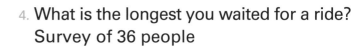 $\frac{9}{36}$ of the people said 15 minutes

 $\frac{15}{36}$ of the people said 20 minutes

 $\frac{12}{36}$ of the people said 30 minutes

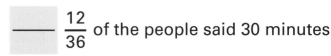

Rainy Days

A rain gauge measures the amount of rain that falls. WRITE each measurement as a mixed number.

1. April 1 $\frac{4}{3}$ in.   _____ in.

2. April 6 $\frac{8}{5}$ in.   _____ in.

3. April 7 $\frac{5}{2}$ in.   _____ in.

4. April 10 $\frac{7}{6}$ in.   _____ in.

5. April 13 $\frac{9}{4}$ in.   _____ in.

6. April 18 $\frac{19}{16}$ in.   _____ in.

7. April 22 $\frac{15}{8}$ in.   _____ in.

8. April 29 $\frac{23}{10}$ in.   _____ in.

Gassing Up

How much gasoline did each person get at the gas station? WRITE the amount as a mixed number.

1. Kate put $\frac{25}{4}$ gallons into her car. _____ gallons

2. Alberto put $\frac{27}{4}$ gallons into his car. _____ gallons

3. Juliet put $\frac{31}{3}$ gallons into her car. _____ gallons

4. Benjamin put $\frac{53}{6}$ gallons into his car. _____ gallons

5. Sheila put $\frac{15}{2}$ gallons into her car. _____ gallons

6. Brian put $\frac{35}{3}$ gallons into his car. _____ gallons

7. Jackie put $\frac{17}{4}$ gallons into her car. _____ gallons

8. Russell put $\frac{83}{8}$ gallons into his car. _____ gallons

Kate's Kitchen

Today in Kate's Kitchen, Kate is showing how to make measurements when you don't have the right kind of measuring cup. WRITE the equivalent measurement as an improper fraction.

1. $1\frac{1}{2}$ cups = $\frac{3}{2}$ cups

2. $3\frac{1}{3}$ cups = $\frac{}{3}$ cups

3. $2\frac{1}{3}$ cups = $\frac{}{3}$ cups

4. $5\frac{1}{2}$ cups = $\frac{}{2}$ cups

5. $1\frac{3}{4}$ cups = $\frac{}{4}$ cups

6. $2\frac{1}{8}$ cups = $\frac{}{8}$ cups

7. $4\frac{2}{3}$ cups = $\frac{}{3}$ cups

8. $1\frac{7}{8}$ cups = $\frac{}{8}$ cups

Leftover Pizza

Each amount of leftover pizza is shown as a mixed number. WRITE the amount of leftover pizza as an improper fraction.

  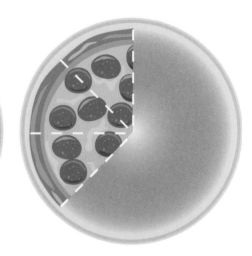

1. $2\frac{3}{8}$ pizzas = _____ pizzas

2. $1\frac{5}{6}$ pizzas = _____ pizzas

3. $3\frac{3}{4}$ pizzas = _____ pizzas

4. $1\frac{9}{10}$ pizzas = _____ pizzas

5. $3\frac{1}{3}$ pizzas = _____ pizzas

6. $2\frac{1}{4}$ pizzas = _____ pizzas

7. $4\frac{1}{2}$ pizzas = _____ pizzas

8. $3\frac{5}{6}$ pizzas = _____ pizzas

9. $5\frac{5}{8}$ pizzas = _____ pizzas

10. $2\frac{7}{9}$ pizzas = _____ pizzas

11. $3\frac{1}{8}$ pizzas = _____ pizzas

12. $6\frac{1}{6}$ pizzas = _____ pizzas

Coin Count

There are 100 coins on this page. WRITE the fraction, decimal, and percent for each type of coin.

HINT: A percent (%) is a way of showing parts of 100. If 67 out of 100 coins are pennies, this can be written as $\frac{67}{100}$, 0.67, or 67%.

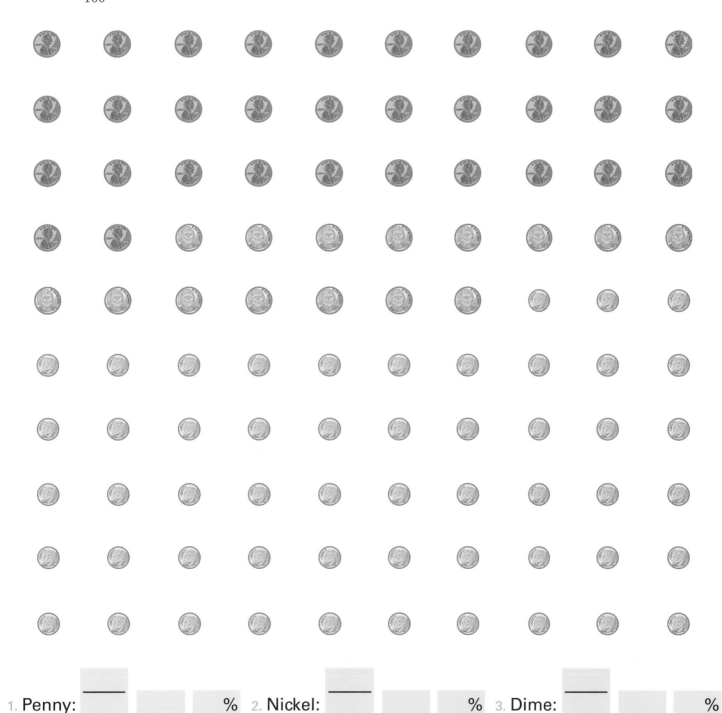

1. Penny: _____   %   2. Nickel: _____   %   3. Dime: _____   %

Fractions, Decimals & Percents

Frosted Cupcakes

WRITE the fraction, decimal, and percent of yellow frosted cupcakes in each row.

Example:

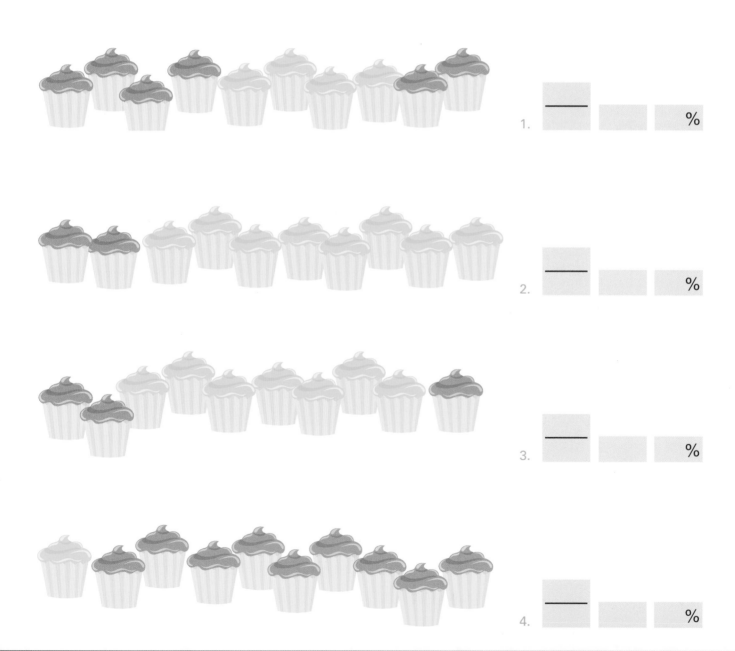

If 3 out of 10 cupcakes have yellow frosting, this can be written as $\frac{3}{10}$, 0.3, or 30%.

1. _____ _____ _____%

2. _____ _____ _____%

3. _____ _____ _____%

4. _____ _____ _____%

Survey Says

A research company surveyed people about things that they have in their homes. WRITE the percent for each survey result.

HINT: Think of each group of people as a fraction and the equivalent fraction that has 100 in the denominator.

1. People who own a television set: 99 out of 100 _____ %

2. People who own a car: 75 out of 100 _____ %

3. People who have at least one pet: 40 out of 50 _____ %

4. People who have more than one computer: 6 out of 10 _____ %

5. People who own a snowblower: 47 out of 100 _____ %

6. People who have a yard with a swing set: 15 out of 50 _____ %

7. People who own more than 50 books: 12 out of 25 _____ %

8. People who own a motorcycle: 2 out of 100 _____ %

9. People who have a home with three bedrooms: 5 out of 10 _____ %

10. People who own a boat: 1 out of 25 _____ %

11. People who have Internet access: 46 out of 50 _____ %

12. People who have a pool: 2 out of 10 _____ %

Skateboard Sort

WRITE each percent.

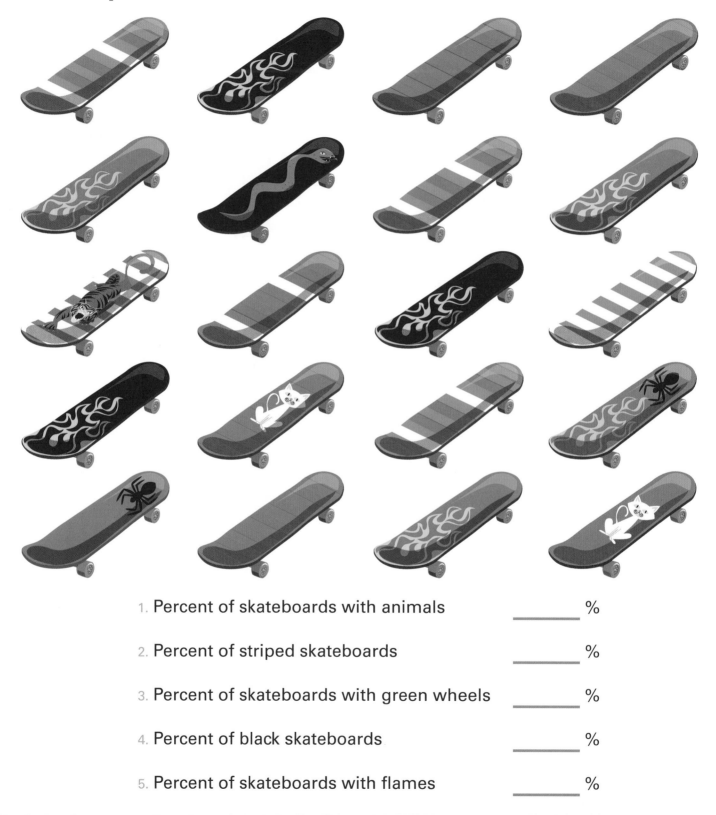

1. Percent of skateboards with animals _____ %

2. Percent of striped skateboards _____ %

3. Percent of skateboards with green wheels _____ %

4. Percent of black skateboards _____ %

5. Percent of skateboards with flames _____ %

Pay the Check

WRITE each tip, and ADD the tip to each of the restaurant checks.

GUEST CHECK

Date	Table	Guests	Server	000945

Hamburger	$4.50
French fries	$1.75
Soda	$1.55
Food Total	$7.80
15% tip	$1.17
Total	$8.97

15% is the same as 0.15, so to find the tip, multiply 7.80 by 0.15.

Then add the tip to the food total, and you have the total cost of the check.

GUEST CHECK

Date	Table	Guests	Server	000946

Meatball sub	$ 6.20
Bag of chips	$ 1.65
Bottle of water	$ 2.35
Food Total	$10.20
10% tip	
Total	

GUEST CHECK

Date	Table	Guests	Server	000947

Chicken club sandwich	$ 8.55
Bowl of soup	$ 3.20
Small coffee	$ 0.85
Food Total	$12.60
15% tip	
Total	

GUEST CHECK

Date	Table	Guests	Server	000948

Grilled ham and cheese	$4.15
Lemonade	$2.40
Cherry pie	$3.30
Food Total	$9.85
20% tip	
Total	

GUEST CHECK

Date	Table	Guests	Server	000949

Garden salad	$10.25
Iced tea	$ 2.60
Chocolate pudding	$ 1.75
Food Total	$14.60
25% tip	
Total	

Fractions, Decimals & Percents

Cool Collections

READ the descriptions of each collection, and WRITE the answers.

Annie has a collection of 50 action figures. Heroes make up 64% of her action figures, while 36% of her action figures are villains.

1. How many of the action figures are heroes? _____

2. How many of the action figures are villains? _____

Richie has 40 video games. His collection is 50% adventure games, 20% arcade games, and 30% sports games.

3. How many of the video games are adventure games? _____

4. How many of the video games are arcade games? _____

5. How many of the video games are sports games? _____

Kurt has a collection of 125 model train cars. Train engines make up 40% of his collection, while 12% of his collection is cabooses, 16% of his collection is passenger cars, and 32% of his collection is boxcars.

6. How many of the train cars are engines? _____

7. How many of the train cars are cabooses? _____

8. How many of the train cars are passenger cars? _____

9. How many of the train cars are boxcars? _____

Vivian has a collection of 1,500 stamps. Animals appear on 34% of her stamps, pictures of famous people on 52% of her stamps, and flags are featured on 14% of her stamps.

10. How many of the stamps have animals? _____

11. How many of the stamps have people? _____

12. How many of the stamps have flags? _____

Library Checkout

Each person is checking out a large number of library books, all on different topics. What's the largest amount of books on a topic that each person is checking out?
WRITE the fraction, percent, or decimal.

1. Rita checked out 10 books. Of the books Rita borrowed, $\frac{1}{2}$ are about Egypt, 30% are mysteries, and 0.2 are about animals.

   $\frac{1}{2}$

2. Carl checked out 15 books. Of the books Carl borrowed, $\frac{1}{5}$ are about auto repair, 20% are about robots, and 0.6 have vampires and monsters in them.

   _____

3. Mei checked out 20 books. Of the books Mei borrowed, $\frac{7}{20}$ are historical fiction, 40% are about Greek mythology, and 0.25 are about wizards.

   _____

4. Walter checked out 15 books. Of the books Walter borrowed, $\frac{3}{5}$ are biographies, 20% are history books, and 0.2 are about the military.

   _____

5. Hazel checked out 10 books. Of the books Hazel borrowed, $\frac{2}{5}$ are knitting books, 50% have sewing patterns, and 0.1 is about needlepoint.

   _____

6. Travis checked out 25 books. Of the books Travis borrowed, $\frac{1}{5}$ are about gardening, 32% are about house repair, and 0.48 are fiction.

   _____

Comparing Amounts

Best Price

CIRCLE the item with the lower price in each row.

1.

$80 $\frac{1}{2}$ off $80   60% off

2.

$142   40% off $142 $\frac{3}{5}$ off

3.
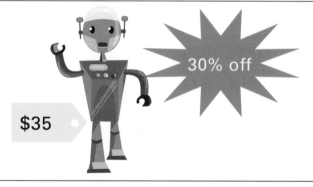

$35 $\frac{1}{3}$ off $35   30% off

4.
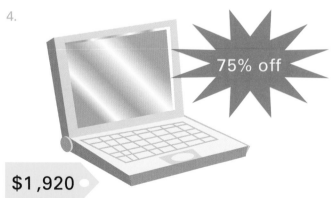

$1,920   75% off $1,920 $\frac{6}{7}$ off

That Does Not Compute!

The Great Roboto is on the fritz and is spitting out some math problems with wrong answers. CIRCLE the incorrect sums.

$$\frac{5}{8} + \frac{2}{4} = \frac{7}{8}$$

$$\frac{4}{9} + \frac{1}{3} = \frac{7}{9}$$

$$\frac{7}{12} + \frac{3}{8} = 1\frac{1}{24}$$

$$\frac{1}{2} + \frac{7}{8} = 1\frac{3}{4}$$

$$\frac{5}{6} + \frac{1}{12} = 1$$

$$\frac{3}{7} + \frac{4}{21} = \frac{13}{21}$$

$$\frac{6}{7} + \frac{3}{14} = 1\frac{1}{14}$$

$$\frac{4}{15} + \frac{2}{3} = \frac{14}{15}$$

$$\frac{3}{5} + \frac{9}{10} = \frac{2}{3}$$

$$\frac{7}{9} + \frac{1}{6} = \frac{17}{18}$$

$$\frac{3}{11} + \frac{17}{22} = 1\frac{1}{22}$$

$$\frac{8}{9} + \frac{2}{5} = 1\frac{2}{9}$$

Adding Fractions

Gassing Up

How much gasoline will each person have after a stop at the gas station? WRITE the fraction in its simplest form.

1. Burt had $2\frac{3}{5}$ gallons of gas in his car, and he added $8\frac{1}{5}$ gallons at the gas station. _____ gallons

2. Marsha had $6\frac{1}{6}$ gallons of gas in her car, and she added $9\frac{5}{6}$ gallons at the gas station. _____ gallons

3. David had $7\frac{3}{4}$ gallons of gas in his SUV, and he added $14\frac{1}{2}$ gallons at the gas station. _____ gallons

4. Teri had $1\frac{3}{8}$ gallons of gas in her car, and she added $12\frac{1}{4}$ gallons at the gas station. _____ gallons

5. Michael had $5\frac{9}{14}$ gallons of gas in his car, and he added $11\frac{4}{7}$ gallons at the gas station. _____ gallons

6. Rebecca had $6\frac{1}{5}$ gallons of gas in her truck, and she added $18\frac{3}{10}$ gallons at the gas station. _____ gallons

7. Peter had $4\frac{5}{6}$ gallons of gas in his van, and he added $14\frac{1}{3}$ gallons at the gas station. _____ gallons

8. Janet had $12\frac{4}{9}$ gallons of gas in her SUV, and she added $16\frac{2}{3}$ gallons at the gas station. _____ gallons

Louisa's Lasagna

Each lasagna has been cut into a different number of pieces, and some of the pieces have been eaten. WRITE the remaining fraction of lasagna as a fraction in its simplest form.

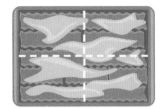

1. Louisa cut her lasagna into 4 pieces, and 2 pieces were eaten.

$$\frac{4}{4} - \frac{2}{4} = \underline{\hspace{1cm}}$$

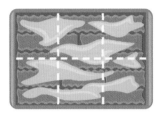

2. Louisa cut her lasagna into 6 pieces, and 4 pieces were eaten.

$$\frac{6}{6} - \frac{4}{6} = \underline{\hspace{1cm}}$$

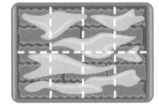

3. Louisa cut her lasagna into 8 pieces, and 5 pieces were eaten.

$$\frac{8}{8} - \frac{5}{8} = \underline{\hspace{1cm}}$$

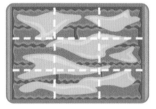

4. Louisa cut her lasagna into 9 pieces, and 3 pieces were eaten.

$$\frac{9}{9} - \frac{3}{9} = \underline{\hspace{1cm}}$$

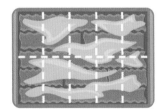

5. Louisa cut her lasagna into 10 pieces, and 8 pieces were eaten.

$$\frac{10}{10} - \frac{8}{10} = \underline{\hspace{1cm}}$$

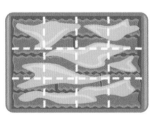

6. Louisa cut her lasagna into 12 pieces, and 4 pieces were eaten.

$$\frac{12}{12} - \frac{4}{12} = \underline{\hspace{1cm}}$$

Rainy Days

The Jones family has a rain gauge in the backyard to measure the amount of rain that falls each day. The chart shows the amount of rain that fell in one rainy week in April. LOOK at the chart, and WRITE each answer as a fraction in its simplest form.

Sunday	Monday	Tuesday	Wednesday	Thursday	Friday	Saturday
$\frac{3}{4}$ in.	$\frac{1}{3}$ in.	$\frac{3}{8}$ in.	$\frac{1}{4}$ in.	$1\frac{1}{2}$ in.	$\frac{7}{8}$ in.	$\frac{3}{5}$ in.

1. How much more rain fell on Friday than on Tuesday? _____ in.

2. How much more rain fell on Sunday than on Wednesday? _____ in.

3. How much more rain fell on Thursday than on Sunday? _____ in.

4. How much more rain fell on Monday than on Wednesday? _____ in.

5. How much more rain fell on Sunday than on Saturday? _____ in.

6. How much more rain fell on Thursday than on Friday? _____ in.

7. How much more rain fell on Saturday than on Monday? _____ in.

8. How much more rain fell on Friday than on Saturday? _____ in.

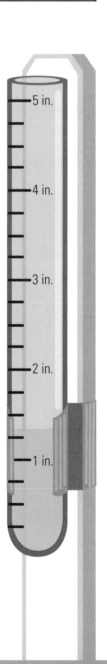

That Does Not Compute!

The Great Roboto is on the fritz and is spitting out some math problems with wrong answers.
CIRCLE the incorrect differences.

$$\frac{5}{6} - \frac{5}{18} = \frac{5}{9}$$

$$\frac{7}{9} - \frac{2}{3} = \frac{1}{9}$$

$$\frac{11}{12} - \frac{1}{4} = \frac{7}{12}$$

$$\frac{3}{4} - \frac{1}{8} = \frac{5}{8}$$

$$\frac{5}{6} - \frac{3}{5} = \frac{2}{6}$$

$$\frac{3}{4} - \frac{2}{3} = \frac{1}{12}$$

$$\frac{9}{14} - \frac{2}{7} = \frac{5}{14}$$

$$\frac{7}{15} - \frac{1}{5} = \frac{2}{5}$$

$$\frac{7}{10} - \frac{1}{2} = \frac{1}{10}$$

$$\frac{8}{9} - \frac{5}{6} = \frac{1}{36}$$

$$\frac{15}{16} - \frac{3}{4} = \frac{1}{4}$$

$$\frac{5}{8} - \frac{1}{24} = \frac{7}{12}$$

Tall Team

READ the paragraph, and WRITE each answer as a fraction in its simplest form.

The Barnaby Basketball team is lucky to have so many tall players. The tallest player, Marco, is $76\frac{3}{8}$ inches tall. The shortest player on the team is Lucy, who is $68\frac{1}{4}$ inches tall. Henry is $72\frac{1}{3}$ inches tall, and Tamara is close to Henry's height at $71\frac{3}{4}$ inches tall. The last player is Jack, who is $70\frac{1}{2}$ inches tall.

1. How much taller is Tamara than Lucy? _____ in.

2. How much taller is Marco than Lucy? _____ in.

3. How much taller is Tamara than Jack? _____ in.

4. How much taller is Henry than Lucy? _____ in.

5. How much taller is Marco than Jack? _____ in.

6. How much taller is Henry than Tamara? _____ in.

Time Well Spent

READ the paragraph, and WRITE each answer as a fraction in its simplest form.

Malcolm follows the same schedule after school every Monday through Friday. He spends $\frac{1}{4}$ hour on the bus to karate class, which lasts $\frac{3}{4}$ hour. His mom picks him up and drives him home, which takes $\frac{1}{3}$ hour. At home he has his $\frac{1}{2}$-hour-long violin lesson, followed by $\frac{2}{3}$ hour of computer time.

Then he relaxes with $\frac{5}{6}$ hour of television.

What is the total amount of time Malcolm spends doing each activity in a five-day period?

1. Riding the bus _____ hours

2. Taking a karate class _____ hours

3. Riding in the car _____ hours

4. Taking a violin lesson _____ hours

5. Using the computer _____ hours

6. Watching television _____ hours

Kate's Kitchen

Today in Kate's Kitchen, Kate is scaling up a recipe. When you scale up a recipe, you multiply the ingredients in the recipe to make a larger number of servings. WRITE the new amount of each ingredient in the scaled-up recipes as a fraction in its simplest form.

HINT: Multiply the ingredients by 2 and by 4 to scale up the recipes.

Very Berry Muffins Serves 6	Very Berry Muffins Serves 12	Very Berry Muffins Serves 24
2 eggs	1. __4__ eggs	9. __8__ eggs
$\frac{5}{8}$ stick of butter	2. _____ stick of butter	10. _____ stick of butter
$\frac{3}{4}$ cup sugar	3. _____ cup sugar	11. _____ cup sugar
$\frac{1}{4}$ cup brown sugar	4. _____ cup brown sugar	12. _____ cup brown sugar
$1\frac{1}{2}$ cups flour	5. _____ cups flour	13. _____ cups flour
$\frac{1}{2}$ teaspoon baking powder	6. _____ teaspoon baking powder	14. _____ teaspoon baking powder
$\frac{4}{5}$ cup blueberries	7. _____ cup blueberries	15. _____ cup blueberries
$\frac{1}{3}$ cup raspberries	8. _____ cup raspberries	16. _____ cup raspberries

That Does Not Compute!

The Great Roboto is on the fritz and is spitting out some math problems with wrong answers.
CIRCLE the incorrect products.

$$\frac{1}{5} \times \frac{3}{4} = \frac{1}{10}$$

$$\frac{4}{5} \times \frac{1}{16} = \frac{2}{5}$$

$$\frac{7}{8} \times \frac{1}{14} = \frac{1}{16}$$

$$\frac{1}{20} \times \frac{5}{6} = \frac{1}{24}$$

$$\frac{1}{2} \times \frac{6}{7} = \frac{3}{7}$$

$$\frac{5}{28} \times \frac{7}{15} = \frac{5}{6}$$

$$\frac{3}{7} \times \frac{14}{15} = \frac{2}{5}$$

$$\frac{7}{12} \times \frac{6}{7} = \frac{1}{7}$$

$$\frac{5}{9} \times \frac{1}{5} = \frac{1}{9}$$

$$\frac{16}{17} \times \frac{15}{16} = \frac{17}{15}$$

$$\frac{2}{3} \times \frac{33}{34} = \frac{11}{17}$$

$$\frac{3}{11} \times \frac{7}{12} = \frac{7}{12}$$

Tough Training

Maxine is training to run a marathon. With each part of her training, she runs longer distances for a fewer number of days. WRITE the total number of miles Maxine will run in each part of the training.

Part	Days	Miles	Total Miles
1	40	$2\frac{1}{2}$	100
2	35	$4\frac{1}{5}$	
3	30	$6\frac{3}{5}$	
4	24	$10\frac{2}{3}$	
5	18	$15\frac{5}{6}$	
6	12	$18\frac{3}{4}$	
7	7	$22\frac{4}{7}$	
8	5	$26\frac{2}{5}$	

Time Slots

WRITE each answer.

1. How many $\frac{1}{2}$ hours are in 24 hours?   48

2. How many $\frac{1}{3}$ hours are in 6 hours?   _____

3. How many $\frac{1}{4}$ hours are in 48 hours?   _____

4. How many $\frac{3}{4}$ hours are in 30 hours?   _____

5. How many $\frac{5}{6}$ hours are in 15 hours?   _____

6. How many $\frac{1}{4}$ hours are in $\frac{3}{4}$ hour?   _____

7. How many $\frac{1}{2}$ hours are in $\frac{5}{2}$ hours?   _____

8. How many $\frac{1}{9}$ hours are in $\frac{2}{3}$ hour?   _____

9. How many $\frac{1}{6}$ hours are in $\frac{1}{2}$ hour?   _____

10. How many $\frac{1}{12}$ hours are in $\frac{3}{4}$ hour?   _____

Part of a Pie

WRITE the size of each piece of pie as a fraction in its simplest form.

1. Pete is cutting $\frac{3}{4}$ of a pie into 6 pieces.
   What size will each piece be?

   $\frac{1}{8}$ of the whole pie

2. Betsy is cutting $\frac{4}{5}$ of a pie into 8 pieces.
   What size will each piece be?

   _____ of the whole pie

3. Don is cutting $\frac{1}{2}$ of a pie into 7 pieces.
   What size will each piece be?

   _____ of the whole pie

4. Joan is cutting $\frac{7}{8}$ of a pie into 7 pieces.
   What size will each piece be?

   _____ of the whole pie

5. Roger is cutting $\frac{8}{9}$ of a pie into 4 pieces.
   What size will each piece be?

   _____ of the whole pie

6. Peggy is cutting $\frac{2}{3}$ of a pie into 10 pieces.
   What size will each piece be?

   _____ of the whole pie

7. Kenny is cutting $\frac{9}{10}$ of a pie into 6 pieces.
   What size will each piece be?

   _____ of the whole pie

8. Trudy is cutting $\frac{6}{7}$ of a pie into 3 pieces.
   What size will each piece be?

   _____ of the whole pie

That Does Not Compute!

The Great Roboto is on the fritz and is spitting out some math problems with wrong answers.
CIRCLE the incorrect quotients.

$$\frac{1}{9} \div \frac{2}{3} = \frac{1}{6}$$

$$\frac{8}{13} \div \frac{3}{26} = 5\frac{1}{3}$$

$$\frac{5}{9} \div \frac{5}{27} = 3$$

$$\frac{7}{8} \div \frac{1}{16} = \frac{1}{14}$$

$$\frac{2}{5} \div \frac{3}{8} = \frac{15}{16}$$

$$1 \div \frac{4}{5} = \frac{4}{5}$$

$$\frac{3}{11} \div \frac{5}{21} = \frac{7}{55}$$

$$\frac{4}{7} \div \frac{8}{9} = \frac{9}{14}$$

$$\frac{5}{3} \div \frac{5}{3} = \frac{6}{25}$$

$$\frac{9}{10} \div \frac{1}{40} = \frac{1}{36}$$

$$\frac{7}{8} \div \frac{21}{24} = 1$$

$$\frac{6}{7} \div \frac{12}{35} = 2\frac{1}{2}$$

Super Stacker

Lela has been busy stacking things she finds around the house. WRITE the number of objects in each stack.

1. Lela made a stack of nickels that is $5\frac{7}{8}$ inches tall. Each nickel is $\frac{1}{16}$ inches tall. How many coins are in the stack? _____

2. Lela has blocks that are $1\frac{3}{8}$ inches tall, and with her blocks she made a stack that is $20\frac{5}{8}$ inches tall. How many blocks are in the stack? _____

3. Lela used cookies that are $\frac{7}{16}$ inches tall to make a stack of cookies that is $9\frac{5}{8}$ inches tall. How many cookies are in the stack? _____

4. Lela made a stack of cups that measures $40\frac{5}{8}$ inches tall. Each cup is $3\frac{1}{8}$ inches tall. How many cups are in the stack? _____

5. Lela made a stack of sugar cubes measuring $21\frac{1}{4}$ inches from sugar cubes that are each $\frac{5}{8}$ inches tall. How many sugar cubes are in the stack? _____

6. Lela used magnets that are $\frac{5}{16}$ inches tall to make a stack of magnets that is $17\frac{1}{2}$ inches tall. How many magnets are in the stack? _____

Lightning Chargers

Gary is really proud of his Lightning Charger action figures. He never takes any of them out of their boxes, and he wants to build shelves to show off his collection. MEASURE the width of the box in inches. Then, ANSWER the questions. Write the answers as fractions.

HINT: Remember, 1 foot (ft) = 12 inches (in.), and 1 yard (yd) = 36 inches.

Gary has 57 of the Lightning Charger action figures that all come in the same size box. He wants to group them in different ways. For each of these groups, how long should he make each shelf?

1. Shelf 1 should have 11 action figures. _____ in.

2. Shelf 2 should have 13 action figures. _____ in.

3. Shelf 3 should have 15 action figures. _____ in.

4. Shelf 4 should have 18 action figures. _____ in.

5. If Gary builds only shelves that are one yard long, how many action figures would fit on a shelf?

_____

6. If Gary builds only shelves that are one foot long, how many action figures would fit on a shelf?

_____

Alien Invasion

The aliens have landed…and they're tiny!
Scientists want to study the little visitors.
MEASURE each alien. Then ANSWER the questions.

HINT: Remember, 1 meter (m) = 100 centimeters (cm).

What is the width of each alien? Write the answers as decimals.

1. green _____ cm

2. blue _____ cm

3. orange _____ cm

Their alien spaceship is one meter wide. How many of each alien standing side to side would be about as long as the spaceship?

4. green _____ cm

5. blue _____ cm

6. orange _____ cm

Angled Alphabet

There are three different types of angles: right, acute, and obtuse. LOOK at the letters, and WRITE the number of right, acute, and obtuse angles that can be found in each letter.

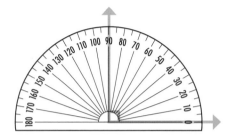

A **right** angle is an angle measuring exactly 90°, indicated by the ⌐ symbol in the corner.

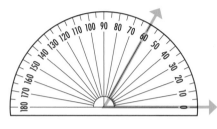

An **acute** angle is any angle measuring less than 90°.

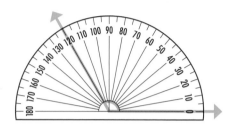

An **obtuse** angle is any angle measuring more than 90°.

1. A
    _____ right
    _____ acute
    _____ obtuse

2. F
    _____ right
    _____ acute
    _____ obtuse

3. H
    _____ right
    _____ acute
    _____ obtuse

4. X
    _____ right
    _____ acute
    _____ obtuse

5. W
    _____ right
    _____ acute
    _____ obtuse

6. Y
    _____ right
    _____ acute
    _____ obtuse

Angle Creator

DRAW an angle to match each measurement.

HINT: If you don't have a protractor, cut out the one in the example.

Example:

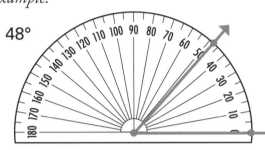

48°

Mark a point on the page. Place the center of the protractor on the point. Place a second point on the paper at zero on the protractor. Place a third point on the paper at the measurement. Then connect the first point to the second point. Finally connect the first point to the third point to form the angle.

1. **15°**

2. **36°**

3. **75°**

4. **142°**

5. **120°**

6. **94°**

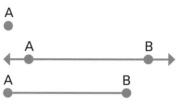
Line Art

Each person was asked to draw the following: A, $\overleftrightarrow{BC}$, $\overline{DE}$, and $\overrightarrow{FG}$. CIRCLE the paper with the correct drawings.

A is a **point**. A point marks a place in space, represented by a dot.

$\overleftrightarrow{AB}$ is a **line**. A line is a straight path that has no end in either direction.

$\overline{AB}$ is a **line segment**. A line segment is the part of a line between two points, called **endpoints**.

$\overrightarrow{AB}$ is a **ray**. A ray is a line that begins at an endpoint and has no end in the other direction.

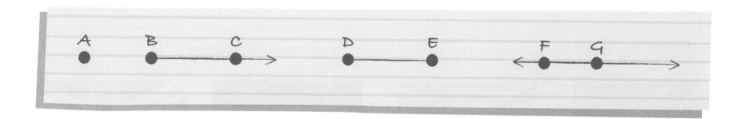

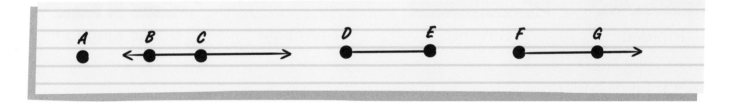

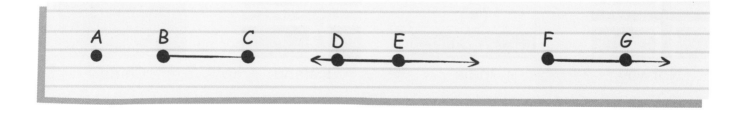

Points, Lines & Rays

Find the Flag

CIRCLE the flags that match each description.

HINT: Do not count the flag edges. Only use the flag pattern.

Intersecting lines are lines that cross one another.

Perpendicular lines intersect to form right angles.

Parallel lines never intersect and are always the same distance apart.

CIRCLE any flag that has at least one pair of intersecting lines in its design.

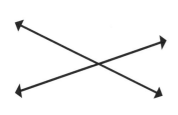 Trinidad
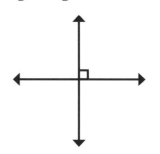 Guyana
 Germany
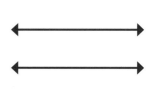 United Kingdom

CIRCLE any flag that has at least one pair of perpendicular lines in its design.

 Norway
 India
 Iceland
 China

CIRCLE any flag that has at least one pair of parallel lines in its design.

 Tanzania
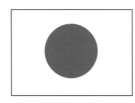 Japan
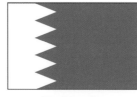 Bahrain
 South Korea

Making Polygons

A polygon is a closed plane shape that has three or more sides. DRAW a shape to match each definition.

1. A quadrilateral has 4 sides.

2. A heptagon has 7 sides.

3. A decagon has 10 sides.

4. A parallelogram is a quadrilateral with two pairs of parallel sides.

5. A pentagon has 5 sides.

6. An octagon has 8 sides.

7. A rhombus is a parallelogram whose sides are all of equal length.

8. A nonagon has 9 sides.

9. A trapezoid is a quadrilateral with only one pair of parallel sides.

Clipboard Check

Heidi has a list of shapes and their descriptions, but some of the descriptions are not correct. CHECK the box next to any description that matches the shape.

HINT: A **vertex** is the point where two sides meet.

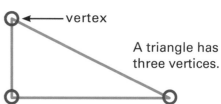

vertex

A triangle has three vertices.

❏ Nine vertices
❏ Shape name: heptagon
❏ Seven obtuse angles
❏ Two right angles
❏ No pairs of parallel lines

❏ No perpendicular lines
❏ Acute and obtuse angles
❏ Six vertices
❏ One pair of parallel lines
❏ Shape name: rhombus

❏ Two right angles
❏ Four vertices
❏ Five sides
❏ Two pairs of parallel lines
❏ Shape name: pentagon

❏ Shape name: parallelogram
❏ Four vertices
❏ Four right angles
❏ Two pairs of parallel lines
❏ Two obtuse angles

That's My Room!

READ the paragraph, and ANSWER the questions.

HINT: To find the perimeter of something, add the length of each side.

Alyssa's family has just bought a new house. Alyssa knows that her parents will get the biggest room, so she wants to find the next biggest room to claim as her room. There are four bedrooms. Bedroom 1 is 18 feet by 16 feet. Bedroom 2 is $16\frac{1}{2}$ feet by $15\frac{1}{2}$ feet. Bedroom 3 is 14 feet by $18\frac{1}{2}$ feet, and bedroom 4 is $17\frac{1}{2}$ feet by $15\frac{1}{2}$ feet. Alyssa has measured the perimeter of each room and knows which one she wants.

1. Which bedroom does Alyssa want? _____

2. Which bedroom will be for Alyssa's parents? _____

3. What is the perimeter of Alyssa's room? _____

Green Acres

The area of one acre is equal to 43,560 square feet or 4,840 square yards. CIRCLE the piece of land that is not one acre.

HINT: Find the area of a rectangle by multiplying the length by the width.

240 ft

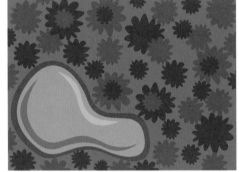

$181\frac{1}{2}$ ft

80 yd

$60\frac{1}{2}$ yd

$75\frac{1}{2}$ yd

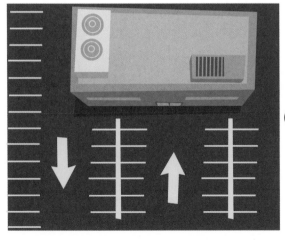

62 yd

$272\frac{1}{4}$ ft

160 ft

Box of Chocolates

WRITE the flavor of each piece of chocolate.

Short Cylinder: Chocolate Cherry

Tall Cylinder: Toffee

Rectangular Prism: Orange Crème

Square Pyramid: Caramel

Cube: Marshmallow

Cone: Truffle

1 _____

2 _____

3 _____

4 _____

5 _____

6 _____

Clipboard Check

Tim has a list of shapes and their descriptions, but some of the descriptions are not correct. CHECK the box next to any description that matches the shape.

HINT: In a three-dimensional shape, a vertex is where three or more edges meet. An edge is where two sides meet. A face is the shape formed by the edges.

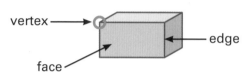

vertex ⟶   ⟵ edge

face ⟶

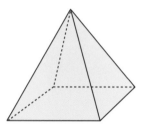

- ❑ Shape name: square pyramid
- ❑ Five vertices
- ❑ Six edges
- ❑ One square face
- ❑ All faces that are triangles

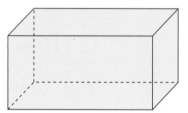

- ❑ Eight edges
- ❑ Shape name: rectangular prism
- ❑ Sides that are parallel
- ❑ Four vertices
- ❑ Six faces

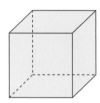

- ❑ Shape name: cube
- ❑ No parallel lines
- ❑ Twelve edges
- ❑ Eight vertices
- ❑ All square faces

- ❑ Eight faces
- ❑ All faces that are rectangles
- ❑ Shape name: cube
- ❑ Twelve edges
- ❑ Eight vertices

Bug Blocks

The latest craze is building bug houses out of bug blocks. Each bug house set has a different volume. **Volume** is the measure of cubic units that fit inside a space. Think of each bug block as a cubic unit. WRITE the volume of each bug house in cubic units.

Example:

1 cubic unit

12 cubic units

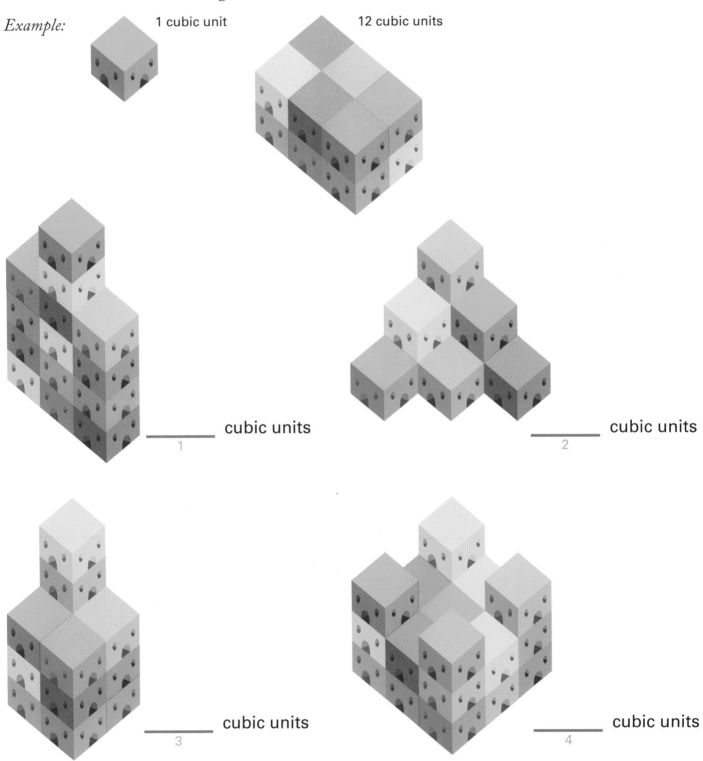

_____ cubic units
1

_____ cubic units
2

_____ cubic units
3

_____ cubic units
4

Volume

At the Farm

Farmer Brown is thinking about buying a neighborhood farm and is gathering some information about it. WRITE the volume of each building on the farm in cubic feet (ft³).

HINT: Find the volume of each building by multiplying the base times the width times the height.

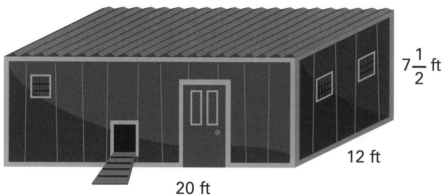

$7\frac{1}{2}$ ft

12 ft

20 ft

Chicken coop: _____ ft³
1

10 ft

$8\frac{1}{2}$ ft

$21\frac{1}{2}$ ft

Greenhouse: _____ ft³
2

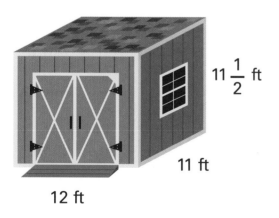

$11\frac{1}{2}$ ft

11 ft

12 ft

Storage shed: _____ ft³
3

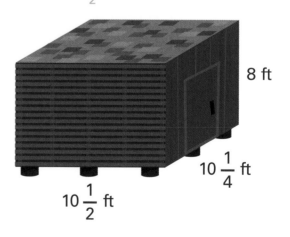

8 ft

$10\frac{1}{4}$ ft

$10\frac{1}{2}$ ft

Corn crib: _____ ft³
4

Budding Musicians

Kids were asked if they play a musical instrument, and their responses are shown in the line plot. Each X represents one kid. LOOK at the line plot, and ANSWER the questions.

Kids Who Play Instruments

Guitar   Trumpet   Drums   Piano   Violin   Flute   Bass   Saxophone

1. How many kids play violin? _____

2. How many kids play drums? _____

3. Exactly four kids play what instrument? _____

4. What two instruments do the same number of kids play?

_____

5. How many more kids play piano than flute? _____

6. How many more kids play violin than bass? _____

7. How many kids play trumpet and saxophone combined? _____

8. If each kid plays only one instrument, how many kids are shown in this graph? _____

Living Situations

Two different groups of kids were asked how many people live in their house. Using the definitions for the line plot on this page to help you, ANSWER the questions about the line plot on the opposite page.

Number of People Living in the House

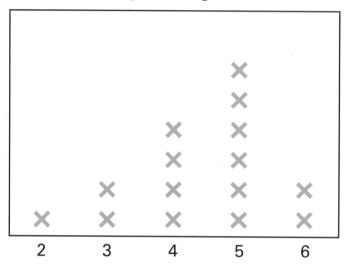

The **range** is the difference between the highest and the lowest numbers of a data set. In this line plot the highest number of people living in the house is 6, and the lowest number is 2. The range of this line plot is 4.

The **median** is the number that is in the middle of a data set. In this line plot, the data set written in order from lowest to highest is 2, 3, 3, 4, 4, 4, 4, 5, 5, 5, 5, 5, 5, 6, 6. The median in this set is 5.

The **mode** is the number or answer that occurs the most. In this line plot, the most kids said that 5 people were living in their house. The mode of this line plot is 5.

The **mean** is the average number in a set of data. It can be found by adding all of the data values together, then dividing by the number of values in the data set. In this line plot, the mean can be found by dividing the total number of people by the number of houses.

First, find the total number of people and houses.

1 house with 2 people = 2 people   2 houses with 3 people = 6 people

4 houses with 4 people = 16 people   6 houses with 5 people = 30 people

2 houses with 6 people = 12 people

There are 15 houses with 66 people. 66 ÷ 15 = 4.4. The mean number of people living in a house is 4.4.

Number of People Living in the House

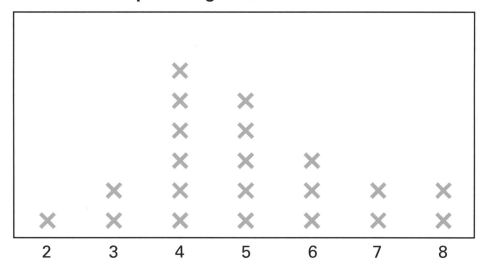

1. The range is _____ .

2. The median is _____ .

3. The mode is _____ .

4. The mean number of people living in the house is _____ .

Graph It

ASK 15 people how many books they have read in the past month. RECORD their answers by marking an X on the line plot. Then WRITE the range, median, mode, and mean of your graph.

Books Read in the Past Month

0   1   2   3   4   5   6   7   8   9   10   11   12

The range is _____.

The median is _____.

The mode is _____.

The mean number of books is _____.

Family Membership

The graph shows the number of family memberships to popular city attractions. LOOK at the graph, and ANSWER the questions.

Family Memberships to City Attractions

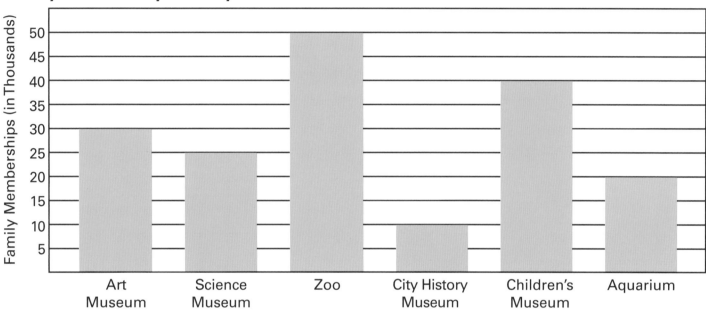

1. How many families have memberships to the science museum? _____

2. How many families have memberships to the children's museum? _____

3. How many more families have memberships to the zoo than to the art museum?

   _____

4. What are the three most popular city attractions for families?

   _____

5. What is the least popular city attraction for families? _____

6. How many family memberships have been sold at the four museums combined?

   _____

7. How many family memberships have been sold at the zoo and the aquarium combined?

   _____

8. What is the range in family memberships in this graph? _____

Game Time

This graph shows the number of points scored in the first six games of the season by the two local soccer teams, the Blazers and the Demons. LOOK at the graph, and ANSWER the questions.

Points Scored in Soccer Games

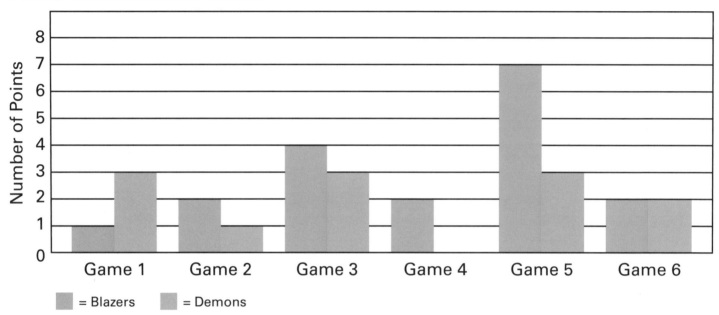

= Blazers   = Demons

1. How many points did the Blazers score in game 3? _____

2. How many points did the Demons score in game 6? _____

3. In what game did the Blazers score only one point? _____

4. In what game did the Demons score no points? _____

5. In one game, the Blazers were playing a team whose best players were all out sick.

   Judging by the scores in this graph, which game was it? _____

6. What is the range of scores in this graph? _____

7. What is the mean number of points scored by the Blazers? _____

8. What is the mean number of points scored by the Demons? _____

The Votes Are In

Three candidates ran for mayor. This graph shows the number of votes each got from men and women voters. LOOK at the graph, and ANSWER the questions.

Mayoral Votes of Men and Women Voters

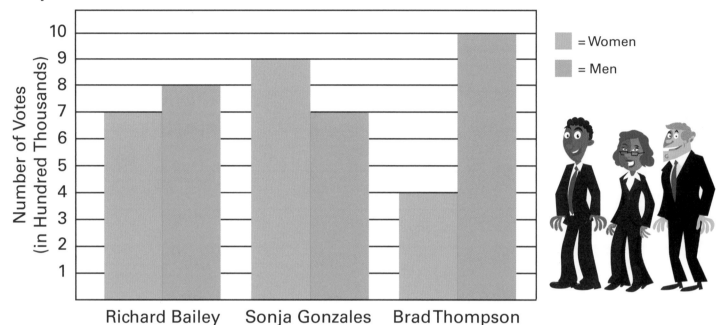

1. How many votes did Richard Bailey get from women voters? _____

2. How many votes did Brad Thompson get from men voters? _____

3. Which candidate was more popular among women voters than men voters?

   _____

4. Who got 1,400,000 total votes? _____

5. How many total votes did Richard Bailey get? _____

6. What is the range of votes from women voters? _____

7. What is the range of votes from men voters? _____

8. Who won the election? _____

Graph It

ASK 10 kids and 10 adults about the type of shows they watch in a week. RECORD their answers with tally marks in the chart, one tally mark for each type of show a person watches. Then DRAW the graph.

	Kids	Adults
Cartoons		
News		
Sitcoms		
Dramas		
Reality		

Favorite Types of TV Shows

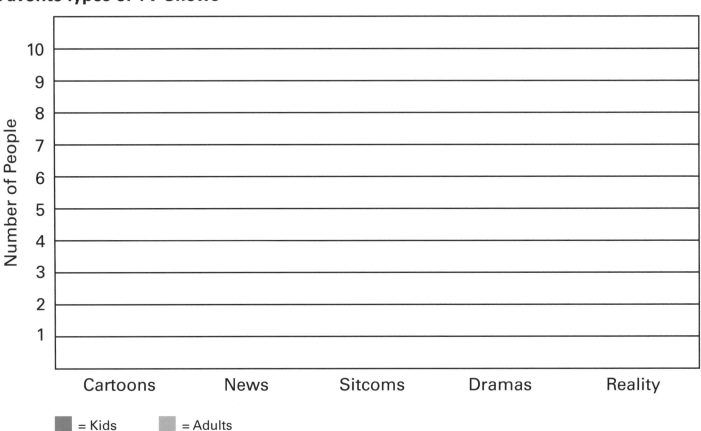

■ = Kids   ▨ = Adults

After-School Sports

The two graphs show the number of sports played by boys and girls after school. LOOK at the graphs, and ANSWER the questions.

Boys Sports

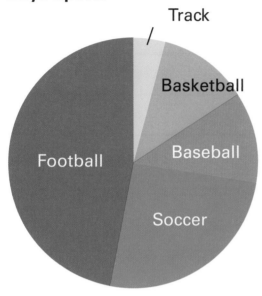

Girls Sports

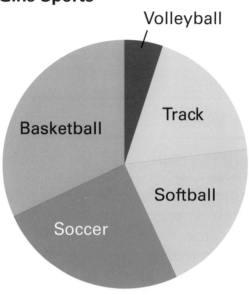

1. About what percentage of boys play football? _____

2. About what percentage of girls play soccer? _____

3. What sport is played by about $\frac{1}{3}$ of girls? _____

4. What sport is played by about $\frac{1}{25}$ of boys? _____

5. Which sport do nearly an equal number of girls and boys play? _____

6. What sport do about 15% more girls play than boys? _____

7. How likely is it that a boy joining an after-school team will join the track team?

    impossible   unlikely   likely   certain

8. How likely is it that a girl joining an after-school team will join the girl's football team?

    impossible   unlikely   likely   certain

Viewing Audience

Television ratings show the percentage of people from different age groups who watched a particular show. The chart shows the ratings for Thursday evening shows. LOOK at the chart, and WRITE the age-group title for each graph.

Show	Ages 9–17	Ages 18–34	Ages 35–49
Family Flies	14%	7%	3%
The B Team	24%	23%	11%
King of the Grill	5%	8%	21%
The Clinging Detective	10%	17%	42%
Miami Mice	46%	10%	4%
Twin Creeks	1%	35%	19%

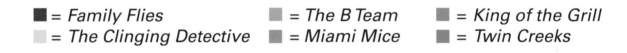

■ = *Family Flies*   ■ = *The B Team*   ■ = *King of the Grill*
■ = *The Clinging Detective*   ■ = *Miami Mice*   ■ = *Twin Creeks*

1. _____ 2. _____ 3. _____

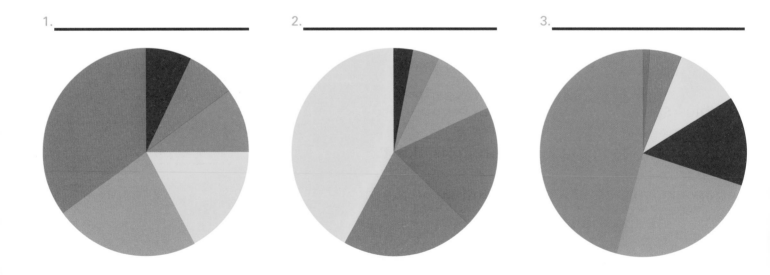

Sandwich Shop

The owners of Sal's Sandwich Shop are changing the menu but want to keep the most popular sandwiches. They graphed the sandwich purchases of 500 customers. LOOK at the graph, and ANSWER the questions.

Sandwich Purchases of 500 Customers

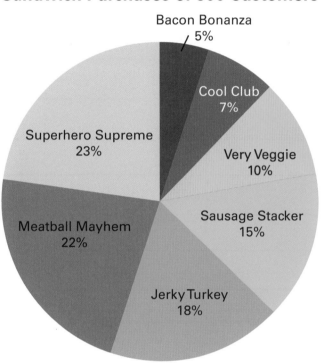

How many people bought each sandwich?

Superhero Supreme _____ 1

Sausage Stacker _____ 2

Meatball Mayhem _____ 3

Very Veggie _____ 4

Cool Club _____ 5

Bacon Bonanza _____ 6

Jerky Turkey _____ 7

8. What are the two most popular sandwiches? _____

_____

9. Based on this graph, what two sandwiches should the owners of Sal's Sandwich Shop replace with new sandwiches? _____

Graph It

ASK 20 people their favorite color. RECORD their answers with tally marks in the chart. Then COLOR the graph according to the favorite colors, and WRITE the percentage of people that like each color.

Color	Number of People	Percent of People

Favorite Color

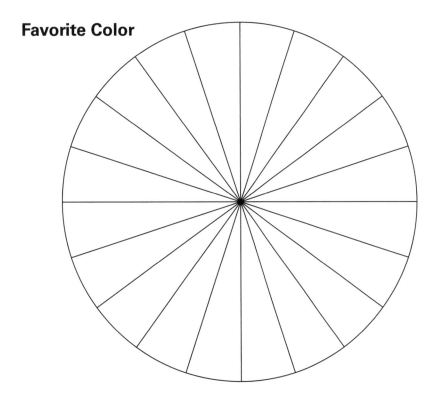

What's in a Name?

This graph shows the popularity of a name as it changed over time. The names are ranked in popularity from 1 to 100. LOOK at the graph, and ANSWER the questions.

HINT: A name only appears on this graph in the years that it was in the top 100 names.

Name Rank by Year

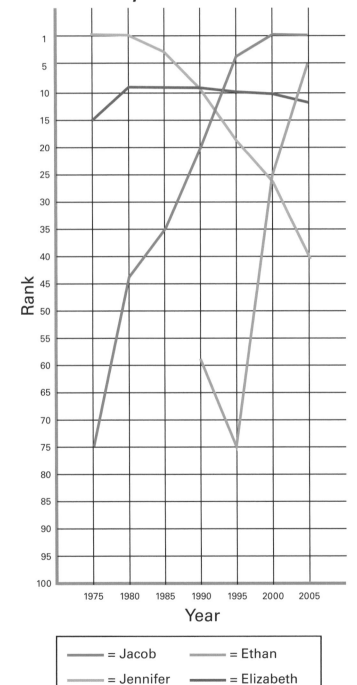

1. What name was ranked number 35 in 1985? _____

2. What name was ranked number 5 in 2005? _____

3. What two names have been ranked at number 1?

_____

4. What two names have been ranked at number 75?

_____

5. What name did not rank in the top 100 until 1990? _____

6. What name has had a rank that remained about the same over this 30-year period? _____

7. In what year were Jennifer and Elizabeth similarly ranked? _____

8. In what year were Jennifer and Ethan similarly ranked? _____

_____ = Jacob   ——— = Ethan
_____ = Jennifer   ——— = Elizabeth

Population Shift

USE the data on this page to DRAW the graph on the opposite page.

HINT: Round the populations to the nearest thousand, and estimate the placement of each point on the graph.

	Miami, FL	St. Louis, MO	Pittsburgh, PA
1930	110,637	821,960	669,817
1940	172,172	816,048	671,659
1950	249,276	856,796	676,806
1960	291,688	750,026	604,332
1970	334,859	622,236	520,117
1980	346,865	453,085	423,938
1990	358,548	396,685	369,879
2000	362,470	348,189	334,563

City Population by Year

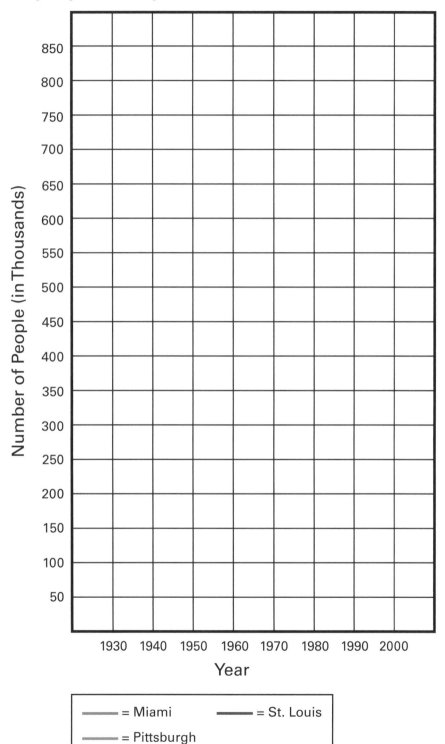

Number of People (in Thousands)

850
800
750
700
650
600
550
500
450
400
350
300
250
200
150
100
50

1930 1940 1950 1960 1970 1980 1990 2000

Year

——— = Miami   ——— = St. Louis

——— = Pittsburgh

On the Phone

This graph shows the number of minutes spent on a cell phone over a six-month period. LOOK at the graph, and ANSWER the questions.

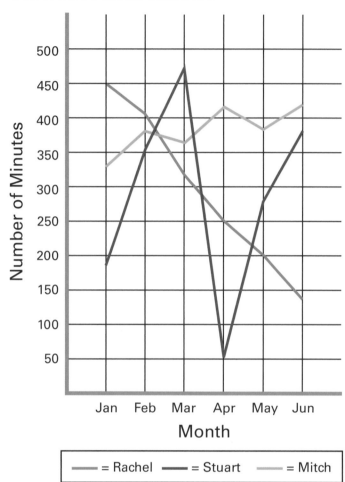

Used Cell-Phone Minutes

1. About how many minutes did Stuart use in February? _____

2. About how many minutes did Rachel use in May? _____

3. Who used the most minutes in April? _____

4. Whose cell phone use is pretty consistent from month to month?

   _____

5. Stuart lost his phone for most of a month but then found it again. Which month was it? _____

6. How likely is it that Rachel will use her cell phone for around 400 minutes in July?
   impossible   unlikely   likely   certain

7. How likely is it that Mitch will use his cell phone for around 400 minutes in July?
   impossible   unlikely   likely   certain

8. Stuart used his phone for 182, 351, 468, 53, 274, and 382 minutes each month over the 6-month period. What is his mean number of minutes? _____

Answers

Page 215

Player 1	
800 × ◆	40,000
70 × ◈	35,000
4 × ◇	20,000
Total Score	95,000

Player 2	
1,000 × ◆	50,000
200 × ◈	100,000
1 × ◇	5,000
Total Score	155,000

Player 3	
90 × ◆	4,500
30 × ◈	15,000
20 × ◇	100,000
Total Score	119,500

Player 4	
2,000 × ◆	100,000
11 × ◈	5,500
9 × ◇	45,000
Total Score	150,500

Page 216

1	1	1
× 3	× 4	× 5
3	4	5
× 3	× 4	× 5
9	16	25
× 3	× 4	× 5
27	64	125
× 3	× 4	× 5
81	256	625

Page 217

1. 375
2. 360
3. 252
4. 160
5. 330
6. 480
7. 192
8. 220
9. 480
10. 340
11. 180
12. 190
13. 225
14. 520
15. 312
16. 200

Page 218

1. 77
2. 120
3. 112
4. 144
5. 175
6. 372
7. 322
8. 708
9. 441
10. 888
11. 616
12. 1,164

Page 219

1. 480, 1,260, 432, 585
2. 408, 828, 828, 1,350
3. 600, 900, 450, 1,125
4. 1,248, 1,368, 1,170, 1,890

Page 220

1. 11,835
2. 10,260
3. 19,850
4. 18,090
5. 20,370
6. 17,640
7. 14,760
8. 36,250
9. 14,700
10. 5,600

Page 221

1. 20,000
2. 9,000
3. 42,000
4. 16,000
5. 15,000
6. 49,000
7. 4,000
8. 15,000
9. 36,000
10. 30,000
11. 12,000
12. 16,000

Page 222

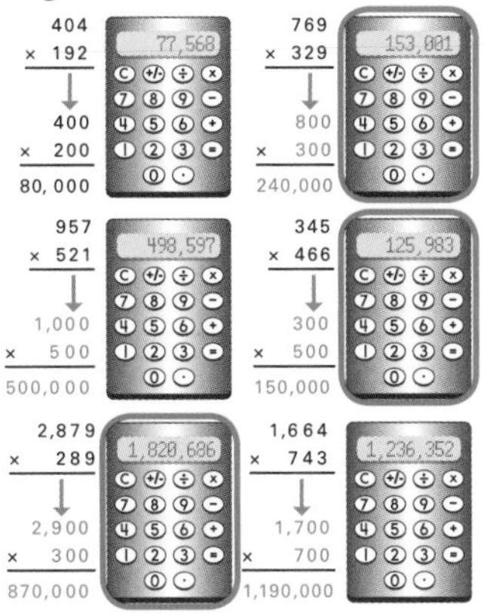
404 × 192
400 × 200 = 80, 000
77,568
769 × 329
800 × 300 = 240,000
153,001
957 × 521
1,000 × 500 = 500,000
498,597
345 × 466
300 × 500 = 150,000
125,983
2,879 × 289
2,900 × 300 = 870,000
1,820,686
1,664 × 743
1,700 × 700 = 1,190,000
1,236,352

Page 223

1. Kenneth: 8, Courtney: 16, Diana: 28, Aaron: 32
2. Joseph: 10, Alyssa: 15, Isaac: 25, Cassandra: 45
3. Alejandro: 18, Victoria: 42, Hunter: 54, Faith: 66

Page 224

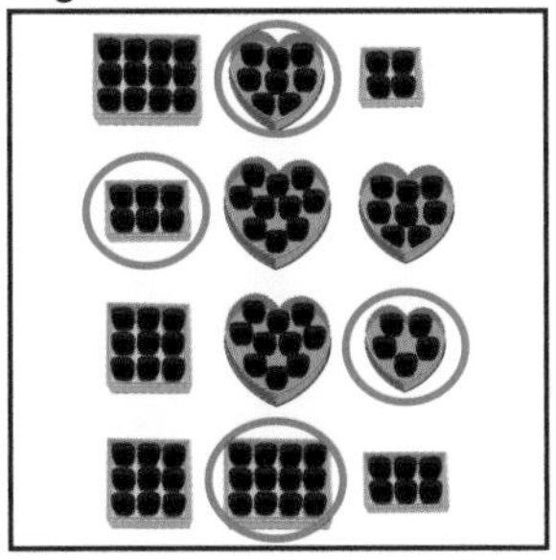

Page 225

1. 60, 50, 40
2. 300, 200, 100
3. 250, 200, 150
4. 4,000, 3,500, 2,000

Page 226

324	512	3,750
÷ 3	÷ 4	÷ 5
108	128	750
÷ 3	÷ 4	÷ 5
36	32	150
÷ 3	÷ 4	÷ 5
12	8	30
÷ 3	÷ 4	÷ 5
4	2	6

Page 227

1. 63
2. 196
3. 223
4. 631

Page 228

1. 9,435
2. 8,128
3. 11,592
4. 10,663
5. 9,008
6. 7,950
7. 13,624
8. 10,708
9. 8,712
10. 12,558

Page 229

1. 7
2. 6
3. 9
4. 11
5. 13
6. 8
7. 5
8. 18
9. 4
10. 9
11. 12
12. 14

Page 230

1. 17, 5
2. 22, 17
3. 15, 3
4. 14, 11
5. 13, 50
6. 9, 45

Page 231

1. 3,000
2. 2,000
3. 9,000
4. 5,000
5. 4,000
6. 35,000

Page 232

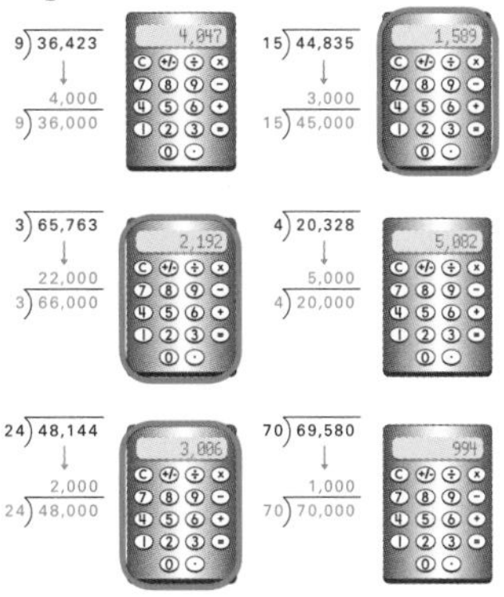
9)36,423
4,000
9)36,000
4,047
15)44,835
3,000
15)45,000
1,589
3)65,763
22,000
3)66,000
2,192
4)20,328
5,000
4)20,000
5,082
24)48,144
2,000
24)48,000
3,006
70)69,580
1,000
70)70,000
994

Page 233

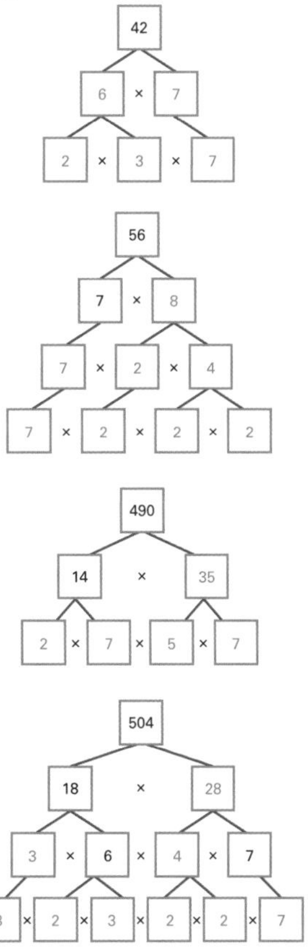
42
6 × 7
2 × 3 × 7
56
7 × 8
7 × 2 × 4
7 × 2 × 2 × 2
490
14 × 35
2 × 7 × 5 × 7
504
18 × 28
3 × 6 × 4 × 7
3 × 2 × 3 × 2 × 2 × 7

Page 234

1	2 ◯	3 ◯	4	5 ◯	6	7 ◯	8	9	10
11 ◯	12	13 ◯	14	15	16	17 ◯	18	19 ◯	20
21	22	23 ◯	24	25	26	27	28	29 ◯	30
31 ◯	32	33	34	35	36	37 ◯	38	39	40
41 ◯	42	43 ◯	44	45	46	47 ◯	48	49	50
51	52	53 ◯	54	55	56	57	58	59 ◯	60
61 ◯	62	63	64	65	66	67 ◯	68	69	70
71 ◯	72	73 ◯	74	75	76	77	78	79 ◯	80
81	82	83 ◯	84	85	86	87	88	89 ◯	90
91	92	93	94	95	96	97 ◯	98	99	100

Page 235

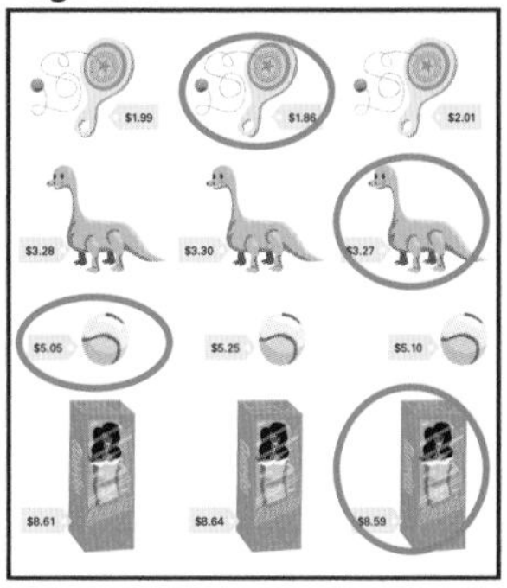
$1.99
$1.86
$2.01
$3.28
$3.30
$3.27
$5.05
$5.25
$5.10
$8.61
$8.64
$8.59

Page 236

1. 7
2. 5
3. 2
4. 3
5. 10
6. 6
7. 1
8. 4
9. 9
10. 8

Page 237

1. 18
2. 53
3. 22
4. 68
5. 1
6. 75
7. 41
8. 100

Page 238

1. 17
2. 23
3. 21
4. 19
5. 20
6. 22
7. 7.2
8. 5.9
9. 6.6
10. 6.0
11. 6.7
12. 7.4
13. 12.93
14. 13.05
15. 12.88
16. 14.22
17. 13.49
18. 12.72

Page 239

1. 89.99
2. 5.83
3. 170.37
4. 613.07
5. 29.48
6. 244.94

Page 240

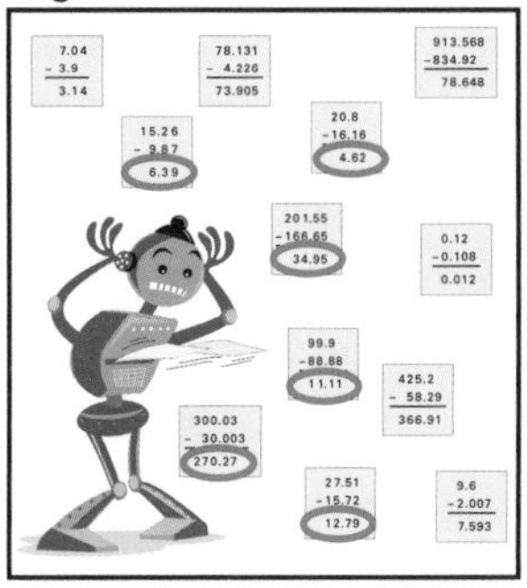
7.04 − 3.9 = 3.14
78.131 − 4.226 = 73.905
913.568 − 834.92 = 78.648
15.26 − 9.87 = 6.39
20.8 − 16.16 = 4.62
201.55 − 166.65 = 34.95
0.12 − 0.108 = 0.012
99.9 − 88.88 = 11.11
425.2 − 58.29 = 366.91
300.03 − 30.003 = 270.27
27.51 − 15.72 = 12.79
9.6 − 2.007 = 7.593

Answers

Page 241
1. 5.60　　2. 0.60
3. 4.80　　4. 8.25
5. 8.75　　6. 67.50
7. 25.68　　8. 66.96

Page 242
1. 18.95　　2. 25.30
3. 26.13　　4. 29.44
5. 32.11　　6. 47.20
7. 62.93　　8. 67.71
9. 38.18　　10. 27.78
11. 24.47　　12. 18.31

Page 243
1. 1.37　　2. 3.36　　3. 1.84
4. 2.49　　5. 1.99　　6. 0.29

Page 244

Page 245

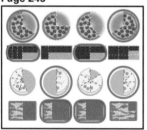

Page 246
1. $\frac{2}{2}$　　2. $\frac{8}{8}$　　3. $\frac{4}{4}$
4. $\frac{6}{8}$　　5. $\frac{3}{3}$　　6. $\frac{2}{4}$
7. $\frac{4}{6}$　　8. $\frac{2}{8}$

Page 247
1. $\frac{3}{4}$　　2. $\frac{2}{3}$　　3. $\frac{1}{3}$
4. $\frac{3}{4}$　　5. $\frac{1}{4}$　　6. $\frac{1}{3}$
7. $\frac{1}{2}$　　8. $\frac{2}{5}$　　9. $\frac{3}{5}$

Page 248
1. $\frac{1}{2}, \frac{1}{3}, \frac{1}{6}$　　2. $\frac{1}{9}, \frac{2}{9}, \frac{2}{3}$
3. $\frac{1}{3}, \frac{1}{6}, \frac{1}{2}$　　4. $\frac{1}{4}, \frac{5}{12}, \frac{1}{3}$

Page 249
1. $1\frac{1}{3}$　　2. $1\frac{3}{5}$　　3. $2\frac{1}{2}$
4. $1\frac{1}{6}$　　5. $2\frac{1}{4}$　　6. $1\frac{3}{16}$
7. $1\frac{7}{8}$　　8. $2\frac{3}{10}$

Page 250
1. $6\frac{1}{4}$　　2. $6\frac{3}{4}$　　3. $10\frac{1}{3}$
4. $8\frac{5}{6}$　　5. $7\frac{1}{2}$　　6. $11\frac{2}{3}$
7. $4\frac{1}{4}$　　8. $10\frac{3}{8}$

Page 251
1. $\frac{3}{2}$　　2. $\frac{10}{3}$　　3. $\frac{7}{3}$
4. $\frac{11}{2}$　　5. $\frac{7}{4}$　　6. $\frac{17}{8}$
7. $\frac{14}{3}$　　8. $\frac{15}{8}$

Page 252
1. $\frac{19}{8}$　　2. $\frac{11}{6}$　　3. $\frac{15}{4}$
4. $\frac{19}{10}$　　5. $\frac{10}{3}$　　6. $\frac{9}{4}$
7. $\frac{9}{2}$　　8. $\frac{23}{6}$　　9. $\frac{45}{8}$
10. $\frac{25}{9}$　　11. $\frac{25}{8}$　　12. $\frac{37}{6}$

Page 253
1. $\frac{32}{100}$, 0.32, 32%
2. $\frac{15}{100}$, 0.15, 15%
3. $\frac{53}{100}$, 0.53, 53%

Page 254
1. $\frac{4}{10}$, 0.4, 40%
2. $\frac{8}{10}$, 0.8, 80%
3. $\frac{7}{10}$, 0.7, 70%
4. $\frac{1}{10}$, 0.1, 10%

Page 255
1. 99　　2. 75　　3. 80
4. 60　　5. 47　　6. 30
7. 48　　8. 2　　9. 50
10. 4　　11. 92　　12. 20

Page 256
1. 30　　2. 50　　3. 15
4. 20　　5. 35

Page 257

GUEST CHECK		000946
Meatball sub		$ 6.20
Bag of chips		$ 1.65
Bottle of water		$ 2.35
	Food Total	$10.20
	10% tip	$ 1.02
	Total	$11.22

GUEST CHECK		000947
Chicken club sandwich		$ 8.55
Bowl of soup		$ 3.20
Small coffee		$ 0.85
	Food Total	$12.60
	15% tip	$ 1.89
	Total	$14.49

GUEST CHECK		000948
Grilled ham and cheese		$ 4.15
Lemonade		$ 2.40
Cherry pie		$ 3.30
	Food Total	$ 9.85
	20% tip	$ 1.97
	Total	$11.82

GUEST CHECK		000949
Garden salad		$10.25
Iced tea		$ 2.60
Chocolate pudding		$ 1.75
	Food Total	$14.60
	25% tip	$ 3.65
	Total	$18.25

Page 258
1. 32　　2. 18　　3. 20
4. 8　　5. 12　　6. 50
7. 15　　8. 20　　9. 40
10. 510　　11. 780　　12. 210

Page 259
1. $\frac{1}{2}$　　2. 0.6　　3. 40%
4. $\frac{3}{5}$　　5. 50%　　6. 0.48

Page 260

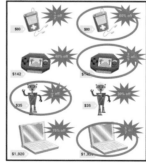

Page 261

Page 262
1. $10\frac{4}{5}$　　2. 16　　3. $22\frac{1}{4}$
4. $13\frac{5}{8}$　　5. $17\frac{3}{14}$　　6. $24\frac{1}{2}$
7. $19\frac{1}{6}$　　8. $29\frac{1}{9}$

Page 263
1. $\frac{1}{2}$　　2. $\frac{1}{3}$　　3. $\frac{3}{8}$
4. $\frac{2}{3}$　　5. $\frac{1}{5}$　　6. $\frac{2}{3}$

Page 264
1. $\frac{1}{2}$　　2. $\frac{1}{2}$　　3. $\frac{3}{4}$
4. $\frac{1}{12}$　　5. $\frac{3}{20}$　　6. $\frac{5}{8}$
7. $\frac{4}{15}$　　8. $\frac{11}{40}$

Page 265

Page 266
1. $3\frac{1}{2}$　　2. $8\frac{1}{8}$　　3. $1\frac{1}{4}$
4. $4\frac{1}{12}$　　5. $5\frac{7}{8}$　　6. $\frac{7}{12}$

Page 267
1. $1\frac{1}{4}$　　2. $3\frac{3}{4}$　　3. $1\frac{2}{3}$
4. $2\frac{1}{2}$　　5. $3\frac{1}{3}$　　6. $4\frac{1}{6}$

Answers

Page 268
1. 4
2. $1\frac{1}{4}$
3. $1\frac{1}{2}$
4. $\frac{1}{2}$
5. 3
6. 1
7. $1\frac{3}{5}$
8. $\frac{2}{3}$
9. 8
10. $2\frac{1}{2}$
11. 3
12. 1
13. 6
14. 2
15. $3\frac{1}{5}$
16. $1\frac{1}{3}$

Page 269

Page 270
Part	Days	Miles	Total Miles
1	40	$2\frac{1}{2}$	100
2	35	$4\frac{1}{5}$	147
3	30	$6\frac{3}{5}$	198
4	24	$10\frac{2}{3}$	256
5	18	$15\frac{5}{6}$	285
6	12	$18\frac{3}{4}$	225
7	7	$22\frac{4}{7}$	158
8	5	$26\frac{2}{5}$	132

Page 271
1. 48
2. 18
3. 192
4. 40
5. 18
6. 3
7. 5
8. 6
9. 3
10. 9

Page 272
1. $\frac{1}{8}$
2. $\frac{1}{10}$
3. $\frac{1}{14}$
4. $\frac{1}{8}$
5. $\frac{2}{9}$
6. $\frac{1}{15}$
7. $\frac{3}{20}$
8. $\frac{2}{7}$

Page 273

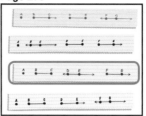
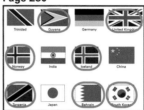

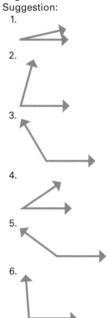

Page 274
1. 94
2. 15
3. 22
4. 13
5. 34
6. 56

Page 275
1. $30\frac{1}{4}$
2. $35\frac{3}{4}$
3. $41\frac{1}{4}$
4. $49\frac{1}{2}$
5. 13
6. 4

Page 276
1. 3.8
2. 2.6
3. 4.2
4. 26
5. 38
6. 23

Page 277
1. 0, 3, 2
2. 3, 0, 0
3. 4, 0, 0
4. 0, 2, 2
5. 0, 3, 0
6. 0, 1, 2

Page 278
Suggestion:
1.
2.
3.
4.
5.
6.

Page 279
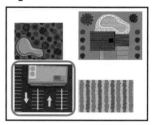

Page 280
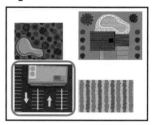

Page 281
Suggestion:
1.
2.
3.
4.
5.
6.
7.
8.
9.

Page 282
- ☐ nine vertices
- ☑ shape name: heptagon
- ☑ seven obtuse angles
- ☐ two right angles
- ☑ no pairs of parallel lines

- ☑ no perpendicular lines
- ☑ acute and obtuse angles
- ☑ six vertices
- ☑ one pair of parallel lines
- ☐ shape name: rhombus

- ☑ two right angles
- ☐ four vertices
- ☑ five sides
- ☐ two pairs of parallel lines
- ☑ shape name: pentagon

- ☑ shape name: parallelogram
- ☑ four vertices
- ☐ four right angles
- ☑ two pairs of parallel lines
- ☑ two obtuse angles

Page 283
1. bedroom 4
2. bedroom 1
3. 66 feet

Page 284

Page 285
1. Chocolate Cherry
2. Truffle
3. Marshmallow
4. Toffee
5. Orange Crème
6. Caramel

Page 286
- ☑ shape name: square pyramid
- ☑ 5 vertices
- ☐ 6 edges
- ☑ 1 square face
- ☐ all faces that are triangles

- ☐ 8 edges
- ☑ shape name: rectangular prism
- ☑ sides that are parallel
- ☐ 4 vertices
- ☑ 6 faces

- ☑ shape name: cube
- ☐ no parallel lines
- ☑ 12 edges
- ☑ 8 vertices
- ☑ all square faces

- ☐ 8 faces
- ☑ all faces that are rectangles
- ☐ shape name: cube
- ☑ 12 edges
- ☑ 8 vertices

Page 287
1. 14
2. 10
3. 14
4. 22

Page 288
1. 1,800
2. 1,827
3. 1,518
4. 861

Page 289
1. 6
2. 2
3. trumpet
4. drums, bass
5. 7
6. 4
7. 9
8. 39

Pages 290–291
1. 6
2. 5
3. 4
4. 5

Page 292
Have someone check
your answers.

Page 293
1. 25,000
2. 40,000
3. 20,000
4. Zoo, Children's Museum, Art Museum
5. City History Museum
6. 105,000
7. 70,000
8. 40,000

Answers

Page 294
1. 4
2. 2
3. game 1
4. game 4
5. game 5
6. 7
7. 3
8. 2

Page 295
1. 700,000
2. 1,000,000
3. Sonja Gonzales
4. Brad Thompson
5. 1,500,000
6. 500,000
7. 300,000
8. Sonja Gonzales

Page 296
Have someone check
your answers.

Page 297
1. 50%
2. 25%
3. basketball
4. track
5. soccer
6. track
7. unlikely
8. impossible

Page 298
1. Ages 18–34
2. Ages 35–49
3. Ages 9–17

Page 299
1. 115
2. 75
3. 110
4. 50
5. 35
6. 25
7. 90
8. Superhero Supreme,
   Meatball Mayhem
9. Cool Club, Bacon Bonanza

Page 300
Have someone check
your answers.

Page 301
1. Jacob
2. Ethan
3. Jennifer, Jacob
4. Jacob, Ethan
5. Ethan
6. Elizabeth
7. 1990
8. 2000

Pages 302–303

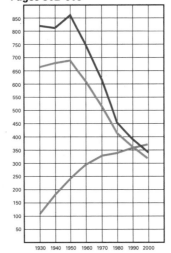

Page 304
1. 350
2. 200
3. Mitch
4. Mitch
5. April
6. unlikely
7. likely
8. 285